DISPATCHES FROM
THE DIASPORA

by the same author

GARY YOUNGE

DISPATCHES FROM THE DIASPORA

FROM NELSON MANDELA TO BLACK LIVES MATTER

faber

First published in 2023
by Faber & Faber Ltd
Bloomsbury House
74–77 Great Russell Street
London WC1B 3DA

Typeset by Ian Bahrami
Printed and bound by CPI Group (UK) Ltd, Croydon, CR0 4YY

All *Guardian* articles reproduced by kind permission of Guardian News & Media Ltd.
'Black bloke' originally published in the *Washington Post*, 6 October 1996.
'Racism rebooted' originally published in *The Nation*, 23 June 2005.
'White history 101' originally published in *The Nation*, 21 February 2007.
'Shots in the dark' originally published in *The Nation*, 14 June 2007.
'The misremembering of "I Have a Dream"' originally published in *The Nation*, 14 August 2013
'In my diction, in my stance, in my attitude, this is Black British' originally published in
   GQ, 5 February 2020.
'We can't breathe' originally published in the *New Statesman*, 3 June 2020.
'What Black America means to Europe' originally published in the *New York Review of
   Books*, 6 June 2020.
'Black like me? *Bridgerton* and the fantasy of a non-racist past' originally published in
   The Nation, 4 April 2022.

*Every effort has been made to trace or contact all copyright holders. The publishers would be
pleased to rectify at the earliest opportunity any omissions or errors brought to their notice.*

A CIP record for this book
is available from the British Library

ISBN 978–0–571–37682–7

MIX
Paper | Supporting
responsible forestry
FSC® C171272

Printed and bound in the UK on FSC paper in line with our continuing
commitment to ethical business practices, sustainability and the environment.
For further information see faber.co.uk/environmental–policy

10 9 8 7 6 5 4 3 2 1

To Pat and Wayne

For the journeys we've taken
and the support you've given me
along the way

Contents

4. Express Yourself

5. Me, Myself, I

Introduction

The night before South Africa's first democratic elections I slept at the home of a family in Soweto so I could accompany them to the polls the next day. A thick fog hung low over the township that morning that was only just beginning to lift as they set off to vote. Beyond those closest to you all you could see were shoes and trouser hems, the number of ankles growing with every step and every block as more joined us on our way to the polling station. Dressed in Sunday best, nobody was talking. Nelson Mandela had described his political journey as 'the long walk to freedom'. This was the final march.

It was a huge day for me personally. As a seventeen-year-old I had picketed the South African embassy in Trafalgar Square with my mother, calling for Mandela's release; as an eighteen-year-old I had set up an anti-apartheid organisation at my university in Scotland. And now here I was, watching the mist burn on the moment.

But it was important for me professionally too. The *Guardian* had sent me to South Africa, aged twenty-four, to 'try and get some of the stories white journalists couldn't get'. I had stayed in Alexandria township for several weeks, and travelled to Moria, near Polokwane, in a minibus with members of the Zion Christian Church for their Easter pilgrimage. But my main assignment had been to follow Mandela on his campaign trail.

There was just one catch: I couldn't drive. Mandela's campaign took him to far-flung areas of a country with precious little public transport. To get the job done I had to organise an elaborate network of favours. I got lifts to rallies with journalists, paying for their petrol and keeping them company. Once there, I would then ask if anyone was heading back to the nearest big town and do the same again. During one of those trips a film crew dropped me off at a petrol station and told me they'd arranged for others to take me the rest of the way.

The people who picked me up were Mandela's bodyguards. We got chatting. They found me amusing (more accurately put, I made it my business to amuse them). We had things to talk about. I had studied in the Soviet Union (my degree was in French and Russian), as had many of them; I had been involved in the anti-apartheid movement; and I was from England, where a number of them had spent some time in exile. They let me hang around with them on a regular basis.

So there I was, an occasional extra in Mandela's extended entourage, with a ringside seat on history. The trouble was, I still had to write the article. It was to occupy the most coveted slot in the paper at the time, and I felt the pressure keenly. Just a day before I had to file I was still lost in the piece and couldn't pull the various strands together. I'd never felt so out of my depth.

I gave it to David Beresford, the *Guardian*'s senior correspondent in South Africa at the time, who went through it slowly, giving precious little away. He handed it back with '&' signs where he thought I should expand it and '£' signs where I should shorten it. 'It's all there,' he said. 'There are some wonderful bits. But you've been working on it so long you can't see them. You need to take a break from it.' I had to file it the next day. 'Let's go and get something to eat,' he said, 'and talk about something else, and then you work on it overnight, and it'll be great.'

I don't know if he really believed that. But I didn't. I spent all night on it, moving things around, chopping bits out and adding information elsewhere, as he'd suggested. When morning came, I sent it over to the paper, convinced I had delivered an incoherent mess and that the notion of sending a young Black journalist to cover a huge story would be forever tarnished. Then I headed for Soweto to stay with a family for the night before going to the polls with them.

Communications back then were relatively basic. I didn't have a mobile phone, so I had no idea how the piece had been received. I spent the day with the family in Soweto as they went to vote. It was only when I went to file that story that I began to receive a number of internal messages, each one coming up separately on my computer, as though on ticker tape: first peers, then desk editors, then the deputy editor and finally the editor (a first), all complimenting me on the article. And so it was that I sat in a house in Soweto with my eyes welling up, feeling a mixture of relief, accomplishment and regret that my mother, who had stood alongside me on those night-time pickets, was not there to read it.

This was the article that launched my career, and within a few months I was offered a staff job at the *Guardian* as assistant foreign editor. It wasn't the career path I had anticipated. Originally I had wanted to be the Moscow correspondent. But in 1996 I was awarded the Laurence Stern Fellowship, which sends one young British journalist to the *Washington Post* every year to work for a summer on the national desk. I fell in love with an American. Within three years I had written a book about travelling through America's Deep South; within seven I was the *Guardian*'s New York correspondent.

This book is a collection of pieces written during that twenty-eight-year-long journalist career, almost half of which I spent in the US. Most are from the *Guardian*, where I spent twenty-five of those years, before becoming a professor at the University of Manchester. But roughly a quarter of them are not. For much of that time I have been the Alfred Knobler Fellow at the Type Media Center based in New York and have written regular articles for *The Nation* magazine. The collection also includes work from *The New Statesman*, *GQ*, the *New York Review of Books* and the *Washington Post*.

Over the span of my career I have covered six UK general elections, seven US presidential elections, the Occupy Wall Street movement, the Tea Party and Brexit. I have reviewed books, films and television shows and commented on the wars in Bosnia, Iraq and Libya, the Arab Spring, migration, gay rights, terrorism, Islamophobia, feminism, anti-Semitism, economic inequality, social protest, guns, knives, nuclear weapons, the Roma in Eastern Europe, Latinos in America, Turks in Germany and Catholics and Protestants in Northern Ireland.

I have examined the impact that McDonald's apple dippers will have on the agricultural sector and why children love spaghetti.

This collection does not draw from all the articles I have written, but only those from or about the African diaspora, including the Caribbean, Zimbabwe, Sierra Leone and Europe, as well as Britain and the US. This is a path that, from the very outset, I was warned not to take. To become too identified with issues of race and racism (Black people, basically) would, some said, find me pigeon-holed.

This advice, which came from older white journalists (pretty much the only older journalists available when I started out), was rarely malicious. They thought they were looking out for me. A fear of being 'pigeon-holed' is one of the most common crippling anxieties of any minority in any profession. Being seen only as the thing that makes you different through the lens of those with the power to make that difference matter really is limiting.

Then there were other, older, white editors who wanted me to write only about race. One of the first columns I wrote for the *Guardian*, about the NATO bombing of Bosnia, was spiked because the comment editor at the time thought I should stick to subjects closer to home. 'We have people who can write about Bosnia,' he said. 'Can you add an ethnic sensibility to this?'

The problem with both of these requests is that they didn't take into account the fact that I might want to write about the things I was interested in and knew about. Race in particular, and Black people in general, were a couple of the subjects I wanted to focus on. They weren't dealt with particularly well or at all comprehensively at the time, so there was lots to write about and improve on. In almost three decades of reporting, no Black person has ever approached me and asked me to write about them less, even if they weren't always in agreement with what I wrote.

But Black people and race were never the only things I was interested in. (Looking back, they are covered in fewer than half of my articles.) My advice to young Black journalists has always been to write about the things they are interested in and passionate about because that's what they'll write about best. If it's race, great. If it's fashion, finance or travel, that's great, too. They'll still be Black.

In his 1926 essay 'The Negro Artist and the Racial Mountain', Langston Hughes writes about a young Black poet who insisted he wanted to be known as a poet, 'not a Negro poet'. 'And I was sorry the young man said that,' reflected Hughes, 'for no great poet has ever been afraid of being himself.' Or as the artist Chris Ofili told me, when I asked him during an interview how he responded to the threat of pigeon-holing: 'Well, pigeons can fly.'

I have no problem being regarded as a Black writer. It's an adjective, not an epithet. It's not the only adjective available, and I have no interest in being confined by it. But I'm not in flight from it either. In the words of the late Toni Morrison, when asked if she found it limiting to be described as a Black woman writer: 'I'm already discredited. I'm already politicised, before I get out of the gate. I can accept the labels because being a Black woman writer is not a shallow place but a rich place to write from. It doesn't limit my imagination, it expands it.'

The Black diaspora has indeed provided an incredibly rich source to write from and about. I got drunk with Maya Angelou in her limousine on the way back from a performance. ('Do you want ice and stuff [with your whisky]?' her assistant asked her. 'I want some ice, but mostly I want stuff,' came Angelou's reply.) I had Archbishop Desmond Tutu nearly fall asleep on me, speech slowing and eyelids drooping, punished by a schedule that would wear out a much younger man. I have had the privilege of chatting to Stormzy in his living room, Angela Davis in her office and of counting Andrea Levy as a close friend.

It has at times been heartening, such as spending election night with African Americans in a bar in Chicago's South Side as Obama emerged victorious, or watching the St Louis suburb of Ferguson rise up in protest against police brutality. At other times it could be incredibly distressing, such as when witnessing the effects of civil war in Haiti and Sierra Leone, or entering New Orleans after Hurricane Katrina.

Some of the pieces in this collection offer not reportage but analysis – attempting to momentarily shift the reader's gaze – so that we might understand the world differently, imagining, for example, how Boris Johnson would fare if he were a Black woman, or what a good White history month might look like. I write both in defence of Uncle Tom, the much-maligned nineteenth-century fictional character, and for the right to riot against state oppression and structural inequality.

The pieces are not all of equal quality. Some bear testimony to the moment. The article about the acquittal of George Zimmerman for the murder of Trayvon Martin was written at an angry, late hour, filed quickly in the hope that it would help shape whatever discussions came afterwards; the account of the night of Obama's victory was written in the early hours of the morning, after no sleep, and as the results were still coming in. But it took me three years to find Claudette Colvin, who was arrested for refusing to give up her seat on a bus in Montgomery, Alabama, in March 1955 – nine months before Rosa Parks – but who had not been championed until relatively recently, and I spent a year shuttling to and from New Orleans after Katrina.

And like that night in Soweto, when my eyes brimmed with a mixture of pride and disbelief at the journey I had taken in order to get to such places, there are personal reflections on what certain moments have meant to me. Like all journalists, I came into the profession with something – my identity. But unlike some, I am happy to own it and share it. I have tampered with the original articles only if it was absolutely necessary for clarity, context, copyright issues, repetition or to conform with Faber house style.

In many ways, the world in which this book lands is hugely different to the one in which the first article was published. South Africa has

Dispatches from the Diaspora

been a stable multiracial democracy for almost three decades; the US has had a Black president, and now has a Black vice president and has trebled the number of people of colour in its Supreme Court. There are now almost eight times the number of Black MPs in the UK parliament than there were then, and Black actors, artists and writers who would once have struggled to gain a platform are now far more prominent. Meanwhile, almost a decade of intermittent Black Lives Matter protests, which reached their most recent global crescendo with the murder of George Floyd in 2020, have raised popular awareness about the issue of racism, to the point where two-thirds of Britons are now aware of the terms 'institutional racism' and 'systemic racism'. The language has changed; the conversation is better. We are not where we were.

And yet despite all that has changed, what is most remark-able is how much has remained the same. South Africa is still the most unequal society in the world, while the gaps in both wealth and unemployment between Black and white Americans rose dur-ing Obama's tenure, as did the Black poverty rate. In Britain, the *Windrush* scandal saw Black citizens deported or deprived of their basic rights because they could not prove they were British to a suf-ficient threshold, Black incarceration grew and young Black men, in particular, found themselves persistently and disproportionately at risk of being stopped and searched in the streets by the police. A YouGov poll from June 2020, the month the Black Lives Matter protests escalated around the world, revealed that the percentage of non-white people in Britain who think racism existed in society thirty years ago is virtually identical to the proportion who think it is present today.

The disproportionate number of Black deaths across the globe dur-ing the Covid-19 pandemic exposed the degree to which racism itself remains a hardy virus that adapts to the body politic in which it finds a home, developing new and ever more potent strains. We are neither where we need to be nor have we travelled quite as far as some think.

Indeed, if the Black Lives Matter protests have taught us anything, it is how little has changed, beyond the urgent realisation that so little had changed for so many for so long.

I am by nature an optimist. But I am not delusional. Over more than two decades spent reporting from the front line of the Black diaspora, I have seen how much change is possible and the potential of humanity to rise to those changes, but I have also witnessed the power systems have to thwart those aspirations, both openly and covertly. But the progress we seek will not come about through benevolence and enlightenment but by will and resistance. It will come, as Mandela arrived and as thousands poured on to the streets to protest more recently, because we demand it.

As I wrote in my final column for the *Guardian*, 'With racism, cynicism and intolerance on the rise, wages stagnant and faith that progressive change is possible declining even as resistance grows, things look bleak. The propensity to despair is strong, but should not be indulged. Sing yourself up. Imagine a world in which you might thrive, for which there is no evidence. And then fight for it.'

1

CHANGE
IS
GONNA
COME

Witnessing transformative moments
which promise, but don't always deliver,
significant progress

The Black knight

I followed Nelson Mandela on the campaign trail, during South Africa's first democratic elections, where each rally brought a heady release for the cheering crowds.

Guardian, 27 April 1994, Johannesburg

'I cannot sell my birthright. Only free men can negotiate. I will return.' So said Nelson Mandela in a message to the people of Soweto in 1985, responding to an offer of conditional release from prison from South Africa's former president, P. W. Botha.

Nine years later, he has returned and negotiated, and today exercises his birthright as the world's most famous first-time voter. I have followed Mandela for the past five weeks on the final stretch of his long march to the South African presidency, watching him address rallies and press conferences, on walkabouts and at official ceremonies.

To call it his 'election campaign' might confuse it with the limp affairs we are subjected to in Britain, where people in sharp suits or wearing shoulder pads convince themselves they are getting audiences worked up over tax bands and EU employment legislation. Mandela's campaign has been more like a series of political orgasms: each rally a passionate climax offering a brief, heady release from deep-seated frustrations.

Thousands of people, squashed into cattle trucks or minibuses, will travel more than a hundred miles and wait for hours in the shelter of a ramshackle stadium just for a glimpse of Mandela. Those who do not have access to a television will only have seen his face on posters and leaflets.

His arrival is signalled by the campaign song, 'Sekunjalo Ke Nako' ('Now Is the Time'). Jean Paul Gaultier would call it 'Afrotrash' – lowest-common-denominator lyrics, part Xhosa, part Zulu, part English, with an irritating tune that will keep you humming for the rest of the day. None of which bothers the crowd. From the old and toothless to the young and barefoot, they all dance along until they spot the first car of his cavalcade. The sighting generates a rush of energy through the crowd. Women ululate, and children cheer. All wave their flags and placards intensely, creating first ripples and then waves of excitement that roll on a sea of black, gold and green.

Mandela has returned . . . on the back of an open truck. He stands tall, straight and dignified: the Black knight on the white horse, slayer of apartheid and harbinger of majority rule. With a mischievous grin on his face and his fist punching the air, he will insist on doing a lap of honour, even if one has not been planned, so that no one will go home disappointed.

If it is just the excitement and atmosphere you have come for, it is best to leave now. By the time he has taken his place on stage, the orgasm is over. The local ANC official who has been charged with giving Mandela a brief introduction – as if he needed one – is eager to cut himself a slice of the glory. He will keep going until the microphone is wrested from his hands. And by the time Mandela rises to speak, after the prayer has been read and '*Viva* ANC' chanted countless times, the momentum has gone and the crowd is worn out by the waiting and excitement.

Mandela's accomplishments are many, but public speaking is no longer one of them. His bodyguards will tell you that during the Rivonia and Treason Trials, when as a qualified lawyer he represented himself and his co-defendants, Black people used to come from miles around to hear him cut the white man down to size with his sharp wit and analytical prowess. His powers of analysis are still sharp, but his slow oratorical style appears laboured and stiff.

His speeches are also unimaginative. He starts off with a factual explanation of the ANC's reconstruction and development programme (RDP) – the liberation movement's answer to Roosevelt's New Deal – and then moves on to voter education. 'Take your ID and go to the polling station. When you get to the first booth, you will be voting for the national parliament. Look all the way down the ballot paper until you see the ANC flag with the wheel, the spear and the *assegai* [the ANC emblem], and the letters "ANC". What letters should you look for?'

'A . . . N . . . C,' the crowd shouts.

'Very good. And there you will see the face of a very handsome young man whose hair has been turned grey by all the worry you have given him.' Laughter. 'There you should put your cross.'

He then goes through exactly the same routine again, using the same joke, but explaining that this time it is for the provincial ballots.

It is all solid stuff, especially in a country where 70 per cent of the electorate have not voted before and many are illiterate. But as one onlooker pointed out: 'It is hardly Martin Luther King.'

The people are then asked to raise their fists for the ANC anthem 'Nkosi Sikelel' iAfrika' ('Lord Bless Africa'). And after the brief reign of silence that follows that soft, powerful song a protracted spell of chaos ensues as Mandela is bundled into his car before the crowd can penetrate the lines of ANC marshals.

For at least half an hour after his departure, the road to the motorway is lined with supporters punching the air and shouting *'Viva'* at every vehicle that passes. By this time Mandela will have been whisked away at high speed to the next venue by either road or air. If he is flying, the ANC hires a different helicopter every time. Using the same one, his security men say, would make him an easy target for terrorists.

In his personal affairs Mandela is a stickler for punctuality, but on the campaign trail he is invariably late. Those close to him say it is his insistence on shaking every hand that makes it over his wall of bodyguards and a genuine desire for human contact that are largely to blame. 'He loves to talk to people and is very polite. He will tell his bodyguards off if he sees them being even the slightest bit rough with anyone,' says Barbara Masakela, the head of staff in Mandela's office.

Not all the rallies are so formulaic. In Cape Town, where the ANC stands a serious chance of losing, no punches were pulled as far as election kitsch was concerned. An inflatable Zeppelin in ANC colours floated next to the stage and white pigeons were released, along with black, gold and green balloons. Then, in what seemed like a mixture of liberation politics and karaoke, two singers led the crowd in a marathon rendition of 'Sekunjalo Ke Nako' and one verse of 'We Are the World', as Mandela danced his way on to the stage.

In Umlazi, Natal, he bored a crowd rigid by taking more than half an hour to read out the new constitutional rights he had proposed to the Zulu king, Goodwill Zwelithini. But he then went on to make an emotive speech which conjured up memories of the Mandela of old: 'I am the father of all of you and I love you like you were my children. It saddens me that I must leave you now . . . I wish I could put you all in my pocket and take you home. And when I am troubled or lonely take you out and see all your smiling faces.'

Once, in the Eastern Cape, he actually turned up on time, and in Durban he turned up an hour early, made his speech to a youth congress and left, much to the frustration of the journalists who arrived shortly afterwards. At another rally, when it started raining he told supporters to go home before they caught pneumonia. He had been speaking for only ten minutes.

The team primarily responsible for the campaign's strategy comprises six activists with varied political histories. Carl Niehaus, the main ANC spokesperson, is an Afrikaner from a very conservative working-class background. Pallo Jordan, the secretary of information and publicity, is a fierce critic of the South African Communist Party who was detained by the ANC's security department for six weeks during the early 1980s as a result of internal rivalry. Gill Marcus, his deputy, spent her years in exile clipping newspapers for the ANC office in London. Barbara Masakela (the sister of jazz trumpeter Hugh) became head of the department for arts and culture while in exile in Zambia. Marcel Golding, former deputy leader of South Africa's mineworkers union, is the bright young thing to watch among the ANC leadership. Jesse Duarte, Mandela's special assistant, is the top woman candidate in one region.

They divided the campaign into three phases. First came the People's Forums, which saw Mandela and other senior ANC members travel the country addressing mass rallies and answering questions. Then they spelled out the party's plans for housing, employment and education as outlined in the RDP and contrasted them with the National Party's record. In the final two weeks they concentrated on 'reassurance', trying to make sure people felt comfortable with change. Throughout, there has been the constant theme of voter education.

It was no accident that Mandela did not evoke painful memories from the past, such as his time in prison, the Sharpeville massacre or the Soweto uprising. Given the ANC's assurance of victory from the outset, it was decided that the campaign would be positive.

'It would be patronising to tell Black South Africans they have had a bad life under apartheid,' says Ken Modise, who is in charge of the account at the ANC's ad agency. 'Everybody knows the ANC was a highly effective liberation movement. But will it be an effective government? South Africans look to the ANC as the incumbent. We had to show people we had the wherewithal to govern.'

As well as their political roles, Duarte and Masakela look after Mandela's personal needs. 'We make sure that he has a jumper packed, that the right food has been ordered if he is staying away and that his schedule is not too exacting,' says Masakela.

For a seventy-five-year-old, Mandela does a good job of looking after himself. He does not drink or smoke. Nor does he eat butter, eggs, cream or anything that would aggravate his high blood pressure. He used to get up at 4.30 every morning, a habit acquired in prison. But age has wound down his body clock, setting his alarm for 5 a.m. He used to jog first thing in the morning, but now that running is considered too much of a security risk he uses an exercise bike. Then he has a light breakfast of fresh fruit or oatmeal with warm milk, before starting work at 6.30 a.m.

He is incredibly self-contained. Ahmed Kathrada, who shared a prison cell with him for seven years, says that he and Walter Sisulu sometimes had to force him to stop reading and talk to them. They also had to stop him jogging around the cell at 4.30 in the morning while they were trying to sleep. Nowadays the little relaxation time he does get he spends watching sport on TV, especially boxing, and reading biographies.

He rarely goes to bed after 10 p.m., but during the campaign his days have been getting longer. At the end of last month, when he contracted laryngitis, there was a concern that he was being pushed too hard. He was taken off the trail and out of the public eye for a week to recuperate.

The very fact that Mandela could do this a month before polling day illustrates how much the election has been a sideshow, with events in KwaZulu/Natal and the numerous efforts at mediation often dominating the political agenda. The situation has turned him into something of a Jekyll and Hyde politician. One minute he is campaigning and calling the country's president, F. W. de Klerk, 'weak and indecisive', the leader of a party that is still racist and guilty of collusion with the Third Force; the next he is negotiating, and de Klerk has become a man of integrity, someone Mandela can do business with. This was most obvious during last week's TV debate. After an hour of sometimes very heated discussion, Mandela offered his hand to de Klerk, saying he was a man he could trust.

And de Klerk is not the only one with whom he blows hot and cold. Two weeks ago, at a rally in Soweto, he ridiculed King Goodwill Zwelithini for having rejected an offer that would have given him the same rights and privileges as Queen Elizabeth II. A week later, in Umlazi, he made a deferential speech in which he claimed to be the king's faithful subject.

These contradictions are partly due to his ambiguous position during the transitional process. For some time now he has been both the de facto leader of the country and the leader of the opposition. De Klerk cannot make any major decisions without his consent, yet Mandela has no say over the day-to-day running of the country. It is an inversion of the dilemma most politicians are used to – he has power without office.

Come his inauguration on 10 May that excuse will no longer hold. During the last two weeks of the campaign there has been some hint of what a President Mandela will look like when he has no one else to blame. At the rallies in Umlazi and Cape Town he told supporters to scale down mass action and to 'settle for industrial peace' whenever possible. In order to give the government of national unity the chance to implement the RDP, 'Mass action won us the vote but now we have the vote we must work together to rebuild the country.'

Both times the audience fell silent, fearing the worst. Could Mandela, in the name of pragmatism and national unity, follow the example of so many other African leaders and put the interests of foreign investors before those of his own supporters?

Maybe. The explanation can be found partly in his background. Born into the Tembu royal family, he is a descendant of a lineage that can be traced back twenty generations to the fifteenth century. At times he still exudes the regal, almost imperious nature of a man convinced he is genetically destined for power.

A freedom fighter he was, but he has never been a revolutionary in the sense that it is commonly understood. If anything, he is quite conservative. During the 1960s, while the rest of Africa's freedom fighters were embracing socialism or developing their own brand of Pan-Africanism, Mandela was singing the praises of his former colonial power. 'I have great respect for British political institutions and for the country's system of justice. I regard the British parliament as the most democratic in the world,' he told Pretoria Supreme Court during the Rivonia Trial.

There is also a paternalistic side to his character, which has come to the fore at times in the campaign. During two rallies in Bophuthatswana, a 'homeland' whose ruler was ousted in a popular uprising last month, he called those who looted at the time 'a disgrace to the ANC'. He gave stern advice to children to 'go to school' and stop 'taking advantage of the chaos', and insisted that the young respect their tribal chiefs, even if they had collaborated with the apartheid regimes.

In one area, where there was an internal dispute in the ANC regional office, he slammed those in the crowd who were waving dissenting banners, saying they 'were not worthy to be called his comrade', and ordered them to explain their grievances to him in front of the rest of the stadium. They came forward, apologised for any embarrassment and then explained their problem. He listened patiently, accepted their apology and said that even though they had not gone about things the right way, they were 'worthy to be called his comrade' after all.

Consensus-building is Mandela's stock-in-trade. He is not an ideologue but a 'One Nation' democrat of the centre left. To his reckoning, almost any question, from the establishment of a *Volkstaat* (an Afrikaner homeland) to the involvement of the International Monetary Fund in policy-making, is worth considering, so long as it will not undermine his efforts to push ahead with national reconciliation.

Sources in the ANC say that his role as president will be largely confined to healing the wounds of apartheid, with the party's vice president getting his fingers dirty with the day-to-day politics. But if his new role earns him the title of 'Father of the Nation', it is due in no small part to his underlying devotion to the ANC, which has come before everything else in his life.

The strain of his political activism destroyed his first marriage to Evelyn Ntoko Mase, with whom he had three children. And it is commonly believed that his separation from Winnie was the result of pressure from the ANC, which regarded her court convictions and radical political stance as liabilities. Asked if he thought Mandela would like to be reconciled with Winnie, Archbishop Desmond Tutu said: 'He doesn't say anything straight out, but I suspect that he wouldn't want to do anything that was detrimental to the party or the cause.'

Winnie has said that ever since he joined the leadership of the ANC he has never really had a life of his own. 'The moment he stepped out of his prison he was national property, and it was as if we were lucky to get ten minutes of his time for the family. I think the family is still waiting for him. Psychologically, he hasn't come out of prison, in the sense that now he is back for the people. It has really been a continuation of the kind of life where the family didn't have access to him.'

Not many people do have access to Nelson Mandela. His friends say that even though they cannot imagine him doing anything else, his nature sits uneasily with the restraints of his high office. He would like to spend more time with his grandchildren, to travel and to read, but simply does not have the opportunity.

Take the ANC away from Mandela, and you are left with a very warm and generous but lonely man, who spent last Christmas on his own on a small island in the West Indies. A man who rarely has time to speak to his friends, and even then only by telephone.

Take Mandela away from the ANC, and you strip the organisation of its greatest asset at the most crucial time in its history. One of the few men capable of helping it complete its transition from clandestine resistance movement to open party of government.

Caribbean at the crossroads

West Indian islands are increasingly asserting a regional identity beyond their colonial legacy.

Guardian, 15 April 1999, Barbados

Nelson's column stands at the mercy of the birds in Trafalgar Square. To his left are the two houses of parliament. Straight ahead, a monument to those who gave their lives in the Second World War. In the distance, behind him, hangs a sign for Barclays Bank. Opposite it is Prince William Henry Street, with a fast-food restaurant called the Beefeater.

Were it not for the warm waves of the Caribbean Sea lapping at his feet and the baking sun overhead you could be forgiven for forgetting that this particular Nelson stands more than eight hours' flight from London, in a country that declared its independence just over thirty years ago.

They don't call Barbados 'Little England' for nothing; here they have red post boxes, drive on the left and watch cricket matches at the Kensington Oval. But soon they may not be calling it that at all. Later this month, on the first anniversary of Emancipation Day (a new national holiday on 28 April), Trafalgar Square will become National Heroes Square – a tribute to the islanders 'whose heroic deeds [Barbadian] society is only now becoming aware of and beginning to appreciate'.

'There is an assertion of Caribbean identity,' says Mia Mottley, the minister for education, youth affairs and culture. 'We are moving into a second generation of those who were born after independence. We now know what it is to determine our own fate, and there is a new confidence that is reflected in everything, from our music to our school curriculums.'

Barbados, like many other islands in the Caribbean, is in a state of flux. Barbadians are keen, on the one hand, to distance themselves from their colonial past. But they are equally eager to express their autonomy from their powerful neighbour, the United States, whose massive cultural influence has not been matched, since the end of the Cold War, by economic support. Caught between the weight of British colonial history and the might of American economic and cultural hegemony, many are now opting to chart their own paths.

Nowhere is this more evident than with the recent row over bananas. On one side are the Americans, protecting the economic interests of their multinationals in Latin America; on the other are the Europeans, weighing up their responsibilities to their former colonies against a possible threat to European unity and punitive tariffs from the US. Neither America nor Europe grow bananas. But the outcome of their battle could have devastating effects for Caribbean islands.

Most of the moves to make a clean break with British rule have their own political logic. Both the Jamaican and Barbadian governments are keen to remove the Queen as head of state. Three countries – Guyana, Trinidad and Tobago, and Dominica – are already republics within the Commonwealth.

All of the above, with the exception of Dominica, want to remove the British privy council – the final court of appeal – by the end of next year, thus severing a link that goes back more than a hundred and fifty years. In its place they plan to establish a Caribbean Court of Justice, partly so that they can reintroduce capital punishment, without deferring to the privy council: the Caribbean has almost four times as many people on death row per capita as America, according to Human Rights Watch. 'In order to complete our independence we need our final court of appeal in the indigenous countries,' says attorney general David Simmons. 'This is about sovereignty and an independence that is both political and psychological.'

The psychological has sometimes verged on the farcical. In 1990 the Barbadian government turned Nelson around so that he no longer looked over the capital's main thoroughfare, Broad Street. Now there is talk of knocking him off his perch altogether. 'Moving Nelson is the best thing the government can do for the social history of Barbados,' says Reverend Charles Morris.

Mottley adds: 'Clearly, we do not feel that Nelson was a national hero of Barbados. But we recognise the contributions he made to British and European colonial history and we have set up a commission to consider a more appropriate place for him.'

Even as many Caribbean nations seek to move away from England, the US is trying to distance itself from the region. American aid to the Caribbean has fallen by an estimated 25 per cent over the past five years. Meanwhile, America's determination to impose punitive sanctions on the EU if it continues to give preferential treatment to Caribbean banana growers has caused anger and dismay. St Lucia's foreign minister, George Odlum, whose economy is heavily dependent on banana production, has termed the policy 'heavy, dangerous and vicious'.

Even those countries which do not grow bananas, such as Barbados, feel the US has sent a strong signal that the Caribbean is no longer of any importance. 'The Caribbean countries did take American support for granted,' says Eudon Eversley, the editor of one national newspaper, *The Advocate*. 'But the end of the Cold War put a stop to that. Before, we could say, "If you don't give it to us, we'll go to Cuba." Now we can't say anything and we have to rely on ourselves.' But the fact that America has turned its back on the region economically does not seem to have halted its culture permeating most aspects of Caribbean life – especially among the young.

In Bubba's restaurant in Hastings, where American football helmets are lined up over the bar, the big screens are showing a baseball match between the Atlanta Braves and the Arizona Diamondbacks and an ice hockey match between the Detroit Red Wings and the St Louis Blues. 'What you are seeing', says Eversely, 'is the recolonisation of the Caribbean.' Outside the Garfield Sobers sports stadium, young men are playing roller-hockey, while inside a two-day basketball tournament is taking place, sponsored by American Airlines. When the West Indies cricket team lost its recent Test match series against South Africa 5–0 – the first whitewash in their history – some commentators said it was because potential cricketing talent was being attracted by basketball.

'There is some truth in that,' says the basketball coach of the national combined schools team, Derek Amey. 'If Michael Jordan comes into your living room every night, then of course that is going to make a difference. Some of my boys have got scholarships to go to study in the United States. There will need to be a lot more investment in cricket before it can compete with that.' Cricket has been relegated to the third most popular sport among young men, after basketball and football. 'Cricket is really for the older generation,' says Terry Boyce, eighteen, of the schools team. 'My dad likes it, but mostly I think it's boring. Basketball is cool.'

But while the breadth of America's influence cannot be denied, its depth has certainly been exaggerated. The nervousness over the impending demise of cricket owes more to moral panic than any actual crisis in the national sport. Despite each ticket for the weekend's basketball games coming with the chance to fly to Miami and see the New York Knicks, the turnout was unimpressive. The standard was also low: one of the saving graces in West Indian cricket is that, recent performances notwithstanding, it is the one sport that the region truly excels at.

Nor is the desire to disassociate Barbados from England as uniform as it might appear. On Sunday, while the West Indies played Australia, Bubba's was packed with mainly Bajan football fans in Newcastle tops watching the FA Cup semi-finals. One newspaper poll in February showed the island evenly split on whether the country should remove the Queen as its symbolic ruler.

Rumours that the government planned to remove Nelson from the island altogether were being met with fierce resistance. One woman, who gave her name only as Peggy, warned: 'You know what will happen if we take him down – we'll have to go somewhere like Prague to see a statue with some history. If each generation simply erased bits of its history it was uncomfortable with, where would we be?' But what all of these issues indicate is an anxiety about how the region should renegotiate its place in a post-colonial era of huge trading blocks and a global culture dominated by Americana.

Pitted against North America, clubbed together in NAFTA, South America, in Mercosur, and Europe, in the EU, countries the size of Barbados, which has a population of just 266,000 living in an area only 166 square miles, have little chance. Most other Caribbean islands are even smaller. But size is not everything. Reggae, carnival, calypso, Red Stripe and Rastafarianism are just a few of the other most obvious cultural examples of how the region has carved a place for itself on the world's landscape.

In a few areas, this has been translated into concrete co-operation between the islands. The University of the West Indies has campuses on several islands. The cricket pitch is another place where the disparate nations have come together for the common good. But while plenty of families comprise people from different islands, an attempt to forge a political and economic union has run into many of the same problems that have almost felled the EU.

There have been several attempts to set up a federal structure for the Caribbean which have foundered because of a mixture of insular chauvinism and uneven economic development. It is incredible that a region of nations that are so small that the inhabitants of each one fit neatly into a phone book can sustain so many heartfelt stereotypes about each other. But they do. Barbadians are regarded as snooty and conservative. Jamaicans as rough and brash. Trinidadians as laid-back party animals. Antiguans as haughty. And so it goes on. Last year, the tiny island of St Nevis tried to secede from St Kitts; had it been successful, it would have become the smallest country in the western hemisphere.

A more crippling handicap has been the considerable disparity in wealth between countries such as Barbados and Trinidad, which are relatively well off, and those like Guyana or Dominica, which are poorer. But in recent years, talk has been revived of a common Caribbean currency, and, after a shaky start, Caricom, the Caribbean common market, has finally been given teeth. Last year, when Fidel Castro toured the region, Grenadian prime minister Keith Mitchell said: 'Our initiative to strengthen ties to Cuba is clearly in the interests of Grenada. Also, it is important in the Caribbean context. Unless you integrate your region appropriately . . . you will not be able to compete.' On Saturday, the sugar cane that surrounds the Seventh Day Adventist Church in Six Roads swayed in the breeze to a sermon about David and Goliath. If it is bananas this time, Barbadians say, it could be sugar – the island's largest crop – next.

But the Caribbean islands are not just feathers for every economic and historical wind that blows. They may be heavily influenced by British and American culture, but they are more than simply conduits for them.

Earlier this week, in Bridgetown, workmen started erecting huge portraits of the ten national heroes – from Bussa, the slave rebellion leader, to Grantley Adams, the country's first premier – in preparation for Emancipation Day. Across the square, over the war memorial on Trafalgar Square, Nelson looks on. But for how much longer?

A year of reckoning

How one document – Sir William Macpherson's report on Stephen Lawrence's murder – shifted the national conversation about racism.
                            Guardian, 21 February 2000, London

Now that the dust has settled and the rubble has been cleared, it is time to check the foundations. The Macpherson report, released a year ago, fell like a bombshell on the British political and cultural landscape. Into what had appeared to be a fairly simple narrative between good (the Lawrence family) and evil (the five young men suspected of killing their son) William Macpherson introduced a new and far more complex character: institutional racism. Suddenly, a term that most of Britain had never heard before was all over the nation's breakfast tables.

Although the specific recommendations of the report were aimed principally at the Metropolitan police, the ramifications were far-reaching. But the inquiry's most radical contribution lay not so much in its content as in its tone and the very process by which it came about.

In the past, to get a report written about the state of race relations in Britain Black people had to either take on the police (the Scarman report) or defend themselves against white thugs (the Salmon report). But Macpherson emerged from an incident prompted by a group of white racist louts, bungled by an overwhelmingly white police force, which sparked an investigation presided over by a white lord. This in itself was a seminal moment in British race relations. This was no longer a debate about how to contain the problems that Black people cause by their very presence. This was white people talking to other white people about the problems engendered by their racism.

All Black people did was, literally and metaphorically, die for it. Stephen Lawrence died for it. Rohit Duggal, Rolan Adams, Michael Menson and many others died for it. The Lawrence family, in their tireless campaigning through the dog years when the mainstream press had lost interest, were dying for it. And the Black community at large was dying for it. This was our Rodney King. At last, here was proof of what Black people have been saying for years – that they have been falling foul not just of the law of the land but of the law of probabilities; evidence that there is a persistent and consistent propensity to shove ethnic minorities to the bottom of every available pile and not only leave them there but also blame them for being there.

And it had the same effect on white opinion in Britain as the videotape of King's beating had on white America. In the face of incontrovertible evidence, white people were no longer able to ignore the deep-rooted and widespread nature of racism in British society, even if they wanted to.

Those living in many urban centres were confronted with the fact that while they lived in a multicultural society, they had been experiencing a completely different reality from Black people, with whom they may have been mixing every day. Suddenly, they had to learn a new language. In the immediate aftermath of the report's release there was no escape. Its message and the saturation coverage it received in the media brought race into the living room, the newsagent's, the boardroom and the canteen.

There were two general responses to this. Among some, it triggered a process of introspection: white people suddenly realised they were white in a way that they had not considered before. And they were confronted with the fact that this whiteness conferred power, privilege and responsibility. Others reacted aggressively, annoyed at the assumption (which only they made) that they were condemned by virtue of their whiteness. Either way, white people were forced into an acute awareness of a matter that had fluttered only on the periphery of their consciousness. If the results of the *Guardian*/ICM poll in today's paper are anything to go by, then the outcome of this introspection has been broadly positive. The large increase in the number of those who would not mind if one of their relatives married a Black person or had a Black boss suggests that the most nefarious aspects of casual racism are in irreversible and rapid decline. The considerable number who would mind indicates the existence of a stubborn, racist rump.

So Macpherson raised the potential of racial debate in this country at a crucial moment, bringing both perception and understanding of discrimination more closely in line with the reality of the Black British experience. Previously, the predominant view in Britain had been that racism was a question of not being nice to certain people who happen to be Black; that racists are impolite, nasty, poorly educated and badly brought up, and that combating racism was just about treating everyone the same. Anti-racism, it followed, was therefore about denying difference rather than embracing it; its key determinant was not political but behavioural.

Macpherson dealt a severe blow to that misconception. By placing institutional racism at the heart of his report he drew a direct link between the racist boot boys and the complacent pen-pushers; between the black shirts and the blue helmets. The report charted a path from the crudest forms of racism to the most well concealed. In short, it exposed the way in which racism affects all areas of Black people's lives and infects the institutions we are all part of. It shifted the focus of the debate from the individual to the institutional; it encompassed not just the obvious but the abstruse as well. It showed that racism does not have one face but many, and sometimes no face at all.

But while it raised the potential of debate, not everyone has risen to the challenge. In the media, it is evident that some are still desperate to tap a popular vein of prejudice. Witness the coverage of the £50,000 in damages Winston Silcott received for malicious prosecution in the Blakelock murder case ('Silcott should rot in prison' – *Daily Mail*); the Mike Tyson visit ('I watched tots flee in terror'

– the *Sun*); the Afghan hijacking ('Oh no! They all want to stay. And we'll have to pay' – the *Star*). A core of white opinion remains in denial.

On the home affairs select committee, Conservative MP Gerald Howarth bemoaned the dispiriting effect the report had on the white psyche. 'Native Englishmen have been encouraged to get involved in a collective exercise of self-flagellation about their inadequacies with regard to race relations,' he said. In the *Telegraph* an editorial accused Macpherson of having such an intimidating effect on the Met that they had scaled down their stop-and-searches on black people. 'What is racist', said the paper in April, 'is reducing action on the street for fear that the colour of the person involved leads to condemnation. That is a climate encouraged by the report.' When crime figures emerged last year revealing an increase in street crime, Macpherson's influence was blamed again. Steven Norris, the Conservative mayoral candidate for London, wants to get rid of 'politically correct' policing: he doesn't care that a disproportionate number of Black men are stopped – so long as the police are polite, he says.

This, so far, is what has passed for a backlash – evidence of how little the right wing has been able to contribute on an intellectual level and how little there was to lash back against. Since the facts of the matter in relation to the Lawrence inquiry are not in dispute, there can only be any integrity in attacking its recommendations if you can come up with alternative suggestions for how to make sure no other family has to go through what the Lawrences went through. Failing to do so is tantamount to arguing for bad policing and inequality.

For in all of this Macpherson is little more than a metaphor. The battle lines between those who support its findings and those who do not are drawn far more deeply. It is not even just about those who feel it is time to develop a new conceptual framework for Britain's race debate and those who want to keep it as it is – although that has a lot to do with it. It has been a discussion between those who are already aware, or at least are prepared to accept, that Britain has changed and those who would or could not. The latter have either failed or refused to grasp that even though this country will always be predominantly white, it is now impossible to imagine it without Black people. Two-thirds of those of Caribbean descent, a third of those of Chinese descent and the majority of children in every minority community were born in Britain. Indian restaurants do not only make the country's most popular dish; they employ more people than shipbuilding, steel and mining put together.

What used to be a slogan among Black protesters – 'Come what may we're here to stay' – is now an undeniable reality. On the whole, Black people no longer have to defend their right to be here because, on the whole, white people are no longer questioning it. A sense of race is no longer in conflict with a sense of place.

So a sizeable minority is stuck in the paradigm of immigration/ integration/repatriation – desperate to maintain a seamless link between Britishness and whiteness. And the rest have moved on to equal rights, economic opportunities and educational advancement. Some are still asking, 'What are we going to do about these Blacks?' Others wonder, 'What are we going to do about the racism in our institutions?'

But just because we are asking the right questions does not mean that we are getting the right answers. Young Black people are still more than twice as likely to be unemployed as their white peers; two-thirds of the Pakistani/Bangladeshi community are still among the poorest 20 per cent of the country; graduates of African descent in their twenties are seven times as likely to be unemployed as their white counterparts. The statistics go on forever, but the grim reality they describe cannot. Macpherson has provided us with sound foundations; we must wait and see what lasting structures will be built on them.

The politics of partying

The roots, history and symbolism of the Notting Hill Carnival,
Europe's largest street party.

Guardian, 17 August 2002, London

As 1958 drew to a close, a despondent mood drew over the offices of the *West Indian Gazette* in Brixton, south London. A decade after the *Windrush* had docked, with the symbolic arrival of the post-war generation of Black Britons, a series of racist attacks in Nottingham had sparked several nights of rioting in mid-August. By the end of the month, the conflict had spread to west London, to Notting Hill, where white youths regularly went 'nigger-hunting'.

The *Gazette*'s founder/editor, Claudia Jones, had had enough. 'We need something to get the taste of Notting Hill out of our mouths,' she said.

'Someone suggested we should hold a carnival,' says Donald Hinds, who was in the room at the time. 'We all started laughing because it was so cold, and carnival is this out-on-the-street thing. It seemed like a ridiculous suggestion.' But Jones had other ideas and set about making arrangements.

A few months later, on 30 January 1959, London's first Caribbean carnival was held in St Pancras town hall. Televised by the BBC for *Six–Five Special* – a forerunner of *Top of the Pops* – it was timed to coincide with the Caribbean's largest and most famous carnival, in Trinidad. The brief introductory statement to the souvenir brochure came with the title 'A People's Art Is the Genesis of Their Freedom'.

More than forty years on, a bright array of oversized peacock feathers made its way down the Mall towards the royal family. Along with the Household Cavalry, in plumes and gleaming breastplates, and the Red Arrows streaking the sky red, white and blue, Notting Hill carnival took pride of place in the Jubilee celebrations. This was a legacy of empire with a difference, not an exhibition of how much has been preserved but a demonstration of how much has changed.

'There was more military involvement last time,' said Michael Lewington, sixty-two, standing in almost the same spot he took for the Silver Jubilee in 1977. 'I certainly don't remember calypso bands.' Here was an irrefutable sign of Black people's permanent presence and cultural contribution in Britain – a fact as widely conceded today as it was contested in the 1950s.

Notting Hill carnival's journey from being a response to race attacks in 1958 to pride of place on the Mall in 2002, passing revelry, riot and resistance en route, is both powerful and painful. It is the tale of how a marginalised community built, protected and promoted what is now the largest street party in western Europe, using the radical cultural politics of the Caribbean to confront Britain's racist political culture.

Either way, it starts with Claudia Jones, a Trinidadian communist who came to London via Harlem, courtesy of the red-baiting senator Joseph McCarthy. Jones moved to New York with her parents when she was seven. It was there, during the campaign to defend the Scottsboro boys, a group of young African Americans framed for rape in the South, that she joined the American Communist Party, in which she was later to play a leading role. Twice interned for her political beliefs on Ellis Island – ironically, the spiritual home for immigrants fleeing poverty and persecution – she was eventually ordered to leave in 1955 and sent to England.

Jones was a turbulent character, manic in her energy, masterful in her skills as a political organiser and chaotic in her personal life. A lifetime of illness, engendered by poverty and exacerbated by prison, was further compounded by overwork.

'She was so full of energy, she exhausted everyone, including herself,' recalls Corinne Skinner-Carter, one of Jones's closest friends. 'She used to chain-smoke, but I never saw her actually finish a cigarette. And she talked like she smoked.'

Her journey across the Atlantic had brought her into a very different racial and political context. She left America at the start of the civil rights era, when African Americans were asserting a new confidence. She arrived in Britain to find a small Caribbean community more divided by the island allegiances they had left behind than united by a racial identity they were coming to share. 'It was only in Britain that we became West Indians,' says academic Stuart Hall.

In March 1958, Jones launched the *West Indian Gazette*, attempting in part to cohere these disparate groups around their common experience of racism. In many ways, it was a period that echoes our own, with the sparks of popular prejudice fanned by a bigoted press, while a complacent and complicit political class allowed the consequent flames to rage.

On 18 August 1958, the Ku Klux Klan sent a letter to the *Gazette* addressed to 'My Dear Mr B Ape'. 'We, the Aryan Knights, miss nothing,' it said. 'Close attention has been paid to every issue of this rag and I do sincerely assure you, the information gleaned has proven of great value to the Klan.'

A fortnight later, Majbritt Morrison, a Swedish woman, was spotted by a gang of white youths. They had seen her the night before, arguing with her Jamaican husband Raymond outside Latimer Road tube station, near Notting Hill, and had started throwing racial insults at him. She had enraged them by turning on them. When the youths saw her again, they followed her, throwing milk bottles and shouting, 'Nigger lover! Kill her.' Later that night, the 'nigger-hunting' started and the area was ablaze.

'1958 was a big moment,' Hall recalls. 'Before that, individuals had endured discrimination. But in that year racism became a mass, collective experience that went beyond that.'

This was the taste Jones wanted to get out of her mouth. Only she, says Marika Sherwood, author of *Claudia Jones: A Life in Exile*, had the combination of New World confidence and political maturity to launch carnival under those circumstances. 'Her experiences of campaigning against racism and McCarthyism in America put her on a different level from other Caribbeans here.'

Trevor Carter, Skinner-Carter's partner and stage manager of the first carnival, agrees. 'Claudia, unlike the rest of us, understood the power of culture as a tool of political resistance. The spirit of the carnival came out of her political knowledge of what to touch at a particular time when we were scared, in disarray.'

There had been concerns that the unruliness of carnival would not translate from the outdoors of Port of Spain to indoors in London. Since many did not have cars, they arrived in their costumes at St Pancras town hall via public transport. 'The bold ones did,' Carter recalls. 'It was our way of saying to the dominant culture, "Here we come – look, we here."'

The evening itself went excellently. There was calypso singing, dancing and lots of souse, peas and rice, and other Caribbean dishes. 'We disrobed ourselves of our urban, cosmopolitan, adopted English ways and robed ourselves in our own visible cultural mantle,' Carter says.

Thus began London's first annual Caribbean carnival, moving the next year to Seymour Hall, and alternating between there and the Lyceum until 1963, growing bigger each year. By the time Jones was found dead on Boxing Day 1964, it was a large, established event. But while it was born out of experiences in Notting Hill, it had yet to return there. For that we must turn to another remarkable woman, Rhaune Laslett. Laslett, who lived in Notting Hill, knew nothing of Jones or the carnivals when she spoke to the local police about organising a carnival early in 1965. With more of an English fete in mind, she invited the various ethnic groups in what was then the poor area of Notting Hill – Ukrainians, Spanish, Portuguese, Irish, Caribbeans and Africans – to contribute to a week-long event that would culminate with an August bank holiday parade.

'The histories of these carnivals are both independent and interlinked,' says Sue McAlpine of the Kensington & Chelsea Community

History Group. 'They were linked by their motivation and the constituencies they were seeking to motivate.'

Laslett, born in the East End to Native American parents, was a community activist who had been a nurse and a social worker. She died in April this year, after suffering from multiple sclerosis for fifty years. Her motivation was 'to prove that from our ghetto there was a wealth of culture waiting to express itself, that we weren't rubbish people'. She borrowed costumes from Madame Tussaud's; a local hairdresser did the hair and make-up for nothing; the gas board and fire brigade had floats; and stallholders in Portobello market donated horses and carts. Around a thousand people turned up, according to police figures.

Steel band player Russ Henderson was among those roped in. Laslett's partner, Jim O'Brien, knew him from the Colherne pub in Earl's Court – a favoured West Indian hangout – and Henderson had played at the first event in St Pancras organised by Jones. At the Notting Hill event, he was playing alongside a donkey cart and a clown, and he felt things were getting flat. 'I said, "We got to do something to make this thing come alive."' So Henderson, now seventy-eight, decided to walk his steel band to the top of the street and back. When that went down well, he got a little bolder, marching them around the area like so many pied pipers. 'People would ask, "How far are you going?" And we'd say, "Just back to Acklam Road," and they would come a little way with their shopping, then peel off, and someone else would join in. There was no route, really – if you saw a bus coming, you just went another way.'

'With the music, people left everything and came to follow the procession,' O'Brien says. 'By the end of the evening, people were asking the way home.'

In the evening, Michael X – radical, hustler and firebrand – turned to Laslett, pointed to the throng and said, 'Look, Rhaune, what have you done?'

'I was in a state of shock,' Laslett said later. 'As I saw the huge crowds, I thought, "What have I done?"'

During the years Laslett ran the carnival, it was identified more with Notting Hill than with the Caribbean, though as word got round more and more Caribbean people started coming. The numbers had grown to around ten thousand, and O'Brien says a mixture of police interference and the growing assertiveness of Black power meant too many different groups had vested interests. 'It was something we didn't want to have responsibility for,' he adds. 'The police didn't want it because they thought they were losing control of the streets for the day, and we'd had enough. So we decided to hand it over to the community.'

Carnival, Trinidad-style, with no entry fee, is truly open to everyone. Blurring the lines between participant and spectator, it thrives on impulse as well as organisation. With its emphasis on masquerading and calypso, it takes popular subjects of concern as its raw material for lyrics and costumes. Massive in size, working class in composition, spontaneous in form, subversive in expression and political in nature – the ingredients for carnival are explosive. Add to the mix the legacy of slavery and it soon becomes clear why so long as there has been carnival, the authorities have sought to contain, control or cancel it.

In 1881, Trinidad's former police chief, L. M. Fraser, submitted a report on the carnival riot in Port of Spain. 'After the emancipation of the slaves, things were materially altered,' he wrote. 'The ancient lines of demarcation between classes were obliterated and, as a natural consequence, the carnival degenerated into a noisy and disorderly amusement for the lower classes.' He had a point. Trinidad was colonised at various times by both the Spanish and English, with a large number of French settlers, and after emancipation in 1834, its carnival lost its elitist, European traditions and became a mass popular event.

'Carnival had become a symbol of freedom for the broad mass of the population and not merely a season for frivolous enjoyment,' wrote Errol Hill in *The Trinidad Carnival*. 'It had a ritualistic significance, rooted in the experience of slavery and in the celebration of freedom from slavery. The people would not be intimidated; they would observe carnival in the manner they deemed most appropriate.'

Similar tensions have emerged here in the UK. The key dynamic within them is ownership. Ask anyone involved who owns carnival, and they will say the same thing: the people. The trouble is, which people? Since Rhaune Laslett handed over responsibility for the carnival, the primary body organising the event has split, reinvented itself, then split again several times. It has been called the Carnival Development Committee, the Carnival Arts Committee, the Carnival Enterprise Committee and, at present, the Notting Hill Carnival Trust, which is itself riven by internal rows. Each group has its own version of the carnival's history and development.

As carnival has outgrown its grass-roots origins, it has brought with it a constant process of negotiation and occasional flash points; there have been inevitable conflicts, over both its economic orientation and its political function. Carnival, wrote Kwesi Owusu and Jacob Ross in *Behind the Masquerade*, is 'the most expressive and culturally volatile territory on which the battle of positions between the black community and the state are ritualised'.

And so it was that less than a century after the disturbances at the carnival in Port of Spain, there were riots at the Notting Hill carnival in 1976. By that stage it had become a Caribbean event – the by-product of Jones's racial militancy and Laslett's community activism – complete with bands and costumes. In 1975, according to police figures, carnival was attracting 150,000 people. It was also the first time most remember an imposing police presence.

The carnival's primary constituency had changed radically. In the mid-1970s, 40 per cent of all Black people in Britain were born here. Having made the long march through the institutions of education, employment and the criminal justice system, many felt alienated in the land of their birth. It was an experience that found its daily expression in the form of the police, whose racist use of the sus laws made for harassment and indignity. In 1958, the first generation used carnival to protest against the racism of the mob, but in the 1970s their children used it to take on the Met. For them, carnival was not a cultural reminder of a distant, different home but a means of asserting their claim to the only home they knew.

It was a claim that, on the one hand, was increasingly under threat, thanks to the rise of the National Front and skinhead culture. But, on the other, it was constantly being asserted thanks to the powerful role music was playing in shaping British youth culture, through reggae, ska and initiatives like Rock Against Racism. Culture had become a key battleground for race, and there was no bigger racially connoted event than the Notting Hill carnival.

'Carnival was their day,' says one Metropolitan police officer in an off-the-record interview. 'For the rest of the year, police would be stopping them in ones and twos in the street, where they would be in a minority. But for one weekend they were in the majority, and they took over the streets.'

The 1976 riot took most people by surprise. 'I just remember seeing these bottles flying,' says Michael La Rose, head of the Association for a People's Carnival, which aims to protect and promote carnival's community roots; he describes it as like watching a relentless parade of salmon leaping upstream. The police were ill-equipped and ill-prepared. Defending themselves with dustbin lids and milk crates, they were also outmanoeuvred. 'That whole experience made the police very sore,' one policeman says. 'They had taken a beating and were determined that it would not happen again, so when the next one came about, there was some desire for revenge.'

From then on, thanks largely to the press, carnival moved from being a story about culture to one about crime and race. For years after, carnival stories would come with a picture of policemen either in hospital after being attacked or in an awkward embrace with a Black female reveller in full costume. The following year, Corinne Skinner-Carter missed carnival for the first and last time, in anticipation of more trouble. There were indeed smaller skirmishes in

1977. At one stage, late on the Monday night, riot police were briefly deployed. The next day, the *Express*'s front page read: 'War Cry! The unprecedented scenes in the darkness of London streets looked and sounded like something out of the film classic *Zulu*.'

Calls for carnival's banning came from all quarters. Tory shadow home secretary Willie Whitelaw said, 'The risk in holding it now seems to outweigh the enjoyment it gives.' Kensington and Chelsea council suggested holding 'the noisy events' in White City Stadium, a mile or more away. 'If the West Indians wish to preserve what should be a happy celebration which gives free rein to their natural exuberance, vitality and joy,' argued the *Mail* on 31 August 1977, 'then it is up to their leaders to take steps necessary to ensure its survival.' The *Telegraph* blamed Black people for being in Britain in the first place, declaring, 'Many observers warned from the outset that mass immigration from poor countries of substantially different culture would generate anomie, alienation, delinquency and worse.' Prince Charles, meanwhile, backed the carnival. 'It's so nice to see so many happy, dancing people with smiles on their faces.'

As recently as 1991, following a stabbing *Daily Mail* columnist Lynda Lee-Potter described the carnival as 'a sordid, sleazy nightmare that has become synonymous with death'. By this time, however, its detractors were in the minority. Like the Black British community from which it had sprung, there was a common understanding that it was here to stay. Latest police figures suggest an attendance of one million; organisers say it is almost double that.

In west London, not far from the carnival route, the Mighty Explorer launches the calypso tent. The first of many older Caribbean men, in pork-pie hats and matching waistcoats and trousers, who hope to become this year's calypso monarch, he sings his home-written lyrics with the help of a small band and some backing singers. Along with women in shiny sequined dresses, they fill a sweltering night with a medley of topical ballads. Almost all of them contain a strong moral message about the danger of drugs, infidelity and prostitution blighting the Black community, from people whose stage names include Totally Talibah, Celestial Star and Cleopatra Johnson.

This is the first of the heats running up to the carnival itself. The standard is higher than a karaoke bar, lower than the second round of *Popstars*. But the evening is more fun than both – accessible, unpretentious, raucous and, above all, entertaining.

Earlier that day, at the Oval House Theatre, south London, the sewing machines ceased humming in anticipation of curried goat and rum punch. It's time to lime (relax) after a day of stitching and cutting to calypso tunes and boisterous banter. South Connections is one of the scores of mas camps (where carnival costumes are put together) around London and beyond, where mostly volunteers come from mid-July to start making costumes for the bands. Some are housed in people's living rooms and back gardens, others in community halls and offices. With only a week to go before carnival, a camp like South Connections will be attracting around a hundred people a night – a rare focal point for relaxed intergenerational mixing. The youngest person to go masquerading with the camp's band is two, the oldest seventy-five.

The preparations started the year before. The riots in Bradford and Burnley provided the theme for this year's designs, entitled 'Massala Dougla: One People, One Race'. 'In this story, the people travel on this earth searching for a better future and an identity,' says Ray Mahabir, the designer. 'Red is for the blood flowing in us and gold is for our golden hearts.'

On the day of the Golden Jubilee celebrations, designer Clary Salandy had trouble getting to the Mall. At first, the police wouldn't let her and the rest of her mas camp over one of London's bridges, even though they were supposed to be leading the procession. Finally, the authorities relented. Chipping down the Mall – that slow shuffle-cum-toyi-toyi of the masquerader – filled Salandy with pride. 'I'm not a monarchist, but this was a recognition by the establishment that we have made an artistic contribution and took carnival to people who would never go to it.'

In the Harlesden offices of her company, Mahogany, in north-west London, Salandy explains her craft. 'The best costumes', she says, 'have to work well from a distance. So they have to be bold and dynamic and have lots of movement. But when you get close up, you have to be able to see the detail. Carnival is a language. Every shape, colour and form is used like words or symbols. And the best costume speaks that language fluently.'

Her favourite costume that day spoke the language of defiance: one person armed with several huge, multicoloured shields defending his back. 'It's called Protector of Our Heritage,' she says. 'It was there to defend carnival.'

Racism rebooted

Attempts to bring one man to justice for a racist murder in Mississippi threatens to overshadow the racial injustice that remains.
The Nation, 23 June 2005, Philadelphia/Mississippi

For Buford Posey, a white man raised in Philadelphia, Mississippi, the Second World War had a civilising influence. 'When I was coming up in Mississippi I never knew it was against the law to kill a Black man,' he says. 'I learned that when I went in the Army. I was seventeen years old. When they told me, I thought they were joking.'

For several decades Posey's assumption about the relative value of Black life was effectively borne out by the state's judiciary. Among others, the murders of fourteen-year-old Chicagoan Emmett Till, in Money in 1955; the state's NAACP chairman Medgar Evers, in Jackson in 1963; the three young civil rights workers – James Chaney (twenty-one), Andrew Goodman (twenty) and Michael Schwerner (twenty-four) – in Philadelphia in 1964; and civil rights supporter Vernon Dahmer, in Hattiesburg in 1966, all went unpunished.

But recently history has been catching up with the Magnolia State. Over the past decade state authorities have been picking up ageing white men one by one and parading them down history's perp walk of shame, complete with orange jumpsuits and handcuffs.

Mississippi is by no means alone in this. Since 1989, twenty-three murders have been re-examined in the South, resulting in twenty-seven arrests, twenty-two convictions, two acquittals and one mistrial, according to Mark Potok of the Intelligence Project, a branch of the Southern Poverty Law Center, based in Montgomery, Alabama. But given that Mississippi was home to some of the most notorious race crimes during segregation, it stands to reason that it would be home to many of the most high-profile cases. In 1990, sixty-nine-year-old Byron de la Beckwith was indicted for the murder of Evers, who was shot dead on his doorstep; four years later, Beckwith was convicted. In 1997, the case of Dahmer, who died when his house was firebombed by the Klan, was reopened. In 1998, the Klan's Imperial Wizard, Sam Bowers, was convicted of the murder. And earlier this year Edgar Ray Killen was formally charged with the murders of Chaney, Goodman and Schwerner. His trial ended on 21 June with a jury verdict of manslaughter.

These developments should, of course, be welcomed. Beyond the importance of the prosecutions to the families of those who died and the communities in which the murders took place, they have a broader symbolic significance. They show that the struggle for justice, while long and arduous, can bear fruit in the most barren soil. They also show that these men, along with the scores of others who perished in the same cause, did not die in vain.

But while symbols are important, they should not be mistaken for substance. In June, the Senate issued an apology for its failure to enact an anti-lynching law. Its chief GOP sponsor was Virginia senator George Allen, who referred to the legislative inaction as a 'stain on the history of the United States Senate'. Allen, who used to display a Confederate flag at his home and a noose in his law office, scored an 'F' on the NAACP's report card in the last session of Congress. Both Mississippi senators, Thad Cochran and Trent Lott, refused to co-sponsor the resolution.

So while the crimes that occurred during segregation were rarely systematic – the individuals who carried them out and the manner in which they carried them out were far too crude for that – they were systemic. They were born from a system of segregation that worked to preserve white privilege in the face of a concerted progressive onslaught – a system in which the white community had to collude in order for it to function. While the scale and nature of those privileges may have changed, the privileges themselves still exist. You can see them in the racial disparities in health, employment and poverty;

you can watch their physical incarnation in the segregated academies to which so many whites send their children; and you can observe them on death row, where so many Black parents see their children being sent.

The work that Chaney, Goodman and Schwerner aimed to do – break the hold of white supremacy – has yet to be completed. Those who hope it never will be would like to use these trials to draw a line under the past and move on, shifting the burden of racist history from the institutional to the individual and travelling light, without the baggage of its legacy. So long as the likes of Killen and Beckwith are held up as the poster boys of that time and place, the mission to rebrand the South as the region that conquered not just racism but history will succeed – distorting our understanding of both what happened then and also what is happening now.

Schwerner's widow, Rita Schwerner Bender, hailed the verdict as 'a day of great importance to all of us'. But, she added, 'Preacher Killen didn't act in a vacuum. The state of Mississippi was complicit in these crimes and all the crimes that occurred, and that has to be opened up.'

This in no way diminishes the importance of ensuring that those responsible for these crimes are brought to justice, argues Carolyn Goodman, the eighty-nine-year-old mother of Andrew. '[Killen] is a symbol. This is not just about one man. It's a symbol of what this country stands for. Whether it is a country of laws or something else, Bush or no Bush.'

But the notion that these crimes had broad approval at almost every level of white Southern society does suggest that there is more to racism in the South than these murders and more to these murders than these trials. 'The question is, what do these symbols mean?' says Charles Payne, the Sally Dalton Professor of History, African American Studies and Sociology at Duke University. The trials are convenient for those who wish to claim that racism was practised only by the poor and ended with segregation, says Payne. 'Some people will say this is the face of racism. So racism becomes a historically congealed phenomenon. It is understood as just being the expression of hateful, poor white people who live in the South.'

The details of what took place on 21 June 1964 have long been known. Some in Philadelphia believe Killen's actions that night have been, too. The three young men, who had joined the Mississippi Freedom Summer, a civil rights initiative to register Black voters in the state, went missing after they had gone to investigate the burning of a Black church nearby. That afternoon deputy sheriff Cecil Price stopped their car near Philadelphia and took them in, ostensibly on a speeding violation. Price, who has since died, used the time while the activists were in custody to alert local Klan members. When they were released later that night, the posse of Klansmen, said to have been organised by Killen, followed them, murdered them and buried them in a nearby earthen dam.

That night, says Posey, who had got to know Schwerner and publicly supported the activists, he got a phone call: 'They said, "We took care of three of your friends tonight. You're next," and hung up. Well, I thought it was Edgar Ray Killen, but you can't see over a telephone.' He left town shortly afterwards. 'Hell, the Klan was boasting about it,' he recalls. 'If you didn't know who committed the murders, you were either blind or hard of hearing.'

In 1967, eighteen men were prosecuted in federal court on conspiracy charges relating to the case; seven were convicted but none served longer than six years. Among those who walked free without a day behind bars was Killen, the beneficiary of a hung jury, thanks to one juror who could not bring herself to convict a preacher.

Since most of this was known or suspected at the time of the murders, there has been no particular legal breakthrough that prompted investigators to revisit the case. 'It wasn't like there was any one thing that happened that said, "Here's the magic bullet,"' Neshoba County district attorney Mark Duncan told the *Arkansas Democrat-Gazette* in January, shortly after Killen was arrested. 'It really was that we had gotten to the end. There was nothing left to do.' Family members and civil rights activists were prompted to step up the pressure after Dahmer's murderer, Bowers, said in an interview with a state archivist in 1999 that 'the main instigator' of the Philadelphia killings had walked free from the courtroom. Those familiar with the case say that at least seven others who were involved in the murders are still alive but not standing trial.

Philadelphia is a small town of 7,300 that is just over half white, just under half Black and the rest Choctaw Indian. It sits ninety-eight miles north-east of Jackson and sixty north-west of Meridian, but is actually on the road to nowhere. Ronald Reagan chose the town for his first major campaign speech in the 1980 presidential campaign, appealing to racist Confederate nostalgia with a call for states' rights. Philadelphia's grim racial history put it on the map. But the faded shop fronts and low income levels (one in four families lives in poverty) suggest its grim economic present could just as soon wipe it off again.

Discussing the situation in the days before the trial began, a few people, like Barney Shephard, spoke up for Killen and said that the Mississippi Freedom Summer was a federally backed incursion masterminded by President John F. Kennedy. 'The guy has been a good neighbour to me,' he said of Killen. 'He's eighty years old. And now to bring this up, after forty years, is beyond me.' Few were as candid or as conspiratorial as Shephard. The rest of the town seemed to have settled on the notion that justice should be done. But they differed, crucially, on what justice actually means and what it could achieve. And like much else in the town, from where you live to where you worship, these differences fall almost exclusively along racial lines.

Over at Peggy's, a soul food restaurant-cum-living room just off the town's main square, you sit where you can, serve yourself when you're ready and leave your money in a basket on your way out. Here the trial had gone from being a decades-long taboo to a frequent subject of debate. 'For twenty or thirty years nobody really talked about it, and then boom,' said Anne, twenty-four, a white waitress at Peggy's. 'Now everybody talks about it.' Anne grew up in Union, just fifteen miles away, but says she knew nothing about the murders until eight or nine months ago, when she saw the film *Mississippi Burning*, which is loosely based on the failed investigation into the murders. 'It just about tore my heart out. If he did it, he deserves to be punished, that's only right . . . But I don't think they should have brought it back up. It is going to cause more problems in town. A lot has changed since then. You didn't see Blacks and whites mingle then. You do now. This is a new generation. This could cause more problems.'

Hope Jones, a twenty-five-year-old African American teacher at the local school, is part of the same generation but could not disagree more. 'We just want to see justice done,' she said. 'If he's innocent, fine, but we want whoever did it. This could turn ugly . . . It could be a racial thing, but it's not. White people should want justice done also.'

Along with the few local whites like Posey who have long campaigned for prosecutions in the case, several others have come around in recent years. Sitting under a huge picture of Ronald and Nancy Reagan's visit to the Neshoba County Fair in the 1980s, Jim Prince, editor of the *Neshoba Democrat*, explained that he used to be against reopening the case but gradually came to see that the town could not move on without some resolution. Philadelphia would benefit, he said, because the trial would be the 'outcome of doing the right thing. There would be some vindication, some redemption, some soul-cleansing. It will be the atonement, really, for this old sin. We have only got the legal system to go by. That's all we've got.' And if there cannot be redemption, then Prince hopes there can at least be remuneration. 'It's a captivating story,' he says. 'The dark of night, the Ku Klux Klan, you know, it's got all the elements for great drama, but it's a true story and it's a sad story . . . I tell people if they can't be behind the call for justice because it's the right thing to do – and that's first and foremost – then they need to do it 'cause it's good for business.'

For some in town, making money may be the first and only reason. At the Philadelphia Chamber of Commerce you can find a glossy pamphlet titled 'Neshoba County, African-American Heritage Driving Tour: Roots of Struggle, Rewards of Sacrifice'. Inside you are invited to join 'a journey toward freedom', complete with a map detailing where the three young men were murdered and buried. Such civil rights tourism would be a difficult sell as long as the perpetrators were still on the streets and everybody knew who they were. So Killen's trial was part of the town's business plan – a bid to capitalise on its ugly past in order to make money, at least in part, by showing how it has improved.

The desire of many Southerners for a makeover is understandable, as is their irritation at the North's continued attempts to caricature them. The smug and superior manner in which the rest of the country has embalmed the region in the 1960s, so as to better patronise it, has echoes of Europeans on an anti-American binge. Like the Europeans, Northerners have a point – but without sufficient humility and self-awareness of their own shortcomings, that point can soon implode under the weight of its own arrogance. According to a census report from 2002, the top five residentially segregated metropolitan areas in the US are Milwaukee, Detroit, Cleveland, St Louis and Newark. According to the Kaiser Family Foundation, you will find higher rates of Black poverty in Wisconsin, Illinois and West Virginia than in Mississippi. And of the senators who refused to co-sponsor the anti-lynch-law apology, more than half were not from the South.

Mississippi shares the South's desire for change, and indeed has changed considerably. Two huge casinos run by Choctaw Indians are now among the largest employers in the Philadelphia area. You can see Black and white youngsters interacting casually at school, and a few Black people have moved into white areas. But these changes have come about not because most white Southerners wanted them to but because many Black people and a handful of whites forced them to. 'I'm happy to see everybody joining forces to make sure that we get this done now,' says Eva Tisdale, fifty-five, a native Mississippian who came to Philadelphia to participate in the Freedom Summer and stayed. Tisdale believes it is the business case, not the moral one, that has won over many of the whites who now back the resolution of the legal case. 'We organised marches and we marched, and there were no white people marching – not from Philadelphia. So I know the reason we came together is not the same reason for all of us.'

For if a lot has changed in Mississippi, an awful lot has also stayed the same. In a state where African Americans constitute 36 per cent of the population, they make up about 75 per cent of prisoners. In a state that is already poor, Black people are poorer still: according to the latest census, Mississippi has the fifth-lowest median income in the US; the per capita income of Black Mississippians is 51 per cent that of their white counterparts. If there are tougher places to be Black than Mississippi, it is because those places are so bad, not because Mississippi is so good. The problem is not that some whites are trying to rebrand the South but that they are now peddling false goods. 'There's a kind of civic religion in asserting that the past is the past and we should put all these problems behind us,' says Payne. 'Some people are using the progress that has been made to wipe out any sense of the past, as though they have conquered the past. The extent to which these convictions can get people to think critically about how privilege is shaped is the extent to which they strike me as being real and useful.' Some would rather not acknowledge that racial privilege exists at all. 'Race is not an issue now for younger people,' says Prince. 'Today, if you're willing to work hard and be honest, then you're able to succeed. There is equal opportunity in Philadelphia.

If Prince is right, then the poverty, low levels of educational achievement, unemployment and high prison rates among Blacks not just in Philadelphia but elsewhere in the state and the country can be explained only by Black people's genetic inability or inherent unwillingness to seize those opportunities. And so it is that even as these trials seek to cure one symptom, the racist infection mutates into an even more hardy strain. Killen may end up behind bars, but the logic and the system that produced him and made him infamous still remain free.

Journey of generations that passed in a moment

The night Barack Obama won the presidency, I joined revellers on Chicago's South Side.

Guardian, 6 November 2008, Chicago

There are times when the usually glacial pace of social progress accelerates to such a degree that you feel you are experiencing it in real time. Stand in the present and history comes rushing towards you, making you feel light-headed.

The second that Ohio fell to Barack Obama on Tuesday evening, effectively handing him the keys to the White House, was one of those dizzying moments. A man born three years before African Americans secured their right to vote had risen by popular acclaim to the highest office in the land before he reached fifty. A political journey that should take generations felt as though it had occurred in a moment.

At the President's Lounge, a bar in Chicago's Black South Side, the soundtrack to that moment gave voice to decades of thwarted dreams. First they crooned soulfully to Sam Cooke's 'Change Is Gonna Come', and then they bellowed boisterously to McFadden and Whitehead's 'Ain't No Stoppin' Us Now'.

Outside car horns beeped and Chicago police shouted Obama's name at passers-by through loudspeakers. They were cheering for their native son, but the festivities were not bound by geography or race. Tens of thousands across the country took to the streets to celebrate. In Harlem, subway trains erupted into spontaneous applause. In Detroit, the home of Motown, they danced in the street.

Like Joe Louis's defeat of Max Schmeling back in the 1930s, this was Black America's gift to a grateful, if not always gracious, nation. 'It was vindication,' said Maya Angelou of Louis's win. 'Some black mother's son, some black father's son, was the strongest man in the world.'

Dispatches from the Diaspora

Now Obama is the most powerful man in the world. Only he is the son of some white Kansan mother and some Black Kenyan father – a biracial man with a Muslim name in a country at war in the Gulf. No matter how long one pores over the electoral map, his victory still seems unlikely, if not implausible. But the very things Republicans hoped would alienate him from the average American apparently made him appealing to some.

As the campaign gathered pace, it seemed as though there was a little bit of Obama for everyone: the immigrant, the Midwesterner, the Hawaiian, the Black, the white single mother, the Christian faith, the foreign schooling, the Ivy League education and the middle-class upbringing. In a period when many Americans were concerned with their insularity, racial tension, social mobility and regional divisions, he embodied a crude form of resolution.

According to exit polls, most of those who said race was a factor in how they voted backed Obama. But if race provides the historic marker for Tuesday's result, it does little to explain its future meaning. This election was not about a change of colour but a change of direction. Of the three-quarters of the country who disapprove of President George Bush's performance, 67 per cent went for Obama. As such, his victory represents an emphatic repudiation of the Bush legacy. In a fundamental realignment of American politics and discourse, he reintroduced the notions of equality, justice, inclusivity and diplomacy to the national conversation, at a time when many feared their extinction. To that extent, there were always two constituencies for this election.

The first was strictly local. On Tuesday night, America slayed its demons of the past eight years. Geographically, demographically, racially and politically, Obama gained the presidency with the broadest of coalitions and with the narrowest of agendas – change. In so doing he has transformed the nation's electoral landscape with wins in Congress as well as the Mountain West, the upper South and traditional Democratic strongholds. In order to achieve this he has reinvigorated the liberal and progressive base, mobilising millions of people to donate money and time. Having invested so heavily in him, they now feel ownership in his victory. They were driven by a long-held and urgent desire to reclaim their country from the clutches of organised religion and big business. After so many disappointments, the results on Tuesday drove many to tears.

The second constituency was global. The world was watching. And they liked what they saw. Obama has emerged as America's more considered, less cavalier response to the post-9/11 world. Engaged where Bush was antagonistic, nuanced where Bush was brash, he regards international dialogue and co-operation as potential strengths rather than weaknesses and is one of the few members of America's political class who do not bear the stain of the Iraq invasion. Yesterday morning, for the first time in a long time, liberal Americans smiled, and the world smiled with them.

While the fact of this transformation, from both below and above, cannot be denied, the scale and scope of it can be overstated. While Obama has pledged to withdraw troops from Iraq, he also seeks to escalate the war in Afghanistan. For all the talk of unity, two of the states that backed Obama – Florida and California – also elected to ban gay marriage. For all his financial and organisational advantage and the perils of the economic crisis, he still won only 52 per cent of the vote against McCain's 47 per cent – the most decisive Democratic win in more than thirty years, but nonetheless evidence that deep-seated division still lingers. Obama's room for manoeuvre, at home and abroad, is severely hampered by the economic chaos bequeathed by his predecessor.

These details are important. Yet they belong to the future. And Tuesday night belongs to history. The day when fear was defeated even in the privacy of the polling booths. The night when progress looked like a Black family taking a stroll on to the world stage and into the corridors of power. The moment when the patrons of the President's Lounge raised a glass and sang a song to history as it raced to greet them and made us all giddy.

Ferguson's Black community must not be given the same justice as Trayvon Martin

Watching the Black Lives Matter movement take off from a St Louis suburb.

Guardian, 22 August 2014, Ferguson, Missouri

Just outside a mall in Ferguson, Missouri, shortly after ten o'clock on Wednesday, a Black man in his thirties was stopped and frisked by around eight white policemen. As he gingerly emptied his pockets, careful not to move too quickly, he yelled at them. It was a soliloquy of pure rage; a fluent, apparently unstoppable oration against not just the men who had apprehended him but the system they represented.

'Yes, I'm angry,' he shouted. 'Four hundred years we been here. We built this place for free and y'all still hate us.' A man filming the incident was told to move on but did not budge. When the police let the pedestrian go (whatever they were looking for he didn't have), the man recording went too. 'I've done my job,' he said.

'All books about all revolutions begin with a chapter that describes the decay of tottering authority or the misery and sufferings of people,' wrote Polish journalist Ryszard Kapuściński in *Shah of Shahs*. 'They should begin with a psychological chapter, one that shows how a harassed, terrified man breaks his terror and stops being afraid. This unusual process demands illuminating. Man gets rid of fear and feels free.'

For the past fortnight, the Black population of this St Louis suburb has been shedding its fear. Since Michael Brown, an eighteen-year-old Black man, was shot six times while raising his hands in a surrender position, they have asserted their humanity in ways big and small, beautiful and ugly. Every night they marched up the main drag in the Black part of town, past militarised encampments of heavily armed police, chanting, 'Hey, hey, ho, ho, killer cops have got to go.' Every day around town impromptu gatherings of anything from four to a dozen people would spring up in the street, like mini town hall meetings, to debate the source of the problem in both Ferguson and the country at large. 'Don't shoot, I'm with a white guy,' one said as he walked towards some policemen with his friend.

For anyone sceptical about what the past two weeks have achieved, it was this. When hundreds of Black protesters faced off against lines of white police armed as though for military combat, they brought the inequalities and inequities in the town into sharp focus and gave themselves the courage to both challenge and expose them.

'That the poor are invisible is one of the most important things about them,' wrote Michael Harrington in his landmark book, *The Other America*. 'They are not simply neglected and forgotten as in the old rhetoric of reform; what is much worse, they are not seen.' Not only do Black people in Ferguson now see themselves differently, the town's white establishment is seeing them for the first time.

While no one could reasonably claim Black people here had previously been living in tyranny – they had the vote, but precious few used it to shape local matters – they had clearly not been ruled by consent either. In this majority Black town, they considered the overwhelmingly white police force hostile and the local government indifferent. With the world's media present, one policeman from a nearby county pointed his semi-automatic gun at a protester and told him, 'I will fucking kill you.' When asked his name, he said, 'Go fuck yourself.' Another struck an eight-year-old with a tear-gas canister. It got so bad that the local police were replaced by the state's highway patrol. If that's how officers behave when they know they're under scrutiny, imagine what they're like when they think no one is watching.

The most remarkable thing about Michael Brown is not that he was killed by the authorities in broad daylight. That, sadly, is not an unusual occurrence in America. Since his death, at least three Black men have been killed by the police. The most recent case was less than ten minutes away, in St Louis itself. Kajieme Powell, a mentally ill man armed with a knife who was standing twenty feet away from police, was shot – a response that bore more resemblance to the work of a death squad than that of a police force.

No, what marks Brown out is that we are still calling his name; that beyond his immediate community there is interest in the circumstances of his death; that the federal government has intervened. Those in the media who slammed the occasionally violent protests must at least concede that were it not for the disturbances, they would never have paid attention. Brown would be one more dead Black kid, and Darren Wilson, the policeman who shot him, would be back on the beat instead of on paid leave.

What the next chapter will bring is not clear. The protests are winding down; the national guard is being withdrawn; the media are leaving. Only the courts can ascertain Wilson's guilt or innocence. But the judicial system that let George Zimmerman, the killer of Trayvon Martin, walk free inspires little confidence in many. The Black community in Ferguson may now be visible, but the justice it seeks may prove more elusive.

'He was here for us all those years; now we are here for him'

Nelson Mandela's memorial service in Johannesburg was a celebration of his life. Not even the rain could dampen spirits.

Guardian, 10 December 2013, Johannesburg

Sipho brought a hamper; Thule took toilet paper and an iPad; Nicky, who had read the weather forecast, carried just an umbrella. Those determined to get a seat in the World Cup stadium for Tuesday's memorial service for Nelson Mandela in Soweto knew it would be a long day, but few could have guessed how wet.

Assuming chaos and a capacity crowd, many arrived early. The service started at 11 a.m., but organisers said they would open the gates at 6 a.m. The first free train laid on for the occasion from Johannesburg town centre left for Soweto shortly after 5 a.m. and was packed. It emerged into the sunrise and the suburbs with its passengers chanting freedom songs and trading jokes.

The day turned out not to be too chaotic at all; there were glitches at almost every point but never major ones. The station guards kept changing their minds about which platform the trains would go from, sending people scuttling up and down stairs or off the platform and across the tracks; the stadium didn't let people in until around 6.30 a.m., leaving them standing in the drizzle; it took about an hour to get a hot dog; and the women's toilets appeared to run out of toilet paper at one point. But these were minor inconveniences and nobody was too put out.

'Relax,' Thule told her friend, who was looking at her watch as she stood in line outside the stadium. 'He was here for us all those years; now we are here for him. We'll get in.'

It wasn't a capacity crowd either. Whether it was the weather – the drizzle soon turned into a downpour – or the threat of chaos that had scared some away was not clear. Because of the large number of foreign leaders arriving the police had shut off the roads nearby, making transport to the event tricky. But there were still several thousand people – certainly enough to ensure a buoyant atmosphere.

The demographics of the crowd were noteworthy. There were relatively few white people – who comprise one in seven in Johannesburg but couldn't have numbered more than one in thirty in the crowd – raising a question mark over the week's platitude that Mandela's death had brought the country together. But it was very multigenerational, with a large number of young people in attendance. 'Of course we know him,' said Sipho Matlane, twenty-six. 'He's always been there. He's like our father and our grandfather. We grew up with him, and the chances I have now I have because of him.'

From that first train until the first speech the chanting never stopped. Thousands, singing as one, in praise of the ANC's military wing, Umkhonto we Sizwe (Spear of the Nation), Mandela, who founded it, and former ANC leader Oliver Tambo, as well as other staples from the struggle for liberation. Pretty much everybody had something – a hat, coat, umbrella, shawl or flag – that bore the colours of the ANC or the likeness of Nelson Mandela, or both. So as they danced, shuffled and swayed the stadium was carried away on waves of black, green and yellow. At times the crowd stomped so hard you could feel the arena shake.

The rain didn't dampen spirits. The mood remained not just boisterous but generous, and people kept themselves warm by dancing. Almost every dignitary whose face popped up on the huge screen, from the United Nations general secretary, Ban Ki-moon, to the last apartheid leader, F. W. de Klerk, got a cheer. Of course some – Raúl Castro, Winnie Mandela, Robert Mugabe, to name a few – got ovations. But even the mention of the prime minister of Trinidad and Tobago got applause where I was sitting. The sole, notable exception was the sight of the current South African president, Jacob Zuma, who was roundly booed, with some rolling their fists over each other as though they were at a 1970s disco – a sign symbolising 'We want change'.

In this the crowd seemed to surprise itself. The booing started off tentatively and dispersed. But once it started others became emboldened, until by the third time he appeared it was reflexive and widespread. But all in all it was about as jovial and high-spirited as a memorial possibly could be, until the actual memorial started. It wasn't just Barack Obama, David Cameron and the Danish prime minister, Helle Thorning-Schmidt, taking selfies; most people were. Indeed, the degree to which grief has effortlessly morphed into jubilation has been one of the hallmarks of the past week.

It's not difficult to see why. A man who made it his life's work to lead a struggle against a brutal racist regime and was imprisoned for his trouble died, peacefully, in his bed, aged ninety-five, as the world's favourite politician. Given the fate of most anti-racist icons, in both South Africa and elsewhere, that is something to celebrate.

But when officialdom took over, much of the energy seeped from the crowd as they sat through several testimonies, from religious leaders, former comrades and select heads of state, about how great and unifying a leader Mandela had been. There was nothing to argue with in any of them. In a sense, that was the problem. Nobody needed convincing of Mandela's moral significance. That's why they were there.

'The speeches are boring,' said Sweet Coke Malema. 'Everybody knows who Mandela is. We know about his life. The whole world knows him. The whole world loves him. It was better when we were singing and dancing.'

One speaker, however, was singled out for a particularly warm reception: the US president, Barack Obama. While paying tribute to Mandela, Obama spoke fluently and compellingly about the modern relevance of the late leader's life, in a manner that kept the crowd gripped. Said Malema with a smile, 'His speech is also too long, but I like it when he speaks, so I don't mind.'

2

THINGS
FALL
APART

For all the progress that has been made,
at times it feels as if we are standing still –
or, even worse, going backwards

Life after Mandela

Seven years after the end of apartheid, the South African government is dogged by factionalism, a failure to deliver substantial change and bizarre allegations of a plot against the president.

Guardian, 15 May 2001, Johannesburg

The route to Black empowerment runs via Empire Road and Jan Smuts Avenue. In the wealthy white suburb of Sandton, a conference, 'Empowerment 2001', is charting the advancement of Black entrepreneurs through South Africa's white corporate sector. The destination implies political progress in the future, but the directions denote the crippling legacy of the past. At times here it feels as though everything and nothing has changed.

In Sandton, the nibbles are impressive, but the news is bleak. 'Empowerment in the corporate sector has reached a new low,' says the author of a report for the conference. 'Deal flow is down, market performance of Black-controlled companies is in crisis and global and economic prospects offer little relief.'

Sakumzi Macozoma wins Black empowerment businessman of the year. His job title, deputy chairman of Standard Bank's investment division, is the latest in a series of reinventions. Born to a Black working-class family in Port Elizabeth, he has been a student activist, a prisoner on Robben Island, an ANC official, an MP and now, at only forty-four, a successful businessman. The man who marched at the head of the student movement now glides along marble floors in the bank's plush downtown offices.

'We are a new elite, and that is an inevitable consequence of transformation,' he says. Macozoma fully understands the contradictions of sitting on the other side of the table from his former allies who remained in the trade union movement. 'It is quite a challenge because people relate to you very differently, although there are a number of us in the same position. We are living in what they call one of the "privileged moments of history",' he says, sounding like a dot. com millionaire before the bust. 'I am a beneficiary of that.'

Such is the power of any transition. The pace of change is such that individuals cease to live in real time. Human journeys that under normal circumstances take decades, if not generations, are completed in a few years, if not months. So the prisoner becomes president; law breakers become law makers; armed guerrillas become arms dealers. The person who slept on your floor only ten years ago, after a wild party, is now a government minister with an entourage.

'It is interesting to see who still carries their own briefcase,' says one former ANC activist. 'These are people I've known for years when we were in the field. Some of them are still great, but some of them have become very pompous. When you have a car and a driver and you're travelling first class, some people change.'

South Africa has been in perpetual motion for more than a decade now. Seven years ago, shortly before the first democratic elections, I celebrated my twenty-fifth birthday in the garden of the *Guardian*'s correspondent in Johannesburg, playing chess and discussing Arsenal's fortunes with Ronnie Kasrils, the former head of the ANC's military wing, Umkhonto we Sizwe. When I returned in 1999 for the second elections, almost every South African I had met five years previously had changed jobs at least once, and most had moved house, too. The day I arrived, Kasrils was there again, watching Arsenal in the FA Cup final. This time I was sharing a beer with the deputy defence minister.

It is easy, and for some convenient, to forget how far and how fast South Africa has travelled in recent times. In 1994, it stood not only on the brink of democracy but also on the verge of chaos. Throughout the province of KwaZulu/Natal political violence raged between the ANC and Mangosuthu Buthelezi's Inkatha Freedom Party. A gun battle between the two parties had left a trail of dead bodies on the streets of central Johannesburg, where, shortly afterwards, disgruntled Afrikaners set off car bombs.

So to return seven years, two general elections and a change of leader later to a row about an alleged plot to discredit the president feels like progress. Those desperate to claim there is no difference between the new South Africa and the old forget two things: the first time F. W. de Klerk went to the polls before the entire country he was defeated heavily; the first time Thabo Mbeki presented himself to the people he increased the ANC majority. And if the people don't like him in 2004, they can get him out. These are the two principal achievements of the ANC – democracy and stability.

Mandela was released just a year before the anti-Gorbachev coup, which signalled the end of the Soviet Union. Yet, unlike Russia, there is no organised political gangsterism, Mafia-inspired contract killings or civil war. There are no state-sponsored death squads, imprisoned politicians or the banning of parties, as there were under apartheid. Both Aids and crime are rampant, as they were to a lesser extent under apartheid, and the government's response to the former has been problematic and to the latter largely ineffective.

But the social meltdown, mass exodus or civil war, on the scale that was predicted, is nowhere in sight. 'I was reading about Berlusconi the other day,' says one ANC veteran. 'It said he had been under investigation for money laundering, complicity in murder, connections with the Mafia, bribing politicians and judges, and all of that. I thought, "God – our president's done some stupid things, and this plot thing is crazy, but imagine what the world would be saying about us if we had someone like that as our leader."'

The alleged plot is more than crazy; it is a mixture of the banal and the bizarre. The security minister, Steve Tshwete, claimed on national television that Black business leaders were raising funds to support candidates within the ANC who would challenge South Africa's President Mbeki and were influencing the media to show him in a bad light. He then went on to name the plotters as Cyril

Ramaphosa, the former ANC secretary general who had negotiated the transition to democracy for the party; Tokyo Sexwale, the former premier of Gauteng; and Mathews Phosa, the former head of Mpumalanga province. The three men, claimed Tshwete, were trying to implicate Mbeki in the murder of the late Chris Hani, a popular and sorely missed ANC leader who was gunned down outside his home in 1993.

Banal because were it true (the murder aside), it would be no more serious than the kind of story that emanates from most political parties. Bizarre because the fact that it is evidently untrue – the source of the allegations is a man under investigation for seventy-seven counts of fraud and embezzlement – casts serious doubts on the judgement of the ANC leadership, including Mbeki, for airing them in the first place. But, for all that, it is important.

The link between governance and competence is often racially connoted. It does not have to be. Ask any commuter or farmer in Britain, and they will point to several examples of incompetent white people. Similarly, talk to a Nigerian who lived under the dictatorship of Sani Abacha, or a Black resident of Washington DC, where the former mayor, Marion Barry, was filmed smoking crack with a prostitute, and you will hear Black people tell you that Black leaders can mismanage affairs, too.

But in countries where Black people were once kept away from the levers of democracy on the grounds that they were intellectually incapable of operating them intelligently, charges of incompetence made by whites have a specific currency. That does not mean that they should not be made or that they may not be valid. One look at recent events in neighbouring Zambia and Zimbabwe indicate that there is a lot to criticise. But those who make such charges should not be surprised if they are met with the accusation that their criticism is informed by racism.

Since he came to power, racism has been Mbeki's retort to almost every attack on his government. When Max du Preez, the editor of an Afrikaner-language anti-apartheid weekly, *Vrije Weekblad*, accused Mbeki of being a womaniser, the ANC's spokesman accused him of 'irresponsible and undermining' behaviour that 'bordered on hate speech'. Often Mbeki's responses are coded. If he lambasts 'enemies of transformation' or those intent on 'subverting the new democracy', he is talking about whites. Mbeki is by no means alone in this. An advert in this weekend's *Sunday Times*, paid for by prominent Black professionals, accused the media of launching an 'apartheid-style disinformation campaign [comprising] rightwing forces made up of white so-called liberals'.

A similar mood is growing in the townships. When I stayed in Alexandra township in 1994, I remember desperately trying to tease out of Black people what they thought of whites, only to be met with blank expressions. It took me a little while to work out that while they were keen to get rid of apartheid, they didn't think about whites at all. They were too busy worrying about feeding their families and keeping their homes. Today, the townships provide fertile ground for the ANC's claims that white interests are behind the criticisms of the president. 'They want to stay on top,' says Elizabeth. 'We don't want to bring them down or make them suffer. But they must share some of the pain.'

It's not hard to see her point. For most white South Africans the new South Africa looks very much like the old one. They have kept their maids, houses and cooks while they travel freely all over the world and watch their national teams compete in international competitions. The price they pay for this is that they have to live in a democracy. But for many even this is too much. They look on 1994 not as the first year of democracy after centuries of oppression but as year zero, after which all slates are wiped clean and all debts cleared. As though the sun had risen at dawn over the rainbow parliament in Cape Town, without ever having set the previous day on the Voortrekker monument. After years of state-sponsored white supremacy, they have belatedly discovered the principle that jobs should be awarded on merit and are bitterly upset by affirmative action and Black empowerment.

Like Blacks, they are upset and scared by the high levels of crime. But unlike Blacks, they have seen a sharp increase, because previously much of it was contained in the townships. Their reaction has been to fortify their homes with higher walls and more powerful electric fences. Over the past ten years, spending on private security has increased twelve-fold to 12 billion rand (£1.1 billion) – more than three times the 1999/2000 housing budget. They have far more than Blacks and they complain far more, too. A private memo, sent by the chief executive of Standard Bank, told senior staff: 'With the current emphasis on transformation I am concerned that the specific views of white male managers are not being taken into account.' White men make up 54 per cent of the management at the bank; they are 7 per cent of the population.

At times it has indeed seemed as though some people would like the new South Africa to fail, since it would fulfil their deep-seated belief that the move to democracy was a bad idea. Given Mandela's iconic status on the international scene, this was a difficult argument to pursue when he was at the helm – as if emerging from twenty-seven years in prison without bitterness was the sole human quality white South Africans could accept for a Black president. So they concentrated on his successor. In 1999, broadcaster Lester Venter published a book, *When Mandela Goes*, which predicted widespread chaos and violence ahead. Meanwhile, emigration consultants did a roaring trade in fear as they set out to facilitate the passage of those who wanted to leave the country at a price. At a meeting for would-be emigrants in 1999, I saw one such consultant hold up Venter's book and tell the hundred-strong audience, 'People, this book is a wake-up call. The bad news is the paw-paw's really going to hit the fan. The good news is the fan won't be working.'

The problem with Mbeki's criticism of whites is not that racism is not a problem – it clearly is – but that his use of it is so blatantly cynical and opportunistic that it debases him far more than it does those whom he accuses.

'It's awful now,' says one long-standing white ANC activist. 'Any time you try to criticise the party or the leadership you are told you're just representing the interests of the whites. If Black people do it, then they're lackeys of the whites. Mandela was too lenient on the whites. He tried to brush everything under the carpet and say everything will be all right and really let them off the hook. Now Thabo's gone to the other extreme.'

It is one more example, says a Black activist, of how Mbeki's heavy-handed leadership is stifling debate in the movement. 'Internally, the ANC used to be a very democratic movement,' he says. 'We used to discuss everything and then abide by the decisions. Now the decisions are made before the discussions even start, and if you don't like it, then you will be chastised on some spurious grounds.'

Others believe his intolerance of opposition stems from his experience in exile. Groomed for the leadership as a young man by the late ANC leader Oliver Tambo, Mbeki rose quickly through the ranks abroad. But he left the organisation for two years after he was accused of being a traitor. Moreover, there has been a long-standing tension between those activists who remained in South Africa and fought and those who campaigned outside the country. The latter had greater educational opportunities but in many ways lacked credibility with their core support, who were living under the tyranny of apartheid. But they had a different political education, too. 'The exiles had to work in tight cells to avoid infiltration by South African security services,' says one former inmate of Robben Island. 'At home we had to lead debate so that we could lead the people. Even in the prisons there was a kind of democracy.' Mbeki's experience could not have been more different. While his contemporaries at Sussex University in Brighton were wearing kaftans and smoking dope, he was clad in tweeds and puffing on a pipe. He may have been a revolutionary, but he was never a rebel.

But the most common explanation given for both his general aversion to criticism and his most recent outburst over the alleged 'plot' is psychological. Aloof and introverted, Mbeki is an awkward man who is apparently never more happy than when surfing the web at night on his own. The only plot you will find in government, say his sternest critics, is the one Mbeki has lost.

The trouble with psychoanalysis, where political leaders are concerned, is that diagnosis is always in the eye of the beholder and tends to be made with their strategic interests in mind. Saddam Hussein was sane when he was fighting Iran and mad when he invaded Kuwait. Mbeki was a suave, Western-educated man the world could do business with seven years ago, when Mandela named him as his heir apparent; now he is paranoid.

The truth is that whatever his state of mind, Mbeki has good reason to fear a challenge from within the ANC. Partly because that is how mature political parties operate in democracies. And partly because, like most political leaders, he has made some serious mistakes. Chief among them is his position on HIV and Aids. The scale of the epidemic which is blighting South Africa can hardly be exaggerated. Roughly 4.7 million of the country's people live with HIV – about one in nine of the population as a whole – and the number of confirmed sufferers is increasing at a rate of twelve thousand a week. Yet despite overwhelming evidence to the contrary, Mbeki refuses to admit that there is a link between the HIV virus and full-blown Aids, claiming instead that the primary cause of Aids is poverty.

Though Mbeki has stopped espousing this view in public, it has attracted sharp criticism not just from his political opponents but also from key allies in the trade union movement, nurses, doctors, gay rights groups and even Mandela himself. 'It's not just his own crackpot ideas that are the problem,' says one senior ANC activist. 'It's the fact that his position makes it very difficult for those who could make a difference elsewhere in government to speak out. It's really dangerous.'

Mbeki has also come under criticism for his handling of last year's land crisis in Zimbabwe, when some believe he could have been more forthright in his criticism of Mugabe. But the key problem for the government is that its core supporters are beginning to get impatient with the slow pace of change. While Macozoma may be enjoying 'a privileged moment of history', those in the townships feel they have waited too long and received too little.

Alexandra township is just a few miles away from the Sandton conference centre where Macozoma collected his award, but it may as well be on another continent. It is Sunday morning, and the voices of the faithful from the Zion Christian church are mixed with the smell of frying fish and chicken from wooden stoves on the roadside and the beeping horns of the minibuses ferrying people to and from town. The self-built corrugated-iron shacks are still there, along with the dogs scavenging on open rubbish tips. It is wash day, and women troop with buckets full of water from standpipes past washing lines that are fit to snap.

Jobs and phone numbers may change in town but here you never need to change your address book – people stay just where they are because they cannot afford to move anywhere else. That is not to say there is no change. The roads are tarmac, new clinics and schools have been built, and over the stream, in what they called the Far East, West Bank and East Bank, new, comfortable houses have been built. There is even a Nando's chicken takeaway on Rooseveld Avenue – heavily fortified with barbed wire and metal bars.

To drive into Alexandra in a minibus is to roll into a different polit-ical and social paradigm. No longer are your doors locked against potential car-jackers, having motored up the highway in your own private domain. You have staggered there, taking three or four times as long, with at least ten others, stopping and starting in order to pick up and drop off people on the roadside on their way to and from work in the white areas. Away from the vast dwellings and high walls of the suburbs, they live cheek by jowl here – what looks like one house's front garden is often the entrance to a yard for six or seven families.

When I first came here in 1994, I quickly realised just how out of touch most liberal whites were with the concerns of the vast majority of the population. While liberals voiced concerns about the propriety of the ANC including Winnie Mandela so high on its electoral list and outrage at the ANC guards' shooting of Inkatha supporters outside the ANC's then headquarters in Shell House, those issues did not come up in Alexandra unless I brought them up. There, Winnie remained one of the most popular figures on the list after Nelson Mandela himself. Ask them about the Stompie Seipei affair, and they would shrug their shoulders. 'Our children have been dying here for years because of poverty or disease or apartheid soldiers. Why are they now worried about this one boy?' they asked.

The same rift between Black and white priorities is evident today. When a provincial committee banned Shakespeare, because his work was 'too gloomy', and Nadine Gordimer, on the grounds of racism – their decision was reversed and immediately condemned by the ANC nationally – the news went all around the world. But it never made it to Alexandra, where those I spoke to neither knew nor cared.

Similarly, the alleged plot against Mbeki is viewed very differently in the townships, a fact illustrated by a recent Harris opinion poll. The poll was split into those who responded online – far more likely to be white – and those who were questioned offline in predominantly Black areas. A total of 60 per cent of those interviewed offline believed that Mbeki had better watch his back as there 'is substance' to the 'plot' against him; the online figure was only 36 per cent. For Mumsey, the mother of the family I stayed with and a former ANC organiser, Mbeki's claims are entirely credible. But their general willingness to believe it also implies a growing cynicism with politics in general. 'They are always up to something,' says Elizabeth. 'They all want the top job or the big car.' At the local elections voter turnout dropped to below 50 per cent, and the ANC vote also nosedived.

It was the first indication that Black voters' loyalty to the ANC and patience with the pace of change were finite.

The ANC did not win a war, they negotiated a peace. The terms of the truce were hammered out with the former apartheid regime. But the true nature of the pact demands an accommodation not with politicians but with international and domestic capital. The ANC has decided that without a substantial injection of capital investment, which is still largely in white hands, there will not be sufficient wealth to redistribute. White businessmen understand that a government committed to a large programme of public investment will have plenty of lucrative contracts on offer.

In that sense the new South Africa is beginning to look much like America's new South, where economics and politics have shifted and culture and society are struggling to keep up. In hotel lobbies and airports the once radical and the still unreconstructed are awkwardly pressing palms and self-consciously rubbing shoulders. For once the deals are done there is little to talk about. 'Sometimes I am taken aback by how backward some of them can be,' says Macozoma. 'Not when you're doing business, because they know better than that. But after a few beers they start to talk more freely, and you realise that a lot of them have really not adapted to the new situation at all.'

But the real problem for the government is that, so far, the deal they thought they had struck has not been honoured. The plan, following liberation, was that a stable, tightly run economy would attract the capital that would, in turn, help to alleviate poverty. But despite their policies of fiscal rectitude, controlled inflation and restrained spending, and the praise heaped upon them by the World Bank and the International Monetary Fund, the investment has not been forthcoming. 'There is a sense of frustration that the government has done everything that international capital has asked of it,' says Macozoma. 'But the political cost of that has not been rewarded and in some ways has even been punished by speculation against the rand. In retrospect I think we were a bit naive.'

For some the political cost is beginning to prove too great. Trevor Ngwane was an ANC councillor in northern Johannesburg when he wrote an article against privatisation in a Sunday newspaper. By the Wednesday he had been suspended from the party. He believes the ANC has put the interests of its investors before those of its own supporters. 'All governments are constrained by the forces of globalisation,' he says. 'But after liberation we had more space to manoeuvre than they were prepared to use. The world would have understood that it would take a huge amount of public investment to get rid of the legacies of apartheid. But the ANC chose a different path.'

The failure to deliver substantial changes to the bulk of the population is putting a serious strain on the ANC's partners in the trade union movement and the South African Communist Party. COSATU, the main union movement, has already threatened to hold national strikes over the government's privatisation plans. 'The alliance should be using its power to tilt the balance of forces in favour of a transforming agenda. But it is not working in the manner that it should, and if it continues in a particular way, it will die a natural death,' says COSATU leader Zwelinzima Vavi. 'There is no consultation, and the other components of the alliance feel that we need to have more say than just encouraging our supporters to vote for the ANC. The ANC alone cannot drive the transformation agenda.'

Here lies the nub of Mbeki's vulnerability: the threat that the broad church of the ANC, which was united by its opposition to apartheid, might split into its component faiths. While this is unlikely to happen any time soon, the very fact that it is being discussed breaks a taboo. The process by and pace at which this might take place contain an element of risk. But the fact that it is taking place at all is not a sign of crisis but of the maturing of a new political democracy.

Comrade Bob

Robert Mugabe once embodied the optimism of a continent. What went wrong?

Guardian, 4 September 2001, Harare

Six years ago, at the opening of the new bridge across the Limpopo river which links South Africa to Zimbabwe, two men who have dominated the African political landscape for forty years stood on ceremony. Nelson Mandela and Robert Mugabe watched as a group of schoolchildren sang their praises. Once they had finished, Mandela took centre stage.

'He did what Mandela does best,' said one dignitary who attended. 'He called the schoolmaster over, had a few words with him and then shook each of the children by the hand. They loved it. It made their afternoon and it made the event.'

Meanwhile, Mugabe looked on, expressionless, from his seat, a spectator in a play in which he was billed as the co-star. His temper was frayed, his ego diminished and his face taut, desperately with-holding any hint of emotion.

'He just sat there, and if you knew him, you could tell that he was mad,' according to one long-standing colleague within Mugabe's Zanu-PF party. 'But there was nothing he could do. He was being upstaged by the world's most popular politician on his home turf.'

Mugabe holds an intense jealousy for Mandela. And it is not diffi-cult to see why. Although it is difficult to imagine it now, Mugabe was once not only the pride of Africa but the toast of the liberal world. In the press he was hailed as 'Southern Africa's Clem Attlee' and 'the thinking man's guerrilla'.

Bob Marley, one of the few artists to be invited to the Zimbabwe independence celebrations in 1980, named a song after the new nation, and when he got there he found that the guerrillas already knew the words. Of course, not all were happy. White Rhodesians and the British government, believing their own propaganda, were convinced Mugabe was a communist, white-hating psychopath who would lose the elections. Just to make sure, they used precisely the same tactics of intimidation and petty harassment that they accuse him of today. In March 1980, the *Guardian* talked of 'the delays in allowing [Joshua] Nkomo and Mugabe to import their election cars, and publicity material, the hold-ups in providing them with telephones, the dawn searches of hotel rooms and campaign offices, the confiscation of pamphlets and posters, the arrests of campaign workers and candidates'. Twice in the run-up to the first elections Mugabe narrowly escaped death at the hands of pro-Rhodesian hardliners, courtesy of British-made landmines.

When he won a resounding victory, the white Rhodesians had no idea what to do. The day after the election, recalls one, some white children were sent to school with bags packed for a flight, in case rumours of his victory were true.

It was 1980 – four years after the Soweto uprisings in neighbouring South Africa had seen hundreds of young Black people killed by the apartheid regime, a year after Margaret Thatcher had come to power in Great Britain, and a year before Ronald Reagan would be sworn in as US president. Not exactly a propitious time for a self-confessed Marxist to take over from a white minority in the mineral-rich, fertile soil of southern Africa. And yet Comrade Bob, as he was affectionately known, had done it.

As reactionaries fled, idealists poured in to help build a new Jerusalem. 'A third of my class, which graduated in 1980, came straight here,' says one Zimbabwean, who was studying in England at the time. 'For anybody who cared about Africa, there was just a huge optimism about the country.'

Mugabe was then the embodiment of that optimism, giving hope to a generation born too late to be carried away by the idealism of the 1960s, but too early to be moulded by the cynicism of the 1980s. Now he is the man whom Desmond Tutu, the former archbishop of Cape Town, once described as 'almost a caricature of all the things people think black African leaders do'. So he accelerates up the league table of international pariahs, a lonely, desperate and ill man. Lonely, because many of those he counted among his friends, at home or abroad, have either retired or died. His first wife and intellectual, political and romantic partner, Sally, who had been with him since before his incarceration and right through to independence, died nine years ago. In her place came Grace, forty years his junior and more dedicated to extravagant shopping than ascetic socialism.

'Sally was really the one he could talk to, and more importantly, one who could talk to him,' says one person who knows him well. 'She used to organise his social life, too, and do all the entertaining. I don't see his relationship with Grace as one of equals.'

Lonely, too – and far more worrying for the country – because his increasingly despotic tendencies have left him isolated. Those he once counted as comrades are now either alienated, cowered into syco-phancy or effectively silenced. Not even the few who have only good things to say about him will speak on the record. 'Bob is an intellec-tual, and he used to love to just talk,' says one former confidante. 'He would talk about anything, particularly to do with the continent, and was open to new ideas. But anything he considers a threat he just shuts out now. You are either with him or against him, and the only people who want a relationship like that are those who need some-thing from him, and they, by definition, can't be trusted.'

While he has not managed to keep the fact that he is ill out of the public domain – he has fainted twice on official visits over the past eighteen months – rumours vary as to the precise nature of the illness, ranging from cancer of the throat to prostate cancer. And this has left him grappling with his mortality and, therefore, his legacy. 'This is the big thing for Bob,' says one well-placed Zanu-PF polit-ician. 'What he will leave the country when he goes. I believe the new constitution was going to be his parting gift, but when the voters rejected that, he turned to land. He does not want to be remembered as the man who ruined the country but just couldn't go. But by staying he becomes precisely that.'

And so he found himself with Mandela on the banks of the Limpopo, sitting where he thought the limelight should be, in a pool of resentment. 'It was a really important moment, that day,' says one of Mugabe's former friends. 'Mugabe had been in power fourteen years, and here was Mandela saying, "I'll only be around for one term." Mandela has retired, and Bob is still there.'

Mugabe was always different from most other African leaders of his generation in two respects: his experience was entirely in Africa, and he was an intellectual rather than a soldier. While others had been educated in exile and sometimes trained in either the East or the West, Mugabe had spent his entire time in Africa. Born in 1924 to a carpenter and domestic labourer in the village of Kutama, sixty miles north of Harare, he was educated at the local Jesuit-run school, where he was remembered as a highly intelligent, industrious plodder. One of the fathers at the mission once said: 'He was one of those quiet, solid workers who used every minute of his time. He wasn't inclined to laugh much even then.'

Back then, the tentacles of Rhodesian racism reached into every crevice of civil society. His childhood friend, Edison Mpfumgo, once recalled being invited to the mission superintendent's house for tea. 'We sat on the sofas, and just as we were walking out, we actually saw his wife come down with a fumigator and fumigating the seats in which we had been sitting just a few moments ago. I went out and cried.'

Mugabe finished his secondary education, and then started to teach, before winning a scholarship to the University of Fort Hare, an all-Black institution in South Africa's Eastern Cape province. Fort Hare was more than just a university; it was a vehicle for a new generation of Black leadership that had been raised under racism but trained to overcome it. Among Mugabe's contemporaries there were Mandela, Mangosuthu Buthelezi and the late Oliver Tambo.

If anything, his education there was political as much as it was academic. 'I came to Fort Hare', Mugabe has said, 'from a country where most Black people had accepted European rule as such. Most of us believed that all that should be done was to remove our grievances within the system. After Fort Hare there was a radical change in my views.'

Shortly afterwards, he headed to Ghana – a country recently liberated by Kwame Nkrumah, a leader from whom Mugabe later professed to have learned much, but clearly not enough. Nkrumah, who had come to power on a tide of enthusiasm throughout the continent, became increasingly autocratic, until he was finally ousted in a coup.

Mugabe was imprisoned in 1964, following his famous 'cowboy' speech, in which he slammed Ian Smith and his entourage as cowboys because of both their wild behaviour and their penchant for wide-brimmed hats. During his ten years in jail, his only son by Sally died of cerebral malaria. His pleas for compassionate leave to be by his son's side during his final hours and at his funeral were denied by the Rhodesian regime.

Mugabe was an intellectual. While others of his generation (such as Mozambique's Samora Machel or Zambia's Kenneth Kaunda) were essentially military men, Mugabe was never a fighter himself. One ex-combatant who knew him during the war of independence recalls that his principal contribution to the military struggle was strategic rather than practical. 'You never knew what he was thinking, but you knew he was always thinking,' he says. 'Then one day he would just decide on some form of action. He would explain – but only once – and then just move. But even in the field he always kept his distance.' Another recalls, 'Militant he certainly was, but a military man, never. Mugabe's arsenal is in his mind. He is a revolutionary theorist, not a soldier.'

During his ten-year stretch in prison courtesy of the Smith regime, he studied for three degrees by correspondence, to add to the two he already had. 'He knew exactly what he wanted to do,' recalls one of his tutors at the London School of Economics, from which he obtained a postgraduate degree in international economic law. 'So much so that it became quite a struggle to impress on him that for the purpose of this exercise, I – not he – was the boss . . . I got the very clear impression that he was equipping his intellect for the tasks that lay ahead.' One speech writer recalled how drafts would always be returned not only with changes in content but also pedantic corrections of grammar.

If he is punctilious about his language, then he is no less particular about other aspects of his life. He drinks neither alcohol, tea nor coffee, and when he is on tour often insists on bringing cooks who can prepare simple African dishes. He is also incredibly fastidious about clothing. Men may not enter a Zimbabwe court or the public gallery in parliament without a shirt, tie and jacket. When some argued that African MPs and spectators should at least be allowed to wear African clothes, such as robes and jellabahs, a minor concession was made – safari suits are now allowed. 'There is no mix and match around Bob,' says one former colleague. 'Everything has to be ironed flat, sharp, co-ordinated and very conservative.'

His recent conversion to a far more lavish lifestyle is said to have arrived shortly after his marriage to Grace. Before, he was fiercely critical of the kind of wanton ostentation that had plundered the public purses of so many other countries on the continent. Back in 1983, he slammed those ministers who, 'under one guise or another, proceeded to acquire huge properties by way of commercial farms and other business concerns'.

One of the more intriguing facets of the British coverage and understanding of Africa is that the focus is not on the needs, experiences and aspirations of the vast majority of those who have always lived there but on the comparatively small number of whites who have settled in the continent over the past four hundred years. And so it is that rivers, towns and mountains do not exist until they have been 'discovered' by white explorers; leaders are judged not by their ability to deliver their election promises to the majority but by their willingness to preserve the privileges of the minority; and events simply do not happen unless they happen to white people. This warped perspective deprives Black Africans of not only their wealth, citizenship and dignity but their history as well.

Not that whites in Africa are unimportant. As the racial group which until relatively recently held a monopoly on political power and which, in much of the continent, still holds a vastly disproportionate amount of wealth, it would be foolish to ignore it. Moreover, as an ethnic minority, they have basic human rights which should be secured and defended.

But the determination to dwell on the needs and priorities of a privileged few at the expense of the impoverished many continues to distort the continent beyond all recognition. And in few places more so than Zimbabwe, where white people make up less than 0.5 per cent of the population, own 70 per cent of the best land and employ 65 per cent of the people. One of the more bizarre upshots of the current spate of trouble in Zimbabwe is that it should take place against a backdrop of the racism conference in Durban, where Britain's strident tone against Mugabe's regime contrasts unfavourably with its weasel words over colonialism and slavery, as though the two situations were not linked.

As the leader of first the liberation and then the country, Mugabe has therefore been through many incarnations, depending on the anxieties and hopes of the white Zimbabweans and the British establishment. In 1978, according to the *News of the World*'s front page, he was the 'Black Hitler' – an analogy which presumably cast the racist white minority who were enforcing their own version of apartheid as Jews. After he won the election and urged reconciliation, the *Daily Mail*'s front page illustrated a changed tone: 'Mugabe – So meek and mild', it read. As long as he preaches 'reconciliation' to, and forgiveness for, whites, he is liked. As long as he expresses rage at their racism and privilege, he is loathed. Nothing else counts. 'Satan or Saviour?' asked the *Sunday Times* in 1980. There is, it seems, nothing in between.

Throughout the years of the *mkuruhundu* – the massacres in Matabeleland in the mid-1980s – we heard precious little, since the thousands that he murdered, with the assistance of the North Koreans, were Black. Rarely did we hear news of the reasonably successful battles against illiteracy, disease and impoverishment which he led that empowered so many Zimbabweans throughout the 1980s and early 1990s.

But now he is back. The supporters of the opposition Movement for Democratic Change (MDC), whom he is intimidating, torturing and murdering, are his true target, but sadly, not the stuff that inflammatory headlines are made of here. Nor, sadly, are the lesbians and gays he has been harassing and incriminating. Instead, the spotlight shines on him and his country only when it turns its ire on whites. And we have an impressive candidate for what Gore Vidal calls 'the enemy of the month club' – the farm-seizing, land-grabbing, white-hating lunatic of the new millennium.

Ask those who know or support him where it all went wrong, and they will shrug. There were signs, particularly during the Matabeleland massacres, which no one wanted to heed. Liberals concede that when reports started to surface of the mass murder of the N'debele in the area, they would not or could not believe it. 'It wasn't just that we didn't want to believe it,' says one London-based expert. 'But his explanation for it – that South African forces were trying to destabilise the country – was completely plausible. The apartheid regime was killing people all over the front-line states during the 1980s, so why not in Zimbabwe?'

In 1985, Zimbabwe, which this year will be forced to import maize to stave off a food crisis, was one of the few African countries in a position to send drought relief to Ethiopia. In 1990, Mandela

Dispatches from the Diaspora

gave Mugabe and his party a clean bill of health, when he arrived during an election campaign. 'Robert Mugabe and Zanu have made Zimbabwe an example for us,' Mandela said on a visit to Harare shortly after his release.

One of Mugabe's sternest critics, Morgan Tsvangirai, the leader of the opposition MDC, who will challenge him for the presidency in March, says that if Mugabe had gone before the last presidential election, things would have been different. 'If Mugabe had left government in 1995, he would have gone with his reputation intact, but the past five years have been a disaster.'

Some within Zanu date his degradation back to his defeat in the referendum for a new constitution early last year. 'That was a real shock to him because he always thought he had the people with him,' says one. 'When they voted no, he decided he would carry on the transformation without them because it was in their interests.'

But perhaps the most plausible explanation is that Mugabe hasn't changed, the rest of the world has. 'You cannot understand what is happening now without taking into account that violence in Zimbabwe's political culture stretches a long way back,' says a professor at the University of Zimbabwe. 'The Smith regime was violent, and the resistance to it was violent as well. What Mugabe is doing is continuing and entrenching a tradition.'

The battle for independence in Zimbabwe was indeed a bloody and bitter one, not only between the state and the guerrillas but also between the various guerrilla factions. Like other freedom fighters in the area, Mugabe had declared himself a Marxist, but unlike them he was closer to China – home of Mao's mantra 'political power grows out of the barrel of a gun' – than to the Soviet Union, which had long since adopted a policy of 'peaceful coexistence' with the West. When it came to alliances with other organisations, Zanu was closer to the Pan-Africanist Congress, which preached revenge under the slogan 'One settler, one bullet', than to Mandela's African National Congress, which advocated multiracial democracy.

Mugabe's relationship with white Zimbabweans has been volatile and informed by mutual suspicion. For if he is unreconstructed, then so are many of them. When fifteen out of twenty seats reserved for whites went to Smith's Rhodesian Front in 1985, Mugabe lashed out. 'The whites are still the racists of the past,' he said. 'We showed them love, they showed us hatred; we forgave them, they thought we were stupid; we regarded them as friends, but they were wicked witches.'

As a liberation leader, Mugabe was at home in the world of vanguardism, tight security and summary justice. Comfortable at a time when those who were not with you were against you and politics meant not coalition-building but action. He assumed control of Zanu in a coup carried out while he was still in prison. During the mid-1980s, he turned on his former mentor and comrade-in-arms, Joshua Nkomo, and forced him into exile. Mugabe's party always had to be nudged to the negotiating table by other southern African leaders and, like their Rhodesian opponents, forever kept a finger on the trigger. When Mugabe was released from jail in 1974 amid calls for détente, he called for his army 'to intensify the war and ignore persistent calls for a ceasefire. An intensified recruitment campaign [has] to be mounted to build up the army.'

This he managed to sustain for a considerable time after independence. His advocacy of a one-party state in the interests of nation-building made sense in a continent where other countries were disintegrating and his was making great economic and social strides.

Like his old foe Thatcher, he had captured a national mood in the early 1980s that had alienated many but enthused most; and, like her, he entered a new millennium clutching to certainties that had long gone. But while Thatcher operated in a long-standing democratic tradition that could get rid of her, Mugabe does not. It is a sign of how steeped Zanu is in a bygone culture that its principal decision-making body is still called the Politburo.

His old friends, such as Kaunda, were forced out. New allies, such as Mandela, outshone him with a new and brighter message for the

Dispatches from the Diaspora

future. Mugabe still talks to, and of, the past. One of the principal constituencies of the MDC is the young – the so-called Born Frees, who knew not the war he fought but the freedom it brought.

By diverting attention away from his democratic deficiencies to the issue of land, he hoped to rekindle the spirit of independence and provide himself with a legacy. By concentrating his ire on a privileged minority and a former colonial power he hoped he could reinvigorate his flagging popularity. But the more he tries, the worse it gets. The country has moved on.

Left to sink or swim

Hurricane Katrina laid bare America's racial and economic disadvantages.
Guardian, 5 September 2005, New Orleans

'Stuff happens,' said the US defence secretary, Donald Rumsfeld, when called to respond to the looting taking place in Baghdad after the American invasion. 'But in terms of what's going on in that country, it is a fundamental misunderstanding to see those images over and over and over again of some boy walking out with a vase and say, "Oh, my goodness, you didn't have a plan" . . . It's untidy, and freedom's untidy, and free people are free to make mistakes and commit crimes and do bad things. They're also free to live their lives and do wonderful things, and that's what's going to happen here.'

The official response to the looting in New Orleans last week was, however, quite different. The images were not of 'newly liberated Iraqis' making away with precious artefacts but of desperate African Americans in a devastated urban area, most of whom were making off with nappies, bottled water and food.

So these are not scenes of freedom at work but anarchy to be suppressed. 'These troops are battle-tested. They have M-16s and are locked and loaded,' said the Democrat governor of Louisiana, Kathleen Blanco. 'These troops know how to shoot and kill, and I expect they will.'

Events on the Gulf coast following Hurricane Katrina have been a metaphor for race in the US. The predominantly Black population of New Orleans, along with a sizeable number of poor whites, was left to sink or swim. The bulging banks of the Mississippi momentarily washed away the racial divisions that appeared so permanent, not in a common cause but a common condition – poverty.

Under-resourced and without support, those who remained afloat had to hustle to survive. The ad hoc means they created to defend and govern themselves under such extreme adversity were, inevitably, dysfunctional. Their plight was not understood as part of a broader, societal crisis but misunderstood as a problem apart from that crisis. Eviscerated from context, they could then be branded as a lawless, amoral and indigent bunch of people who can't get it together because they are in the grip of pathology.

Katrina did not create this racist image of African Americans; it has simply laid bare America's ahistorical bigotry, and in so doing exposed the lie of equal opportunity in the US. A basic understanding of human nature suggests everyone in New Orleans wanted to survive and escape. A basic understanding of American economics and history shows that despite all the rhetoric, wealth – not hard work or personal sacrifice – is the most decisive factor in who succeeded.

In that sense, Katrina has been a disaster for the poor, for the same reason that President Bush's social security proposals and economic policies have been. It was the result of small government – an inadequate, privatised response to a massive public problem. And if there was ever any bewilderment about why African Americans reject such an agenda so comprehensively at every election, then this was why.

'No one would have checked on a lot of the black people in these parishes while the sun shined,' Mayor Milton Tutwiler of Winstonville, Mississippi, told the *New York Times*. 'So am I surprised that no one has come to help us now? No.'

The fact that the vast majority of those who remained in town were Black was not an accident. Katrina did not go out of its way to affect Black people; it destroyed almost everything in its path. But the poor were disproportionately affected because they were least able to escape it and endure its wrath. They are more likely to have bad housing and less likely to have cars. Many had to work until the last moment, and few have the money to pay for a hotel out of town.

Nature does not discriminate, but people do. For reasons that are particularly resonant in the South, where this year African Americans celebrated the fortieth anniversary of legislation protecting their right to vote, Black people are disproportionately represented among the poor. Two-thirds of New Orleans is African American, a quarter of whom live in poverty.

In the Lower Ninth Ward area, which was inundated by the flood-waters, more than 98 per cent of the residents are Black and more than a third live in poverty. In other words, their race and their class are so closely intertwined that to try to understand either separately is tantamount to misunderstanding both entirely.

'Negro poverty is not white poverty,' explained President Lyndon Johnson in a speech to Howard University in 1965. 'Many of its causes and many of its cures are the same. But there are differences – deep, corrosive, obstinate differences, radiating painful roots into the community and into the family and the nature of the individual. These differences are not racial differences. They are solely and simply the consequence of ancient brutality, past injustice and present prejudice. They are anguishing to observe. For the negro they are a constant reminder of oppression.'

Daily scenes of thousands of African Americans being told to be patient even as they died; their children wailing as they stood stranded and dehydrated on highways; their old perishing as they festered in filthy homes full of faeces; their dead left to rot in the street – it was a reminder too many for some.

By Friday night, rapper Kanye West had finally had enough. On a live NBC television special to raise funds for the victims, he lashed out. 'I've tried to turn away from the TV because it's too hard to watch,' he said. 'Bush doesn't care about Black people. It's been five days [waiting for help] because most of the people are Black. America is set up to help the poor, the Black people, the less well-off as slow as possible.'

While West's comments expressed a blatant truth that all with eyes could see, to some they were more outrageous than watching thousands of people dying from neglect live on television in the wealthiest country in the world. NBC made it clear he had stepped off the reservation. 'Kanye West departed from the scripted comments that were prepared for him, and his opinions in no way represent the views of the networks. It would be most unfortunate if the efforts of the artists who participated tonight and the generosity of millions of Americans who are helping those in need are overshadowed by one person's opinion.'

The fact that this person's opinion, shared by so many, explains why those in need require so much help is, it seems, irrelevant. Perhaps NBC executives should have read that Black radical magazine *Time*, published just a week before Katrina hit, where West graces the cover. The title? 'Why you can't ignore Kanye: More *GQ* than gangsta, Kanye West is challenging the way rap thinks about race and class.'

Shots in the dark

The shooting of a sixteen-year-old in Detroit by an off-duty cop should have been a national scandal. It didn't even make the local papers.
The Nation, 14 June 2007, Detroit

Brandon Martell Moore left the world in a shower of bullets, followed by deafening silence. Brandon, sixteen, was looking at video games in National Wholesale Liquidators on 8 Mile Road in Detroit the Sunday after Thanksgiving when an off-duty cop moonlighting as a security guard kicked him and his friends out of the store, claiming they were not accompanied by an adult. The altercation that followed did not involve Brandon but ended in his death.

It was the middle of the afternoon in broad daylight; Brandon was unarmed; he was shot in the back.

The way Brandon's brother, who was there at the time, describes it, the guard was ruthless in his execution. 'He put one arm on top of the other arm and started aiming at us,' says John Henry Moore Jr. 'He was shooting to kill. It looked like he wanted to kill all of us. Brandon wasn't even involved in anything. He was the last one to take off running, I guess.'

Brandon was a quiet boy. According to his sister Ebony, the only time he made any noise was when 'he was seeing a girl or making jokes'. He and his younger brother were such devotees of *Beavis and Butt-Head* that their mother had to hide the video so they wouldn't keep playing it.

'At the funeral lots of girls I didn't even know came up to me crying and said, "I was his girlfriend,"' says his mother, Susie Burks, laughing. 'There was a whole row of them there.'

He had never been in trouble with the law before. But the man who killed him had. In 1971, Eugene Williams was involved in a fatal hit-and-run accident while under the influence of alcohol. In 1979, Williams shot a thirty-one-year-old man dead during a neighbourhood fracas. Five years later, he shot his wife in the side during a domestic dispute, but she lived. Williams is also a Detroit cop. His badge number is 4174. At the time of writing, he was still on the force. By any standard, you would think this would have been a scandal. But apparently not in Detroit. It took the city's two main newspapers less than two hundred words to finish with the story, in which they failed even to mention Brandon's name.

'We're deemed not reportable,' says Clementina Chery, who runs the Boston-based Louis D. Brown Peace Institute, which assists the families of victims as well as perpetrators in the immediate aftermath of shootings and works in schools to educate people about gun violence. 'Black children are dispensable. Violence is expected to happen in these communities.'

The Detroit police refuse to talk about it. The office of the mayor – the 'hip-hop' mayor Kwame Kilpatrick, who struts around with 'mayor' embroidered on his French cuffs – has not uttered a word and won't return calls. When Brandon's father, John Henry Moore Sr, asked for the police report, the officer told him, 'I'm not fucking giving it to you.'

'Why would I want to live in a place where my son can't even be remembered?' says Brandon's dad, who has since moved. 'That means he didn't mean nothing to this city.'

The police version of the story is, of course, quite different from that of Brandon's friends. The police say Brandon was part of a gang of young men making trouble in the store, when one of the staff asked them to leave. 'One teenager took off his coat and rushed the off-duty police officer,' claimed Detroit police spokesman James Tate. 'The others then got involved.'

Given everything I know about Brandon and everything I know about Williams, I know who I believe.

An investigation into the killing in January ruled that it was justifiable homicide. When I called Williams at his desk on Detroit's traffic enforcement unit at Mount Elliott, he denied ever having heard of Brandon.

Thanksgiving was a big weekend for police shootings. In the early hours of the previous morning, Sean Bell, twenty-three and unarmed, was leaving a strip club in Queens on his wedding day when five police officers unloaded fifty bullets into his car. They call it 'contagious shooting'. One cop fires. Then the others, believing the shooting is itself evidence of a threat, follow suit. Bell's death made headlines. For a young Black man to be killed in cold blood by cops does not raise an eyebrow. Only the inordinate number of bullets makes it newsworthy.

'One of the reasons they can do that is because the press has written off the poorer parts of the city,' explains Diane Bukowski, a reporter for the Black newspaper the *Michigan Citizen*, without whose dogged reporting none of this would have been known. 'A child can just disappear.'

So in some ways Brandon's murder was just another banal fact in the life and death of America, where eight children aged nineteen and under are killed by firearms every day – more in a year than the number who perished in the World Trade Center. Yet there is no war on this terror. The demand for substantive political change withers because it cannot find root in the legislative process.

The statistically relentless nature of these deaths creates an air of political inevitability about their cause. Just a few weeks before Brandon was killed, the Democrats took over Congress. Detroit congressman John Conyers, who became the Democratic chair of the House Judiciary Committee, pledged he would not 'support or forward to the House any legislation to ban handguns'.

Gun control may have been removed from mainstream political conversation, but the guns are still out there. Some of the mobsters and madmen who wield them have badges; some don't. To those they kill it is a distinction without much of a difference. When guns claim lives in areas where any middle-class child might be – schools, universities, upscale malls – America mourns. When they are used in projects, barrios and trailer parks, it yawns. The shots ring out just the same. But no one can hear them in a moral vacuum.

Open season on Black boys after a verdict like this

The acquittal of Trayvon Martin's killer was shameful and sickening, but not surprising.

Guardian, 14 July 2013, Chicago

Let it be noted that on this day, Saturday 13 July 2013, it was still deemed legal in the US to chase and then shoot dead an unarmed young Black man on his way home from the store because you didn't like the look of him.

The killing of seventeen-year-old Trayvon Martin last year was tragic. But in the age of Obama, the acquittal of George Zimmerman offers at least that clarity. For the salient facts in this case were not in dispute. On 26 February 2012, Martin was on his way home, minding his own business, armed only with a can of iced tea and a bag of Skittles. Zimmerman pursued him, armed with a 9 mm handgun, believing him to be a criminal. Martin resisted. They fought. Zimmerman shot him dead.

Who screamed? Who was stronger? Who called whom what and when and why are all details to warm the heart of a cable news producer with twenty-four hours to fill. Strip them all away and the truth remains that Martin's heart would still be beating if Zimmerman had not chased him down and shot him.

There is no doubt about who the aggressor was here. It appears that the only reason the two interacted at all, physically or otherwise, is that Zimmerman believed it was his civic duty to apprehend an innocent teenager who caused suspicion by his existence alone.

Appeals for calm in the wake of such a verdict raise the question of what calm can there possibly be in a place where such a verdict is possible. Parents of Black boys are not likely to feel calm. Partners of Black men are not likely to feel calm. Children with Black fathers are not likely to feel calm. Those who now fear violent social disorder must ask themselves whose interests are served by a violent social order in which young Black men can be slain and discarded thus.

But while the acquittal was shameful, it was not a shock. It took more than six weeks after Martin's death for Zimmerman to be arrested, and then only after massive pressure both nationally and locally. Those who dismissed this as a political trial (a peculiar accusation in the summer of Bradley Manning and Edward Snowden) should bear in mind that it was politics that made this case controversial.

Charging Zimmerman should have been a no-brainer. He was not initially charged because Florida has a 'stand your ground' law whereby deadly force is permitted if the person 'reasonably believes' it is necessary to protect their own life or the life of another, or to prevent a forcible felony. Since it was Zimmerman who stalked Martin, the question remains: what ground is a young Black man entitled to and on what grounds may he defend himself? What version of events is there for that night in which Martin gets away with his life? Or is it open season on Black boys after dark?

Zimmerman's not guilty verdict will be contested for years to come. But he passed judgement on Trayvon that night summarily.

'Fucking punks,' Zimmerman told the police dispatcher that night. 'These assholes, they always get away.'

So true it's painful. And so predictable it hurts.

Yes, he tried: what will Barack Obama's legacy be?

Obama was elected on a tidal wave of optimism, promising to heal America's wounds. Did he deliver?

Guardian, 19 March 2016, Marshalltown, Iowa

When Ohio fell on election night 2008, the President's Lounge, a bar in Chicago's overwhelmingly Black South Side, erupted in jubilation. As I scanned the faces at the bar, one woman looked at me, beaming, raised her margarita and shouted, 'My man's in Afghanistan. He's coming home!' Barack Obama had never said anything about ending the war in Afghanistan. Indeed, he had pledged to ramp up the US military effort there. But she had not misunderstood him; she had simply projected her hopes on to him and mistaken them for fact.

Obama had that kind of effect on people, back then. Often they weren't listening too closely to what he was saying, because they loved the way he was saying it. Measured, eloquent, informed – here was a politician who used full sentences with verbs. He was not just standing to be the successor to George W. Bush; he was the anti-Bush.

And they loved the way Obama looked when he said it: tall, handsome, Black – an understated, stylish presence from an under-represented, marginalised demographic. The notion that this man might lead the country, just three years after Hurricane Katrina, left many staring in awe when they might have been listening with intent. Details be damned: this man could be president.

Earlier on election day, I saw a grown man cry as he came out of the polling station. 'We've had attempts at Black presidents before,' Howard Davis, an African American, told me, 'but they've never got this far. Deep in my heart, it's an emotional thing. I'm really excited about it.' His voice cracked and he excused himself to dry his eyes.

Dispatches from the Diaspora

I first heard about Obama from my late mother-in-law, Janet Mack, who lived in Chicago and joined his campaign for the Senate in 2003. That was the year I moved to the US as a correspondent for the *Guardian*, first in New York and later in Chicago, before moving back to London last August.

Janet had seen Obama on local television a few times and thought he spoke a lot of sense. She attended the demonstration where he spoke, as a state senator, against the invasion of Iraq. When he first ran, she feared he would be assassinated, but became accustomed to him as a prime-time fixture. 'It's like living in California and the earthquakes,' she told me. 'You just can't worry about them all the time.'

We went to the South Side of Chicago together to hear Obama's nomination speech in 2008, watching with a couple of hundred others on a big screen at the Regal Theater. People wept and punched the air. On the way home, Janet, a Black woman raised in the Jim Crow South, punched my arm and laughed. Usually, she chatted a lot, but for most of the thirty-minute ride she kept saying, to nobody in particular, 'I just can't believe it.'

In many ways, Obama's campaign for the presidency was unremarkable. He had voted with Hillary Clinton in the Senate 90 per cent of the time. He stood on a centrist Democratic platform, promising healthcare reform and moderate wealth redistribution – effectively, the same programme that mainstream Democrats had stood on for a generation. But his rise was meteoric. His story was so compelling, his rhetoric so soaring, his base so passionate – and his victory, when it came, so improbable – that reality was always going to be a buzz kill.

Obama had long been aware that voters saw what they wanted in him. 'I serve as a blank screen on which people of vastly different political stripes project their own views,' he wrote in *The Audacity of Hope* in 2006. 'As such, I am bound to disappoint some, if not all, of them.' But he was hardly blameless. He claimed to stand in the tradition of the suffragettes, the civil rights movement and the union organisers, evoking their speeches and positioning himself as a transformational figure. On the final primary night in June 2008, he literally promised the Earth to a crowd in St Paul, Minnesota: 'We will be able to look back and tell our children that this was the moment . . . when the rise of the oceans began to slow and our planet began to heal.'

There was a lot of healing to do. When Obama came to power, the US had lost one war in the Gulf and was losing another in Afghanistan. In a poll of nineteen countries, two-thirds had a negative view of America. Americans didn't have a much better view of themselves. The banking crisis had just sent the economy into free-fall. Poverty was rising, share prices were nosediving and just 13 per cent of the population thought the country was moving in the right direction.

This was the America Obama inherited when he strolled, victorious, on to the stage in Chicago's Grant Park with his family on election night in 2008 – a vision in black before a nation still in shock.

In Marshalltown, Iowa (population 27,800), on 26 January this year, a crowd waits in sub-zero temperatures for several hours to see Donald Trump, while the hawkers enjoy a brisk trade. There are 'Make America Great Again' hats (made in China) and badges stating 'Bomb The Shit Out Of Isis' and 'Hillary For Prison 2016'. One man is carrying a poster with a picture of Hitler holding up a healthcare bill and saying, 'You've gone too far, Obama!' Across the road are protesters, most of them Hispanic. Over the previous six months, Trump has branded Mexicans as rapists, promised to exclude all Muslims from the country and insulted the Chinese, disabled people, women and Jews.

Inside, Sheriff Joe Arpaio from Arizona, an anti-immigrant zealot who still insists that Obama's birth certificate is a forgery, introduces Trump, who emerges from behind a curtain as though walking out on to a game show. 'Heeeeere's Donald!' As the crowd grows into the hundreds, they open up the bleachers on the upper level for the overflow. For the most part, Trump blathers like a drunk uncle at a barbecue. He calls Glenn Beck, who has endorsed his principal rival Ted Cruz, a 'nut job'. He brags about his wall to keep out the Mexicans. 'It's going to be a big wall,' he says. 'A big, beautiful wall. You're gonna love this wall.' Afterwards, Brian Stevens, thirty-seven, tells me he thought Trump was impressive. 'I don't agree with everything he says. But I think he'll make a difference. He has to. Someone's got to stand up for America. We need him.'

Obama rocketed to national fame on the promise that there should be no more days like these. At the 2004 Democratic Party convention, he described the nation's partisan divide as though it had been imposed from the outside by cynical operatives and a simplistic media – 'spin masters and negative ad peddlers who embrace the politics of anything goes'. Back then, just over a year into the Iraq War, it looked as if America couldn't get much more polarised. But it did.

When Obama stood in 2008, one of the central pledges of his campaign was that he would rise above the fray in a spirit of bipartisan co-operation. That's not how it worked out. In 2010, the then Senate minority leader, Mitch McConnell, said the Republican Party's 'top political priority over the next two years should be to deny President Obama a second term'. Republican congressmen, who refused to co-operate even with their own leadership, repeatedly threatened to bring the US to the brink of default, or simply to shut the government down, unless Obama backed down from promises he'd made or repealed laws that had already been passed. A few years ago, as the Republican-led House of Representatives engineered a brief government shutdown, congressman Marlin Stutzman illustrated how petulant Obama's opponents had become: 'We have to get something out of this,' he said. 'And I don't know what that even is.'

Regardless of what he said or did, President Obama was always going to be a lightning rod for political polarisation. Some argued that this was because the right could not come to terms with a Black president, and there's probably something to that. At times, such as when the Republicans refused to return his calls or refer to him as president, or when someone shouted 'Liar!' during a presidential address, they appeared to refuse to recognise Obama as the legitimate holder of the office.

But the issues went way beyond race. In all sorts of ways, he embodied the anxieties of a section of white America. He is the son of a Kenyan immigrant at a moment when America is struggling to come to terms with the impact of immigration and foreign trade. He is the son of a non-observant Muslim who came to power as the country was losing wars in predominantly Muslim lands. He is the product of a mixed-race relationship at a time when one of the fastest-growing racial groups in the nation is made up of those who identify as 'more than one race'. He is a non-white president who ends his term at a time when the majority of children in America aged five and under are not white.

Demographically and geopolitically, being a white American no longer means what it used to. Obama became a proxy for those who could not accept that decline and who understood his very presence as both a threat and a humiliation. Trump, in many ways, is their response.

In his final State of the Union address, in January, Obama conceded that he had not come close to achieving his dream of a more consensual political culture. 'It's one of the few regrets of my presidency', he said, 'that the rancour and suspicion between the parties has gotten worse instead of better. I have no doubt a president with the gifts of Lincoln or Roosevelt might have better bridged the divide, and I guarantee I'll keep trying to be better so long as I hold this office.' With nine months left in an election year, it is difficult to see what would break the logjam.

By the end of Obama's first term in 2012, there was a general sense that things hadn't moved fast enough, that he had caved in to his opponents too easily. It was as though he negotiated with himself before reaching across the aisle, only to have his hand slapped away in disdain anyway. Having been elected on a mantle of hope, he seemed both aloof and adrift. Having moved people with his rhetoric, he was now failing to connect.

At a televised town hall meeting two years after his election, Obama was confronted by Velma Hart, an African American mother of two who articulated the disappointments of many. 'I'm exhausted,' she told him. 'I'm exhausted of defending you, defending your administration, defending the mantle of change that I voted for, and deeply disappointed with where we are right now.'

A few months later, Hart lost her job as chief financial officer for a veterans' organisation. By the time I met her, in the summer of 2011, she was re-employed but still far from impressed. 'Here's the thing,' she told me. 'I didn't engage my president to hug and kiss me. But what I did think I'd be able to appreciate is the change he was talking about during the campaign. I want leadership and decisiveness and action that helps this country get better. That's what I want, because that benefits me, that benefits my circle and that benefits my children.'

'Do you think he's decisive?' I asked.

'Ummm, sometimes . . .' she said. Like many, Hart wanted to support Obama but felt he wasn't making it easy. 'Not always, no,' she added, after a pause.

The notion that strong individuals can bend the world to their will is compelling. It is also deeply flawed. 'That's what we're taught to believe from an early age,' Susan Aylward, who used to work in an Ohio food co-op, told me. 'We're taught that one man should be able to fix everything. Abe Lincoln, George Washington, Ronald Reagan – history's told as though it were all down to them. The world is way too complex for that.'

I first met Susan in 2004, coming out of the opening night of Michael Moore's *Fahrenheit 9/11* in Akron. Back then, she said she intended to vote for John Kerry because he wasn't Bush, but she didn't love him. Four years later, we had breakfast just a week before Obama was elected, and she could barely contain her excitement. She made her two-year-old granddaughter, Sasha, who's mixed race, sit up with her on election night. 'We wanted her to be able to say she saw it that day, even if she didn't really know what she was seeing.'

But when we caught up in 2012, Susan was processing her disappointment. 'It's not going to change my vote,' she said. 'I just wish he could have been better. I don't even know how, exactly. If you're going to be president, then I guess you obviously want to be in the history books. So what does he want to be in the history books for? I don't quite know the answer to that yet.'

When it comes to Obama, people have to own their disappointment. That doesn't mean it's not valid, just that it often says as much about them as it does about him. No individual can solve America's problems. Most radical change in the US, like elsewhere, comes out of huge social movements from below. Poor people cannot simply elect a better life for themselves and expect that vested interests won't resist them at every turn: that's not how Western democracy works.

I supported Obama against Hillary Clinton because he had opposed the war in Iraq at a time when that could have damaged his political career; she had supported it in order to sustain her own. I thought he was the most progressive candidate that could be elected, and while even his agenda was inadequate for the needs of the people I most care about – the poor and the marginalised – it could still make a difference. I got my disappointment in early, to avoid the rush.

I appreciated the racially symbolic importance of Obama's victory and celebrated it. But I didn't fetishise it because I never expected much that was substantial to emerge from it. He leveraged his racial identity for electoral gain, without promising much in return. As a candidate, race was central to his meaning but absent from his message. When I read the transcript of the nomination speech I saw with my mother-in-law in the South Side that night in 2008, I realised he had quoted Martin Luther King but had declined to mention him by name, referring to him instead as the 'old preacher'. 'If a Black candidate can't quote Martin Luther King by name,' I thought, 'who can they quote?' I jokingly referred to him as the 'incognegro'.

Obama never promised radical change, and given the institutions in which he was embedded, he was never going to be in a position to deliver it. You don't get to become president of the United States without raising millions from very wealthy people and corporations (or being a billionaire yourself), who will turn against you if you don't serve their interests. Congress, with which Obama spars, is similarly corrupted by money. Seats in the House of Representatives are openly and brazenly gerrymandered.

This excuses Obama nothing. On any number of fronts, particularly the economy, the banks and civil liberties, he could have done more, or better. He recognised this himself, and in 2011, shortly before his second election, produced a list of issues he felt he'd been holding back on: immigration reform, poverty, the Middle East, Guantánamo Bay and gay marriage.

By 2011, even those closest to Obama could see he was losing not only his base but his *raison d'être* as an agent of change. 'You were seen as someone who would walk through the wall for the middle class,' his senior adviser David Axelrod told him that year. 'We need to get back to that.'

Back then, Obama's prospects looked slim. His campaign second time around was a far cry from the euphoria of the first. The president's argument boiled down to 'Things were terrible when I came to power, are much better now than they would have been were I not in power, and will get worse if I am removed from power.' What started as 'Yes, we can' had curdled into 'Could be worse'.

But Obama has always been lucky in his enemies. The Republican Party effectively undermined and humiliated their nominee, Mitt

Romney, who then proved a terrible candidate. In 2012, I accompanied Howard Davis, the man I'd met weeping at a Chicago polling station back in 2008, who voted for Obama again. There were no tears this time. In the words of Sade, it's never as good as the first time.

As Obama comes to the end of his tenure, we are no longer confined to discussing what it means that he is president; we can now talk in definite terms about what Obama did. Indulging the symbolic promise of a moment is one thing; engaging with the substantial record of more than seven years in power is quite another.

Everybody has their list. None is definitive. Obama withdrew US soldiers from Iraq (only to resume bombing later), relaxed relations with Cuba, executed Osama bin Laden, reached a nuclear deal with Iran and vastly improved America's standing in the world. Twenty million uninsured adults now have health insurance because of Obamacare. Unemployment was 7.8 per cent and rising when he came to power; today, it is 4.9 per cent and falling. He indefinitely deferred the deportation of the parents of children who are either US citizens or legal residents, and expanded that protection to children who entered the country illegally with their parents (the Dream Act). Wind and solar power outputs are set to triple; the automobile industry was rescued. He eventually spoke out forcefully for gun control. He appointed two women to the Supreme Court: Elena Kagan and Sonia Sotomayor, the first Latina. When those on the left question Obama's progressive bona fides, this is generally the list that is read back by his defenders, who mock them as though his critics are mimicking John Cleese in *Life of Brian*, when he asks, 'What have the Romans ever done for us?'

There are, of course, other facts to contend with. Obama escalated fighting in Afghanistan, and the troops are still there; deported more people than any president in US history; used the 1917 Espionage

Act to prosecute more than twice as many whistle-blowers as all previous presidents combined; oversaw a 700 per cent increase in drone strikes in Pakistan (not to mention Yemen, Somalia and elsewhere), resulting in between 1,900 and 3,000 deaths, including those of more than a hundred civilians; saw both wealth and income inequality grow as corporate profits rocketed; and led his party to some of the heaviest midterm defeats in history. In Syria, he drew a red line in the sand, and then claimed he hadn't; he said he wouldn't put boots on the ground, and then he did.

The discrepancies between Obama's campaign promises and his record in office have been most glaring in matters of civil liberties. 'This administration puts forward a false choice between the liberties we cherish and the security we provide,' he said as a candidate on 1 August 2007. 'You can't have 100 per cent security and then 100 per cent privacy and zero inconvenience,' he said on 7 June 2013, during the Edward Snowden affair. 'We're going to have to make some choices.'

And finally, there are the things Obama didn't do. He didn't pursue a single intelligence officer over torture; he didn't pursue a single finance executive for malfeasance in connection with the 2007/8 crash; he didn't close Guantánamo Bay.

But a legacy is not a ledger. It is both less substantial than a list of things done and more meaningful. 'At some point in Jackie Robinson's career, the point ceases to be how many hits he got or bases he stole,' Mitch Stewart, who played a leading role in both Obama campaigns, tells me. 'As great and important as all these stats were, there was a bigger picture.'

Legacies are about what people feel as well as what they know, about the present as much as the past. Aesthetically, there has always been something retro about Obama's public profile: the original campaign posters announcing 'Hope' and 'Change'; the black-and-white video clips in will.i.am's 'Yes We Can' video. With his family at his side, his brand offered not glamour exactly but chic. Like John

F. Kennedy, he projected an image that enough Americans either wanted or needed, or both: a young, good-looking family; a bright future. He offered Camelot without the castle: no ties to the old; all about the future.

Photographs of Obama at the White House suggest both he and Michelle grew into this role quite happily. Whether it was Michelle dancing with kids on the White House lawn or Barack making faces at babies and chasing toddlers around the Oval Office, they returned a sense of playful normality to the White House, an unforced conviviality that did not detract from the gravity of office.

'It's important to remember that he was more recently a more normal person than most people at that level,' one veteran member of his team told me. 'For the 2000 convention, he couldn't even get a floor credential. In 2004, he introduced the presidential nominee. In 2008, he was the nominee. It's tough to see him and Michelle and not give him that benefit of the doubt. He's had small kids in the White House. I think people will remember that as a moment and an era.'

When Virginia McLaurin, a 106-year-old African American woman, was granted her lifelong wish to visit the White House earlier this year, the president and his wife danced with her quite unselfconsciously. 'Slow down now, don't go too fast,' Obama joked. As the second term has progressed, they have seemed happy in their skin – and, for many, the novelty that it is black skin has not worn off. 'I thought I would never live to get in the White House,' McLaurin said, looking up at her hosts. 'I am so happy. A Black president, a Black wife, and I'm here to celebrate Black history.'

Legacies are never settled; they are constantly evolving. A few years before he died, almost two-thirds of Americans disapproved of Martin Luther King because of his stance both against the Vietnam War and in favour of the redistribution of wealth. Yet within a generation, his birthday was a national holiday; when Americans ranked the most admired public figures of the twentieth century in 1999, King came second only to Mother Teresa.

Ronald Reagan is now hailed as a conservative hero, even though he supported amnesty for undocumented migrants and massively inflated the government deficit. During the final year of Bill Clinton's presidency, most guessed that his legacy would be one of scandal. Instead, he was hailed for presiding over a sustained economic recovery. But as his wife seeks the Democratic nomination, he has had to recant key parts of that legacy: the crime bill, welfare reform, financial deregulation – those elements which have disproportionately impoverished African Americans and enriched the banks.

'History will be a far kinder judge than the current Republican Congress,' Stewart tells me. 'It will rest on the untold successes that this administration has had. Energy efficiency, carbon efficiency. He reformed the student loan programme, which is going to have an impact on a generation of students. He's catapulted the US forward in ways that will continue to pay dividends long after his presidency. His legacy will be about these smaller, unsung accomplishments that will have a generational impact.'

Paradoxically, the element of Obama's legacy for which he will be best remembered – being the first Black president – relates to an area that has seen little substantial headway: racial equality. The wealth gap between Black and white Americans has grown, as has the unemployment gap and Black poverty; Black income has stagnated. That's not to suggest he has done nothing. He has appointed an unprecedented number of Black judges, released several thousand non-violent drug offenders, reduced the disparity in sentencing for crack and powder cocaine offenders. Anything he did that helped the poor, like Obamacare, will disproportionately help African Americans.

But, broadly speaking, Obama's racial legacy is symbolic, not substantial. The fact that he could be president challenged how African Americans saw their country. The fact that their lives did not radically improve as a result did not shift their understanding of how America works. When Obama was contemplating a run for the White House, his wife asked him what he thought he could accomplish if he won. 'The day I take the oath of office,' he replied, 'the world will look at us differently. And millions of kids across this country will look at themselves differently. That alone is something.'

The imagery did not, in the end, translate quite so neatly. True, when Trayvon Martin was shot dead by George Zimmerman in 2012, Obama was able to say what no other president could have said: 'Trayvon Martin could have been my son.' Nonetheless, it is unlikely that Zimmerman looked at Trayvon and thought, 'There goes the future president of America.' Thanks to Obama, Americans see racism differently; they do not, however, view Black people differently.

Obama will leave office during a period of heightened racial tension over police shootings. 'His presidency was supposed to pass into an era of post-racism and colour blindness,' Keeanga-Yamahtta Taylor, Princeton professor and author of *From #BlackLivesMatter to Black Liberation*, tells me. 'Yet it was under his administration that the Black Lives Matter movement erupted. In many ways, it's the most significant anti-racist movement in the last forty years, and it happens under the first Black president. The eruption of this movement can be interpreted as a disappointment in the limitations of the Barack Obama presidency. And some of those limitations can be explained externally, by the hostility with which he's been met by the mostly Republican Congress. But some of it lies in the limitations of his own policies.'

Over the past couple of years, the Black Lives Matter debate has taken place almost without reference to Obama. It suggests that, on one level, his relationship to some of the key issues surrounding Black life is almost ornamental. He is the framed poster in the barbershop or the nail salon, the mural on the underpass, the picture in the diner or bodega – an aspiration not to be mistaken for the attrition of daily life. The question of whether America can elect a Black president has been answered; the issue of the sanctity of Black life, however, has yet to be settled.

At the Col Ballroom in Davenport, Iowa, on 29 January, it is difficult not to feel nostalgic. Built in 1914 and listed on the National Register of Historic Places, the chandeliers both illuminate and illustrate the regal atmosphere of an old music hall, while the posters bear witness to the greats who have played there, from Duke Ellington to Jimi Hendrix.

So when the swing band stops playing and Bill Clinton steps on stage to present his wife, Hillary, the sense that you have stepped back in time feels complete. Hillary has become a far more animated candidate since she lost to Obama here eight years ago. Heather Johnson, a precinct captain whose job is to rally support in her area, has been knocking on doors, calling supporters and galvanising the local faithful for months now. 'After she lost last time, I decided if she ran, I'd do everything I could to make sure she didn't lose again,' she says. 'Who else has her experience?'

It's just a few days before the caucuses, and this mostly older crowd is energised. But Hillary still suffers from the same vulnerabilities as in 2008. She is seen as an insider, when the voters want change. She remains dogged by scandal – her emails sent via a private server – and voters find her untrustworthy. She promises progress by increments, rather than transformation. She even tries to make a selling point of the fact that her platform is not exciting. 'I'd rather under-promise and over-deliver,' she tells the crowd. She is effectively running for Obama's third term, asking for the opportunity to continue what he started.

A few days earlier, at Grinnell College, Bernie Sanders offered a younger crowd a future that is more radical and bold – free health-care, no tuition fees, a $15-an-hour minimum wage – and a clear departure from a political culture corrupted by money and corporate influence. Sanders has reservations about Obama's legacy; he recently endorsed a book called *Buyer's Remorse: How Obama Let Progressives Down*. But on the stump he knows there is no mileage in criticising the president.

This crowd likes Obama. His second term has been more sure-footed than his first. Following the Sandy Hook shootings, when twenty-year-old Adam Lanza killed twenty schoolchildren, six adult staff, his mother and himself, Obama finally vowed to challenge the legislative inertia on gun control and has not stopped since. As the Republicans have proven themselves incapable of compromise, Obama has felt more licence to stamp his authority on the political culture. A few months after the midterms, he signed the Dream Act; last November, he vetoed the Keystone Pipeline, from Canada to the Mexican Gulf, because of environmental concerns. While other presidents use the lame-duck portion of their tenure to get to work on their presidential libraries, Obama has been tying up loose ends. 'He'll be a blueprint for how you have a second term,' Mitch Stewart thinks. 'Every day there is an hourglass mentality.'

Karen Sanchez, a nineteen-year-old Sanders supporter in Marshalltown, Iowa, tells me she thinks Obama has done a great job. 'He did what he could. I think he would have done more, but they kept blocking him.' A Hillary supporter at an event in Adel, Iowa, who did not want to give her name, agreed. 'He gave it his best shot,' she said. 'I don't think anyone could have done better when you're up against people who just want to stonewall you.'

This was the standard response at any Democrat event when I asked how people thought Obama would be remembered. Effectively a phantom legacy; not what he actually achieved, but what he might have done if the other side wasn't so unreasonable. As endorsements go, this seemed like faint praise. Like the 1986 World Cup England might have won were it not for Maradona's Hand of God, or the Gore presidency that might have been were it not for hanging chads and the Supreme Court, the case for Obama's legacy was in the subjunctive – what might have been. Yes. We. Tried.

But as the primary season has drawn on, what looked like a partial, qualified stamp of approval has been developing into something more complete and adulatory. Compared with the front-runners, carnival barkers and showmen, Obama is starting to walk taller and appear smarter than ever.

The day after a recent Republican debate, CNN ran the headline, 'Trump Defends Size of His Penis', after Trump objected to Marco Rubio's allusion that because Trump has small hands, he has a small penis. 'Look at these hands; are they small hands?' Trump asked a cheering crowd. 'I guarantee you, there's no problem.'

When the political tone is set this low, when so little is expected of the candidates and the choices are this poor, the fact that Obama tried – and the way that he tried – starts to eclipse the fact that he so often failed. Like a dutiful doctor, he performed triage on a reluctant patient and didn't give up even when the prospects looked bleak. He did his job.

As his term comes to an end and the fractured, volatile nature of the country's electoral politics is once again laid bare, Americans may be coming to realise that, in Obama, it had an adult in the room. As violence erupts at election rallies and spills over into the streets, they may come to appreciate the absence of scandal and drama from the White House. As their wages stagnated, industries collapsed, insecurities grew and hopes faded, he tried to get something done. Not much, not enough – but something. It is possible to have serious, moral criticisms of Obama and his legacy and still appreciate his value, given the alternatives.

In Obama, Americans are losing someone who took both public service and the public seriously; someone who stood for something bigger and more important than himself. This is the end of the line for a leader who believed that facts mattered; that Americans were not fools; that their democracy meant something and that government had a role; that America could be better than this.

The boy who killed and the mother who tried to stop him

In 2017, I led a year-long series on knife crime in Britain.
, 19 September 2017, London

On 23 March 2015, Shirley (not her real name) sent an email to her MP with the heading 'PLEASE HELP ME SAVE MY SON!!!' She described how the behaviour of her thirteen-year-old son Sean (not his real name) was '[deteriorating] rapidly, involving himself with the wrong crowd', and her fears for the impact this could have on his siblings. She detailed how she had enrolled herself in parenting classes, consulted with social workers and psychologists, sought referrals for mental health assessments, requested to move him from his school and asked for help to move her family out of London, but felt she was getting nowhere.

She ended the email: 'All I want is for my [children] not to become another statistic and would like all the help possible to stop this from happening.'

A few months later, she warned a meeting of social workers in the London borough where they lived, 'If we don't do something, he's either going to end up dead or someone's going to end up in a body bag.'

Two weeks ago, Sean, now fifteen, was sentenced to fourteen years in prison for stabbing to death Quamari Serunkuma-Barnes, also fifteen. Sean had been waiting near Quamari's school in Willesden, north-west London, with a knife on 23 January; when he saw Quamari leaving school, he started to chase him. Taller and faster, Sean caught up with Quamari and stabbed him three times, including one fatal blow that pierced a rib and punctured a lung. Quamari died that evening, the fifth of twenty-six children and teenagers to have been killed by knives in Britain this year.

After Sean was convicted in July, I wrote: 'It is difficult to know what justice looks like when one fifteen-year-old is dead and another is on trial for their murder . . . One thrashes about, mostly in vain, for an institution, service or agency to blame; for an intervention that could have helped or a moral safety net with smaller holes that might have caught him.'

It turns out, in this case, that such a search would not be in vain. Shirley, thirty-three, can document, in painstaking detail, requests for help that were either not answered, not met or where the response was inadequate even as she warned of the possible consequences.

There's no saying if this tragedy could have been prevented. What is clear is that more could have been done to try to prevent it. 'My son is totally responsible for his actions,' Shirley says. 'But the preventative measures that should have been put in place were not there. I'm not blaming [the council] to say: "You held my son and made him do this." Ultimately, he's responsible. Ultimately, there's a family that is broken.'

For the most part, fatal knife crime is reduced to a crude morality play, in which the young perpetrators are all but invisible. Abstracted from parents or community, we meet them in the dock, where they are defined by their crime. They are not children who have killed but killers; not people who have done something monstrous but monsters. They stand reduced to this one act: they killed a child. Their anonymity protected by law, we do not see their pictures or hear from their parents. By the time the trial is over, we have no idea where they have come from, why or how, only where they're going – prison. Without faces, families or friends, they are not children, they are cautionary tales.

But in order to heed the caution in these tragic crimes, we must first restore the humanity of those who commit them. Failing to do so is not only morally problematic, it is counter-productive. The best chance we have of sparing the next child from an early death is finding out why the last one died. There are lots of lessons. But none can be learned if they do not start from the fact that this murder was committed by a boy, not a metaphor.

Sean has a narrow, handsome face and a lanky frame. From the words of his mother, his barrister and the judge, one builds a picture of an impulsive teenager with a keen sense of grievance, as desperate for affection as he is clueless how to earn it. Every day of the trial he would wrap his long arms around his mother and, whenever he could, touch his barrister's hand before he was led away. Lost, angry and responding intensely to slights, real or imagined, he has struggled to connect actions to consequences, and his sense of vulnerability seems intimately connected to his episodic bursts of violence.

Much of this is standard teenage fare – only with far greater stakes than most teenagers are used to. Shirley has done her best to guide and protect him from the cruelty of the streets, the negligence of the state and, for much of his short life, himself. Moments after Sean was convicted of murdering Quamari, I saw her emerge from court and bump into Quamari's father, Paul Barnes. Both tearful, they clung on to each other.

'I'm sorry,' he told her. 'I just wanted justice for my son.'

'I'm sorry,' she said. 'I'm sorry.'

'I wish I could have spoken to him more,' she tells me, two months later. We have peered into three coffee shops, looking for somewhere not too crowded so she might cry and not make a scene, settling on a cafe in Morrisons. 'But at the same time, what could I say? I'm probably the last person he wants to see. That's why I have to give him a massive amount of credit for actually taking the time to say something to me.'

Every day of the trial, she travelled to the Old Bailey wondering whether her fellow passengers would move away if they knew where she was going and why.

'Whenever [Sean] was judged – and he was judged a lot as a child – I was judged. But I had to sit with him through that. I wouldn't have it any other way. And that's one of the reasons I didn't want anyone with me. Because I didn't want them to feel they were being ridiculed. That they were being judged. This is a burden I had to bear on my own.'

Shirley raised Sean on her own for most of his life. She separated from his father when he started dealing drugs, but his father and paternal grandmother played an active role in his life. A happy kid, he watched *Finding Nemo* so often that Shirley knew the film by heart. Then he graduated to *The Lion King*, deciding early on that he wanted to be a vet. Shirley is religious and took him to church. A very active child, in later years he became an accomplished athlete and footballer who gained the attention of professional scouts.

When Sean was in primary school, his dad was deported. This was the first time Shirley noticed Sean getting angry and withdrawn. She tried to get help from Child and Adolescent Mental Health Services (CAMHS) at the time, but was told he didn't meet the threshold. At secondary school he seemed to be doing well academically, but before long he was expelled after an altercation with a teacher. From there he was sent to a Pupil Referral Unit, which Shirley considered not an alternative academic environment but a dumping ground for children with behavioural challenges. She tried to get him moved.

'This is not the environment for my child,' she told them. 'I know my child. If he is around people who are bad, he's going to want to be the best at being bad. If he's around good people, he's going to want to be the best at being good.'

Soon Sean was getting into trouble alongside kids she thought were a bad influence. This was when Shirley enrolled herself in a parenting course and requested help to be rehoused outside London, where her son might find a more positive peer group. She was supported by a Safer Schools police officer working with Sean, who wrote: 'It would be highly beneficial . . . as a preventative measure and a chance to give him and his family a fresh start.'

The request was denied. Shirley had him assessed again by CAMHS, but she says that after a twenty-minute interview he was declared fine. 'I'm not a professional,' she says, 'but I don't think you can assess in that short space of time.' Unable to move her family, she took the difficult decision of moving Sean after he and a friend were threatened with their lives unless they returned some stolen goods. She put him in care, asking for him to be placed outside London, away from temptation. Instead, he remained in the capital and started getting into more serious trouble, including street robberies. She complained and lobbied. Emails received no response. It was around this time that she first appealed to her MP to 'HELP ME SAVE MY SON!!!' Further emails to the council over the next couple of years carried subject lines including 'I HAVE HAD ENOUGH' and 'UTTER DISAPPOINTMENT'.

'Every time my son gets in trouble it's for something more and more sinister,' she recalls telling them in one meeting. 'So you're waiting for something to be broken that can't be fixed in order to come to some kind of resolution. I'm asking you to prevent the item from breaking.'

Brent council says: 'An independent multi-agency review is now taking place. The council, along with other agencies involved, has been participating fully in this process to help us agree how lessons can be learned . . . it would not be appropriate to comment further on any aspect of the case until this review is concluded later in the autumn.'

The way Shirley sees it, the problem is not that the council did nothing. It's that what it was doing wasn't working and, she felt, lacked urgency and focus. 'The local authority failed him,' his barrister told the court during sentencing. Eventually, Sean was moved to one care home in a rural area in the north that he kept running away from, before being transferred to another, where he was racially abused, provoking him to physical retaliation. He was eventually returned to London. Shirley asked for anger management classes for him but didn't get them, and they were offered family therapy only when he was living four hours away. On the day of the murder, she says, she called the council to express her concern that Sean was not getting any educational provision.

'If I was in denial, that would be one thing,' she says. 'But if you're open and you're going to the foot of the cross, where the mercy's supposed to be, where they're supposed to help you and give you those multi-agencies to come into your life, if you've gone there and they can't turn around and help you but say, "It cannot meet the threshold," or "The budget is not there," then what are you supposed to do?'

At one point Shirley asked for Sean to be put in a rehabilitation unit that he wouldn't be able to leave. But, she claims, the council said they thought the request would be denied by the courts because it would take away his freedom, and even if he could have a place, it would be too expensive. 'But I didn't ask them how expensive it was,' she says, tearing up. 'Can you go to Quamari's parents now and give them £10 million or £100 million for them to feel better? You can never fill that void because their child is gone.' Two months before the murder, she asked again.

In the TV series *Six Feet Under*, Brenda tells her undertaker boyfriend, 'You know what I find interesting? If you lose a spouse, you're a widow or a widower. If you're a child and you lose your parents, then you're an orphan. But what's the word to describe a parent who loses a child? I guess that's just too fucking awful to even have a name.' When one fifteen-year-old is dead and another is in prison, there is no need to compete for sadness. There's more than enough grief of every kind to go around. On the day of the sentencing, an impact statement from Quamari's mother, Lillian Serunkuma, was read out. It was addressed not to the court but to Sean. 'You have a future regardless of your sentencing. You stole our son's future when you felt entitled to take his life for no reason other than to gratify your own self-worth and ego, which evidently is misplaced and nonsensical,' it read.

'You are a child but your actions were pure evil and for this we cannot imagine our words will do anything to make you see the hurt and pain you have caused . . . Your actions were indefensible and it should have been recognised and flagged up, the danger you are to yourself and to the people around you.'

The sentencing would bring one more shock. Less than an hour before the court sat, the judge received Sean's confession, which his barrister read out in open court. Nine days before the murder, Sean explained, he had been beaten up by members of a gang. When he went to visit a friend, he was offered not a salve for this adolescent wound but salt. His friend's mother said, 'I've never known you take a beating,' while his friend asked whether he would 'take the violation'.

That same friend gave him the knife, ski mask and gloves. Sean took them to his foster home and left them under his bed. He nursed the grudge for more than a week. One rival in particular kept mocking him online, taunting him as Sean rapped on social media just a couple of days before the murder, calling him a 'wasteman'.

What emerges is an account of a boy in an almost semi-delirious fugue state on the day he killed Quamari, his mind racing from grievance to revenge, incapable of finding solace or calm. 'When I woke on 23 January, I felt frustrated and vexed. I still had a knife . . . I called my nan [his father's mother] . . . I wanted to see her because I thought that if I saw her she would calm me down. I was angry and upset.' He tried to visit his nan, but she wasn't in. 'I went to the school. By then the words about taking the violation were ringing in my ears.'

Sean planned to confront his rival but saw Quamari first. Quamari had nothing to do with any gang or the beating Sean had suffered. But Sean recognised him and associated him with an incident in which he had been humiliated two years earlier.

'I am telling the truth now for Quamari's mum and dad,' Sean concluded. 'I had a dream that I was in their house and allowing them to speak to me for me to tell them what happened and that I am sorry. I am sorry. I didn't mean Quamari to get so hurt. I'm not a murderer. I'm not a wasteman. I didn't want him to die. I wish I'd

Dispatches from the Diaspora

told the truth before. I listened to someone close to me I shouldn't have listened to. I didn't trust anyone else. They always let me down. I want to have a different life, but I don't know how. I am trying and am SIP (serving in peace). I am doing well in education and got an award last week. I am sorry.'

Shirley says he seemed lighter after the conviction. 'Mum, I'm tired of this life,' he told her. Finally he has anger management classes and a more regular education. A few days after the murder, Shirley and her family were at last moved out of London. The night before we met, Sean called home. 'Mum, I've got some good news for you,' he told her. 'They've put me forward for my GCSEs.'

And with this, Shirley cries again. 'I'm so happy for him. But on the other hand, when I think about the background, I just crawl back in my shell. For the longest time I couldn't even bring myself to say Quamari's name. I didn't even allow myself to mourn Sean's situation because I didn't think I was worthy of feeling anything because my child was still here. I had to get myself out of that mode because I was about to break down. It's still a loss for me as well.'

And so Shirley is destined to hover between anger and grief, regret and recrimination, asking and answering the three essential questions that act as pillars for her tender emotional state, as though in an incantation, even as they offer neither closure nor comfort. 'Is he responsible for his actions?' she asks, rhetorically. 'Yes. Did I try everything I could? Yes. Were we failed? Yes.'

Hounding Commonwealth citizens is no accident. It's cruelty by design

The Windrush *scandal revealed how anybody could become a border guard and how every Caribbean-born Briton of a certain age was vulnerable.*

Guardian, 13 April 2018, London

On 4 April, Prince Charles opened the Commonwealth Games on Australia's Gold Coast with a brief reminder of the historical ties that bind. 'The ancient stories told by the indigenous people of Australia remind us that, even though we may be half a world away, we are all connected,' he said. 'Over the years, these Friendly Games have shown the potential of the Commonwealth to connect people of different backgrounds and nationalities.'

Five days later, the *Guardian* published an article about Michael Braithwaite that illustrates how fragile and selective those connections are. Braithwaite, a Barbadian-born Briton who arrived here in 1961, when he was nine, was educated here, has worked here his entire life, married here and has three British children and five British grandchildren. He had been a special needs teaching assistant at a north London primary school for over fifteen years when his employers launched a 'routine' immigration status check. Braithwaite, sixty-six, assumed, correctly, that he was British.

But now he had to prove it, providing up to four pieces of documentary evidence to the Home Office for every year he had been here. He lost his job when the Home Office failed to issue him with the documents to verify that he was in the country legally. Trying to prove he was who he was, and who nobody ever seriously doubted he always had been, made him ill. 'It made me feel like I was an alien. I almost fell apart with the stress,' he said.

Within minutes of the article about Braithwaite going online the

Home Office had emailed his lawyers to say the documents had been approved. Welcome to the United Kingdom. With the exception of Northern Ireland, our existence as an island means our physical border is, for the most part, well defined. We stop and start at the water's edge. The entry points, be they at ports or airports, are heavily fortified and highly militarised.

But our administrative borders are invisible and omnipresent, dividing communities and generations at whim and will. These borders represent not a physical space but a political one that can be reproduced without warning in places of learning and healing. At any moment almost anyone – your boss, doctor, child's headmaster or landlord – can become a border guard – indeed, they may be legally obliged to do so – and on the basis of their judgement you may be denied your livelihood, family, home and health.

Incredibly, this is not a glitch in the system. It is the system. Braithwaite has become ensnared in a deliberate government policy, set out by the prime minister, Theresa May, when she was home secretary, to create a 'really hostile environment for illegal immigrants'. The aim was to make life in Britain so onerous for immigrants that those who could not produce the documents at any random point in their daily life would find their life so difficult that they would, in the words of Mitt Romney, 'self-deport'.

The policy, set out in the 2014 and 2016 Immigration Acts, demanded that employers, bank staff, NHS workers, private landlords and a range of other bodies (I have been asked to produce my passport in order to do a book reading at a literary festival) require evidence of people's citizenship or immigration status. It also introduced a 'deport first, appeal later' policy for thousands facing removal who face no 'risk of serious irreversible harm'. This, we may assume, is how a South African woman was accused of faking an illness to avoid deportation, only to die five days later.

The acts, first implemented in the year that UKIP won the European elections and then again in the year of the Brexit referendum, were red meat to the grievances of a base that the Tories were losing. We should not be surprised that they are adversely affecting Black Britons who have every right to be here, any more than we should have been surprised when there was a rise in Islamophobic attacks following Brexit – even though precious few Muslims in Britain come from elsewhere in Europe.

And so it is, seventy years after *Windrush* brought the symbolic arrival of post-war Caribbean migrants, that Braithwaite is one of many who now struggle to justify their existence. There's Renford McIntyre, sixty-four, who came to Britain from Jamaica when he was fourteen to join his mum, worked as a tool setter and is now homeless and unemployed, after he was fired when he couldn't produce papers to prove his citizenship. Or sixty-one-year-old Paulette Wilson, who used to cook for MPs in the House of Commons. She was put in Yarl's Wood Immigration Removal Centre and then taken to Heathrow for deportation, before a last-minute reprieve prevented her from being sent to Jamaica, which she last visited when she was ten and where she has no surviving relatives. Or Albert Thompson, a sixty-three-year-old who came from Jamaica as a teenager and has lived in London for forty-four years. He was evicted from his council house and has now been denied NHS treatment for his cancer unless he can stump up £54,000, all because the hospital questions his immigration status.

Caribbean diplomats have once again called for the Home Office to show compassion. 'This is affecting people who came and gave a lifetime of service at a time when the UK was calling for workers and migrants,' explains Barbados high commissioner Guy Hewitt. 'They came because they were encouraged to come here to help build post-Second World War Britain and build it into the multicultural place that it is now.'

But if compassion is lacking, common sense would do. Even as citizenship tests aim to impart to newcomers the 'values of toleration and fair play', the immigration laws have sent long-standing citizens, who have paid their taxes and raised their families here, to homeless shelters or deportation centres because they have not been able to provide paperwork issued more than forty years ago, when they were kids.

For, lest we forget, this is also the fiftieth anniversary of Enoch Powell's 'rivers of blood' speech: a moment that revealed the galvanising force of populist racism. This mood bleeds effortlessly into immigration policy: the Commonwealth Immigrants Act 1968 was passed the same year, further restricting the future right of entry for former citizens of the empire and loosening the connections about which Prince Charles waxed so lyrical. Braithwaite was one of those 'charming, wide-grinning piccaninnies' to which Powell so disparagingly referred.

Arriving in 1961 (in the same year as my parents and coming from the same place), when Barbados was not yet independent, Braithwaite was effectively a British subject when he arrived, and his parents would have had passports to that effect. To find himself treated in this way is not just a violation of natural justice – it is an abdication of Britain's historical responsibility. Since he arrived before 1973, he has an automatic and permanent right to remain. He has violated no law; it is the law that is violating him.

We can't breathe

Even as the Black Lives Matter demonstrations took place, the issues they were raising were evident in mortuaries and hospital beds, where minorities were disproportionately impacted by the coronavirus.
New Statesman, 3 June 2020, London

I had been spending a fair amount of time reporting from the Caribbean when Hurricane Katrina devastated New Orleans in August 2005. Making my way to the Crescent City from Kingston, Jamaica, I arrived to see US troops stationed outside the Harrah's casino, as mostly Black people were plucked from trees and roofs and bodies floated down main streets and started decomposing in houses.

It wasn't just the levees that had been breached but the facade of a First World nation: one of the United States' most celebrated cities appeared like Port-au-Prince, only with skyscrapers.

The hurricane had not created the inequalities of race and class so evident in the aftermath; it had simply laid them bare. When Katrina struck, more than 44 per cent of New Orleans's residents were functionally illiterate; close to one in three African Americans in Louisiana lived in poverty; rates of Black infant mortality in the state were worse than infant mortality in Sri Lanka, and Black male life expectancy was the same as that for men in Kyrgyzstan. African Americans were less likely to leave town before the storm came because they were less likely to have cars or cash. As thousands of people, most of them Black, flocked to the convention centre, in search of shelter and sustenance, the head of the Federal Emergency Management Agency, Michael Brown, said, 'We're seeing people that we didn't know exist.'

Witnessing coronavirus disproportionately devastate minority communities, in Britain and elsewhere, feels a lot like being in New

Orleans shortly after Katrina. The pandemic is exposing broader inequalities, systemic injustice and official denial.

At the outset the disparities were impressionistic and anecdotal. The roll call of the deceased suggested something more than a pattern. The first ten doctors to die from Covid-19 in the UK were Black or Asian.

'At face value, it seems hard to see how this can be random,' the chair of the British Medical Association, Dr Chaand Nagpaul, said on 10 April. 'We have heard the virus does not discriminate between individuals but there's no doubt there appears to be a manifest disproportionate severity of infection in BAME [Black, Asian and minority ethnic] people and doctors. This has to be addressed – the government must act now.'

The snapshots appearing in the media merely confirmed what people were experiencing on the ground. Community activist and retired lecturer Hesketh Benoit, who is based in Haringey, north London, recalls chatting to reggae singer Delroy Washington, sixty-seven, one morning in late March; by the evening, Washington was dead. 'We'd been joking on the phone,' says Benoit. 'He seemed fine. He had high blood pressure. But he'd been a martial arts expert for forty years.'

Washington was the first person to die that Benoit knew. But before long a few others – elders who used to come and 'big him up' while he ran courses for the young; a couple of guys who were security guards – also fell. 'I remember thinking, "Hang on a minute. Something's going on here."' Today he can count twenty-eight people – all Black – he knows of who have perished, of whom five or six were close friends. That's about two a week. The youngest was only forty-two.

Statisticians and data journalists were soon able to quantify this lived experience. According to the Office for National Statistics (ONS), adjusting for age Black people are over four times more likely to die from Covid-19 than white people. Pakistanis and Bangladeshis are more than three times as likely, and Indians more than twice as likely. BAME people account for 13.4 per cent of the population and 34 per cent of the patients admitted to intensive care units.

A *Guardian* data analysis in April revealed that a high proportion of BAME residents was found to be the strongest predictor of a high Covid-19 death rate: for every 10 per cent increase in ethnic minority residents there were 2.9 more Covid-19 deaths per 100,000 people. (British Jews are also over-represented among the dead, although theories as to why that might be – which include religious practices among certain groups and an older-than-average population – are quite different from those relating to racial minorities.)

Carers have it worst. One in five of the NHS's nursing and support staff are BAME, but they comprise two-thirds of coronavirus deaths among such workers. In late April, Sky News discovered that 72 per cent of all health and social care staff who have died with Covid-19 were BAME.

Two urgent questions emerge from these grim statistics. The first is: why should this be? At first glance, the answer appears straightforward. Put bluntly, minority communities are more likely to be poor, and poor people are, in a range of ways, more likely to be vulnerable. For example, the ONS's analysis of English Housing Survey data from between 2014 and 2017 found that Bangladeshi families were fifteen times more likely to experience overcrowding than white British households, while Pakistanis were eight times more likely and Black people six times more. All three groups were more likely to live in deprived neighbourhoods and to experience higher unemployment, higher poverty and lower incomes than white people.

More than two decades after the 1999 Macpherson report into the Stephen Lawrence case – which found the police to be 'institutionally racist' – minorities remain more likely to fall foul of both the law of the land and the law of probabilities. Wherever there is a pile of deprivation, BAME people are over-represented at the bottom of it.

Material deprivation may not be the whole story. The ONS concludes that even when adjusting for deprivation, age and other factors,

Dispatches from the Diaspora

Black people, Pakistanis and Bangladeshis are almost twice as likely to die as white people.

There is speculation that this disparity may be explained genetically. Black people are more likely to suffer from cardiovascular disease and diabetes, which would, it is said, make them more susceptible to succumbing to the virus. Scientists at the DataLab at Oxford University have ruled that out. Others claim that a deficiency of vitamin D, common among some BAME communities, could be the cause. Thus far it remains only speculation, though the government started formally recommending vitamin D supplements in late April.

One need not dismiss these claims summarily to see that there are sufficient grounds to question their logic. Pakistanis and Bangladeshis are dying at a similarly disproportionate rate to Black people but share little in the way of an ethnically related genetic relationship. Meanwhile, Indians, who until relatively recently were part of the same country as Bangladeshis and Pakistanis, have suffered far lower death rates. The one thing that Black people, Pakistanis and Bangladeshis do have in common is that they are the poorest ethnic groups in the UK, concentrated in the kind of jobs where you might contract the virus. Indians, meanwhile, tend to be wealthier.

Elsewhere, the picture is similar. In Michigan, African Americans comprise 14 per cent of the population, 33 per cent of the reported infections and 40 per cent of the deaths. In Kansas, they are seven times more likely to die of Covid than whites. In New York City, Latinos have a higher death rate than African Americans; in Illinois, they have a higher infection rate. In Arizona and New Mexico, Native Americans are becoming infected at a far greater rate than Latinos.

African Americans, Native Americans, Black Britons, Latinos and British people of Pakistani and Bangladeshi origin do not have a culture or ethnically specific genetic material in common. What they do share is an experience of poverty, low pay and poor housing – and all the things that go with that, including ill health – that would make them susceptible to coronavirus.

There are further plausible explanations for the disparity in mortality rates. For historical reasons, related to migration, some groups are more likely to be concentrated in the health service, public transport and care work, while the modern economy has created significant concentrations of certain ethnicities in cleaning, taxi driving and security. For example, about 12.8 per cent of workers from Bangladeshi and Pakistani backgrounds are employed in public-facing transport jobs such as bus, coach and taxi driving, compared with 3.5 per cent of white people. These are all areas where workers are most at risk. Two Black employees in London – a taxi driver and a transport worker – have now died after being deliberately spat on by people who, it is believed, had Covid-19.

Though it adjusted for other factors, the ONS did not weight its findings to take into account the sectors where minorities are over-represented. 'This is something we want to explore further in our next release,' a spokesperson said. 'We see it as a crucial gap in the evidence to fill.'

Then there are a range of experiences that cannot be adjusted for in raw data, but certainly have an effect on behaviour and outcomes. A 2014 report by Roger Kline of Middlesex University for the NHS revealed BAME staff faced discriminatory treatment in recruitment, career development, membership of trust boards and disciplinary action. They were also more victimised if they were whistle-blowers, concluded the report, which was titled 'The "Snowy White Peaks" of the NHS'.

Other surveys show Black and Asian doctors are often treated as 'outsiders' by their bosses and peers. They are significantly more likely than their white colleagues to be referred to the General Medical Council by their NHS employers for an investigation that could damage or end their careers. They are twice as likely not to raise concerns because of fears of recrimination, and complain of often feeling bullied and harassed. Health workers who are migrants may have no recourse to public funds if they are fired, and a disproportionate number are on zero-hours contracts. Add all this together and it becomes clear why they might be more compliant when put on certain shifts and less insistent in demanding personal protective equipment (PPE).

This is what systemic discrimination looks like. Not isolated incidents but a range of processes built on presumption, assumption, confidence, ignorance and exclusory institutional, personal and professional networks, all buttressed by the dead weight of privilege.

Race is a construct. 'Marble cake, crazy quilt and tutti-frutti', the sociocultural anthropologist Roger Sanjek once wrote, 'are all better metaphors of human physical variability than is the x number of races of humankind.' But racism is real. It's not the virus that discriminates; it is society.

The jury is out on whether more vitamin D would make a difference. But the case on whether more jobs, better pay and better housing would make a difference is closed. Inequality is killing us: being Black is a pre-existing condition. 'You already know enough,' wrote the late Sven Lindqvist in his book about European imperialism in Africa, *Exterminate All the Brutes.* 'So do I. It is not knowledge that we lack. What is missing is the courage to understand what we know and to draw conclusions.'

These deaths are the collateral damage of British racism – the indirect consequence of decades of exclusion that have corralled Black and Asian people into the kinds of jobs, housing and health situations that would make us particularly vulnerable. And yet, because our lives literally depend on it, we are forced to make the obvious explicit in the hope that some will cease to regard the obscene as inevitable.

The police lynching of George Floyd in Minneapolis on 25 May was a clear and brutal manifestation of racial violence. Obscenities such as this, caught on camera, with a clear villain sporting a badge and a number, have become a distressingly familiar occurrence that can distort the vast scope and scale of the racial challenge we all face. It is this incident that has driven tens of thousands to the streets, in occasionally violent clashes with the police across the US, and brought people out in solidarity across Europe. But it is not the only thing keeping them there.

Covid-19 has demonstrated how racism can kill in far less dramatic ways and in far greater numbers, without offering a morality play that might be shared on social media. When the police and politicians order the protesters to go back to their communities, there seems little recognition that that is where they were dying in such disproportionate numbers; that in the slogan 'I can't breathe' – among George Floyd's last words as the police officer knelt on his neck – there is the connective tissue between the most brazen forms of state violence and the more banal tribulations of the ailing pandemic patient.

'Part of the reason these are systemic inequalities is that they transcend not only party, but time,' Stacey Abrams, an African American politician from Georgia who is being vetted by Joe Biden as a potential vice-presidential running mate, told the *New York Times*. 'We have to be very intentional about saying this is not about one moment or one murder – but the entire infrastructure of justice.'

One need not crudely transpose the US racial landscape on to Britain's to see how the issues raised by Floyd's killing could pollinate across the Atlantic and find a receptive home here. We do not have the US's levels of gun ownership or its Black middle class, its centuries-old Black institutions or its degrees of segregation. Our inequalities operate differently. But they are recognisable. And most pertinently, where the virus is concerned, they keep operating. Across the Atlantic, the manner of collecting the data on coronavirus deaths differs – but the racial disparities are, at the very least, comparable. Since we didn't get to this place by accident, we won't get out of it by chance.

The second question is: what can we do about it? In the short term, the answer is fairly straightforward. Just as minorities are disproportionately affected by the disease, they are disproportionately assisted by any efforts to combat it. The more PPE there is for health workers and care workers, the more that people avoid public transport, and the more that testing and tracing is available, the more that racial and ethnic disparities will be reduced. Just as the government's negligence has left us more exposed, government vigilance would make us considerably safer.

Tackling the racial inequalities emerging from the pandemic is not a sectional interest that will benefit just Black people, any more than civil rights or community-sensitive policing do; in a public health crisis anything that helps a significant section of the population will help everyone.

It follows that in the medium term there should be a full, independent public inquiry into the racial disparity in the number of deaths. The government's own review simply established what we already knew – the prevalence of ethnic disparities – even if its findings differed substantially from the ONS on which groups were most vulnerable. The review adjusted the death rate for deprivation, among other things, but made no plans to do anything about it and offered no analysis of why this deprivation might be.

It now plans a further review, led by the equalities minister Liz Truss, focusing on co-morbidities and obesity. Since conditions such as obesity and hypertension are also related to socio-economic factors, the government could be accused of chasing its tail. One need not gainsay Truss's conclusions to see the trajectory in this line of inquiry: to leave the system that produces certain health inequalities unscrutinised, while shifting the burden of vulnerability on to the individual – their lifestyle, diet and general health regimen – as though those things existed beyond the influence of race and class.

A proper inquiry would not only seek to establish accountability, where that is appropriate, but also to examine the pressures, decisions, contexts and environments that got us into such a calamitous state of affairs. Such an inquiry could do for systemic racism what the Macpherson report of 1999 did for institutional racism – map out the complex and at times invisible relationship between power and discrimination that often traps well-meaning people in oppressive structures and Black people in desperate circumstances. A group of BAME public figures have already called on the government to produce a 'Covid-19 race equality strategy'.

None of this will heal the sick or bring back the dead. But it could help us develop a more sophisticated and nuanced understanding of how race is experienced and how racism operates. For the left, it would help end the futile attempts to engage with race and class separately. They do not exist in silos but are two interdependent forces, among many, and they are either understood in relation to each other or are misunderstood completely.

A public inquiry also offers the opportunity to cement human experience as part of politics, as opposed to something distinct and even antagonistic to it. The effort to relegate race, gender, sexual orientation, disability – the list goes on – to mere 'identity politics' has ramped up of late. The disproportionate number of deaths among minorities, the spike in domestic violence during lockdown, the manner in which disabled people were marginalised at every step – all these factors exemplify the degree to which we have experienced this moment differently, in material ways that are not, solely, about class. Acknowledging that doesn't undermine solidarity, it informs it.

We will need this shift in understanding because there's every chance that all of the disparities that made BAME communities so vulnerable are about to get worse. We are barely out of the last economic crisis, which affected Black people (particularly women) more heavily, and are about to enter another economic depression.

It does not follow that because the pandemic has illustrated a range of inequalities and inequities, the state will address them. Indeed, if anything, the government will desperately try to exploit them to reshape the world in its own ideological image. It wouldn't be the first time we demanded an overhaul of 'the entire infrastructure of justice' and ended up with more injustice.

This is precisely what happened in New Orleans after Katrina. There was a brief acknowledgement of how racism and poverty had shaped the identity of the victims. But before long, the cameras left and the corporate interests and the city establishment applied themselves to the task of reordering the city with great prejudice.

The public schools were auctioned off to private entities, and public housing that wasn't even damaged by the hurricane was torn down anyway. More than a third of the Black people who left the city never came back. 'We finally cleaned up public housing in New Orleans,' said Republican congressman Richard Baker, only two weeks after the storm. 'We couldn't do it, but God did.'

I returned to New Orleans a year after the hurricane to see how things had progressed. I was driving through the Lower Ninth ward with a resident, Antoinette K-Doe, in the hearse she bought so that she could evacuate the city. She kept stopping and staring at the dystopian sight of the neighbourhood where she grew up. Whole houses had been washed off their moorings and into the road; cars had been washed into the houses; trees had been blown on to cars. And there they were still. 'We're the richest country in the world,' K-Doe said. 'I don't understand how we can't fix this up.'

3

WAYS
OF
SEEING

Issues aren't always black and white.
Sometimes it's important to shift our gaze,
adopt a different lens or flip the script
in order to understand things differently

Don't blame Uncle Tom

The hero of Harriet Beecher Stowe's novel has become a byword for subservience. But such insults say more about the accuser than the literary figure.

Guardian, 30 March 2002, London

This is suicide. As a politically engaged Black writer I might as well pen my own obituary. Or at least sentence myself to a life in purdah – for the words will almost certainly be taken down in evidence and used against me at a later date. But we cannot always espouse fashionable causes. So hang it. It is time that someone spoke up for Uncle Tom.

This month sees the 150th anniversary of the publication of *Uncle Tom's Cabin*, and it is time that Uncle Tom was rehabilitated. Not the Uncle Tom of popular insult; not the 'neutralised negro', 'non-practising Black' or 'Reverend Pork Chop' charged with undermining Black freedom struggles by ingratiating himself with his white over-seers. Not the Tom of racial slur, but the Tom of literary history: the original Tom, husband of Chloe, father of Mose, Peter and Polly, and creation of Harriet Beecher Stowe. It is time to save the signifier from the sign. *Uncle Tom's Cabin* is one of those books which is more likely to be cited in anger than to have been read at leisure. So while most people think they 'know' Uncle Tom as the Stepin Fetchit of planta-tion politics, few have actually met the man who lived on the page and whose good name has been so thoroughly traduced.

So let me introduce you. We first see Tom in his cabin in Kentucky, where his slave master, Mr Shelby, is forced to sell two of his slaves to clear his debts. Shelby chooses Tom and Harry, the young son of fellow slave Eliza. Preferring the risk of being caught to the certainty of being split up, Eliza makes a run for it with her child. But Tom, to whom Shelby had promised freedom, refuses to flee.

Later, separated from his wife and family, Tom heads deeper down south in the hands of a slave trader, while Eliza makes it to Canada with her son and husband, who has also fled from another owner, and eventually settles in Liberia.

Tom, meanwhile, is floating on a passenger boat down the Mississippi, under the watchful eye of the slave trader, when he sees a white girl, Eva, fall overboard and dives in to save her. Eva persuades her father to buy him, and Tom becomes the property of Augustine St Clare, a wealthy planter from Louisiana. St Clare also offers Tom his freedom, but he dies suddenly, before it is granted. His wife refuses to honour the promise and sells Tom to the vicious Simon Legree. Legree admires Tom's diligence but is frustrated by his refusal to do his bidding. When he orders Tom to whip a fellow slave, Tom refuses and is beaten himself.

When two other slaves go missing, Legree threatens Tom with death unless he tells his master where they are. Tom says he knows but won't say and is fatally thrashed. As he lies, dying, the son of Mr Shelby arrives with the money to honour his father's promise of freedom – in time to see the family's once favourite slave perish at the hands of a brute.

The story was originally run in an anti-slavery newspaper. But when it was released in book form, in March 1852, it was an immediate sensation. In the US alone, it sold 300,000 copies in a year, and more than two million copies by the end of the decade.

What is now commonly regarded as a sentimentalist, racist text was at the time received as a vicious polemic against slavery in general and against the fugitive slave law in particular. In an America divided at the time between the slave-owning South and the 'free states' of the North, the law demanded that northerners returned slaves who had escaped back into the bondage of the South.

In a nation bitterly split and destined for civil war on this very issue, the book's publication, not to mention its success, provoked a vicious reaction. '*Uncle Tom's Cabin* was the epicentre of a massive cultural phenomenon,' writes Richard Yarborough, a California-based academic, in his essay 'Strategies of Black Characterization in *Uncle Tom's Cabin* and the Early Afro-American Novel', 'the tremors of which still affect the relationship between blacks and whites in the United States.'

In the nineteenth century, the editor of the *Southern Literary Messenger* instructed his reviewer: 'I would have the review as hot as hellfire, blasting and searing the reputation of the vile wretch in petticoats who could write such a volume.'

Within two years, pro-slavery writers had answered *Uncle Tom's Cabin* with at least fifteen novels, similarly polemical in style but arguing that slaves in the South were better off than free workers in the North. One of these novels was called *Uncle Robin in His Cabin in Virginia and Tom Without One in Boston.*

When Abraham Lincoln met Stowe in 1862, one year into the American civil war, he greeted her with the words: 'So you're the little woman who wrote the book that made this great war.' But the novel's impact was global rather than national. Among those who hailed it as a masterpiece were Ivan Turgenev, Victor Hugo, Leo Tolstoy and George Eliot. The British prime minister, Lord Palmerston, read it three times and admired it not so much for the story as 'for the statesmanship of it'.

It was Lenin's favourite book as a child. 'When we try to trace the origins of Vladimir's political outlook, we often look to what he read in his late adolescence and early manhood,' wrote Robert Service in his biography of Lenin. 'But we need to remember that, before these Russian and German male authors imprinted themselves upon his consciousness, an American woman – Harriet Beecher Stowe – had already influenced his young mind.'

Within the confines of its age, then, *Uncle Tom's Cabin* was a progressive text, exerting an influence which few works of literature have had before or since on the political debate of the time. The problem is that the confines of its age are very narrow indeed. Written by a white woman principally for other white people, when Black people were still regarded as chattels, its failure to transcend its age is what made it vulnerable to caricature and criticism at a later date. 'Although Stowe unquestionably sympathised with the slaves,' writes Yarborough, 'her commitment to challenging the claim of black inferiority was frequently undermined by her own endorsement of racial stereotypes.'

For in terms of any broader sense of universal humanism or anti-racism, let alone radicalism, the book is deeply problematic. Stowe likes her 'mulattoes' tragic and handsome and her Africans wild and brawny. The Black characters are stock types, with only three means to confront their enforced degradation: submission, brutalisation or banishment.

'Uncle Tom must be killed; George Harris exiled! Heaven for dead Negroes! Liberia for living mulattoes,' an unnamed Black writer argued. 'Neither can live on the American continent. Death or banishment is our doom.'

The one thing Stowe could not imagine, even though real-life heroes like slave rebel Nat Turner and underground railroad organiser Sojourner Truth existed to fuel her imagination, was that some might want to stay and fight. 'In order to appreciate the sufferings of the negroes sold south, it must be remembered that all the instinctive affections of that race are peculiarly strong,' she writes in the book. 'They are not naturally daring and enterprising, but home-loving and affectionate.' In another work, she describes Black people as 'confessedly more simple, docile, childlike and affectionate than other races'.

Like most liberals, she believed that support for the downtrodden demanded sympathy rather than solidarity. Like most liberals, she thought that liberation could only be granted by the good grace of the powerful rather than achieved by the will and tenacity of the powerless. In one polemical passage, Stowe asserts: 'There is one thing that every individual can do [about slavery] – they can see to it that they feel right.' To that extent, Tom must also be rescued from Stowe as well.

So if you are looking for a revolutionary role model, someone who remains master of his own destiny in the most humiliating of circumstances, then Uncle Tom is not your man. But then few people are. His sense of duty, even in bondage, depresses. When his wife encourages him to escape with Eliza, he tells her: 'Mas'r always found me on the spot – he always will. I never have broke trust . . . and I never will.' His inability, or unwillingness, to adapt his principles to a greater good frustrates. Encouraged by another slave to murder the vicious Legree while the latter lies in a drunken stupor, Tom says: 'No! good never comes of wickedness. I'd sooner chop my right hand off . . . The Lord hasn't called us to wrath. We must suffer, and wait his time.'

If ever there was a character to illustrate Marx's most famous quote that '[Religion] is the opium of the people,' it is Uncle Tom, who would rather wait for freedom in the afterlife than fight for it on Earth. But the less famous part of that same quote better sums up Tom's morality and provides the cornerstone for his defence: 'Religion', wrote Marx, 'is the sigh of the oppressed creature, the heart of a heartless world and the soul of soulless condition.' For when Tom is apparently at his most supine, he is, nonetheless, motivated by a desire to remain true to his Christian faith rather than to ingratiate himself with his master.

It is from these deep pools of self-belief and moral absolutes that he manages to preserve his humanism, despite conditions which degrade him daily. It is in this consistency that we find Tom's integrity. It is through it that he is able to assist and defend his fellow slaves and, at times, stand his own ground and still keep himself from loathing whites.

When St Clare asks him if he would not be better off a slave than a free man, Tom responds with a straight 'No'. 'Why Tom, you couldn't possibly have earned, by your work, such clothes and such living as I have given you,' says St Clare. 'Know's all that Mas'r,' says Tom. 'But I'd rather have poor clothes, poor house, poor everything and have 'em mine, than have the best, and have 'em any man else's.'

Picking cotton alongside a woman whose health is failing, he dumps handfuls that he has picked in her bag. 'O, you mustn't! You donno what they'll do to ye,' she says. 'I can bar it!' said Tom, 'better 'n you.' Shortly afterwards, Legree offers him an easier life, if he will whip the woman. 'I mean to promote ye, and make a driver of ye; and tonight ye may jest as well begin to get yer hand in. Now, ye jest take this yer gal and flog her.'

Tom is punched when he refuses but finally tells Legree, 'I'm willin' to work, night and day, and work while there's life and breath in me; but this yer thing I can't feel it right to do . . . t'would be downright cruel . . . if you mean to kill me, kill me; but as to my raising my hand agin anyone here, I never shall, – I'll die first.' He isn't killed, although he is beaten senseless, and has scarcely recovered when Legree finds out that two other slaves have fled. He asks Tom to tell him if he knows anything about it and threatens him with death if he refuses.

'I han't got nothing to tell, Mas'r,' he says. 'Do you dare to tell me, ye old black Christian, ye don't know?' asks Legree. 'I know, Mas'r, but I can't tell anything. I can die.' And die he does.

To discover just how this literary figure of passive resistance becomes a byword for betrayal and subservience, we must look to theatre, film and politics. Stage adaptations removed any remotely radical anti-slave messages and turned the book into a minstrel show. 'Tom troupes' toured the country and characters sang songs like 'I Am but a Little Nigger Gal' and 'Happy Are We Darkies So Gay'. Tom provided the role for the first Black film lead in 1914. Elsewhere, white actors occasionally blacked up. Those performing in film adaptations of the novel included Shirley Temple, Judy Garland, Bill 'Bojangles' Robinson, Abbott and Costello. Felix the Cat even played Tom in an animated version.

By the Second World War, Uncle Tom had become a byword for lickspittle subservience in the face of racial oppression. Richard Wright called his collection of short stories about Black life in the

American South *Uncle Tom's Children*. The protagonist in his most renowned work, *Native Son*, is called Bigger Thomas – an eponymous northern descendant of Uncle Tom. The oldest and most moderate civil rights organisation in America, the National Association for the Advancement of Colored People, tried to proscribe the book and ban its dramatisations.

The fictitious Tom's actual attributes and flaws soon became incidental. Black America had another use for him in real life. He was to represent the lackey, the moderate, the conciliator and the sell-out. If Stowe had not invented him, African Americans would have had to. True, he might not have been called Tom. It could have been Uncle Ben of long-grain rice fame (Tom's female counterpart is Aunt Jemima, the grand matron of pancake mix). Black radical Malcolm X once said: 'Just as the slavemaster in that day used Uncle Tom to keep the field negroes in check, he was the same old slavemaster who today has negroes who are nothing but modern Uncle Toms – 20th-century Uncle Toms – to keep you and me in check.' But the truth is, it was the term 'Uncle Tom' itself that was really designed to keep Black people in check. As a defensive response to racism, those who use it seek to enforce allegiance and cast out dissent purely on grounds of race.

Black people are not alone in this desire to police their borders in this way. Many cultures that feel embattled on some level will attempt to proscribe behaviour deemed equal to betrayal. That is how Zionist Jews get to brand anti-Zionist Jews 'self-haters' – 'They're people of Jewish extraction who've had most of the Jewishness extracted,' one academic explained to me recently. Similarly, those not deemed to be sufficiently Irish become 'West Brits'.

Malcolm X was not talking about Uncle Tom the character but Uncle Tom the construct. The Tom of the novel had preferred to die than oversee his fellow slaves. But to Malcolm X, and many others before and since, Uncle Tom was the man preaching reform when others were preaching revolution; the one who advocated peace instead of war; the person who urged others to stay at home instead of taking to the streets; the leader who preached racial equality instead of Black power.

In short, Uncle Tom is whoever you want him to be. Arbitrary in application – who decides who is an Uncle Tom, and on what basis? – and prohibitive in nature, the term exemplifies the very limits of race-thinking. Even though it is an insult that falls most readily from the lips of self-avowed radicals, it is in fact a reactionary form of psychological and behavioural racial policing within Black communities.

Nowhere is this more obvious than in the *American Directory of Certified Uncle Toms*, released earlier this year. The book comes with the subtitle 'Being a review of the history, antics and attitudes of handkerchief heads, Aunt Jemimas, head negroes in charge and house negroes against the freedom of the black race'. It was published by the self-appointed Council on Black Internal Affairs, which was set up after the Million Man March and cast itself as the supreme arbiter of Black authenticity. The council set the lofty target of '[monitoring] the progress of the black race toward its inevitable freedom'. The book, wittily written as it is, remains a landmark document in the history of internal race regulation.

It ranks over fifty Black leaders, past and present, according to a five-star Uncle Tom rating, with five being the worst. Michael Jackson, who has had plastic surgery that has left many of his Black features destroyed, gets one star; Bayard Rustin, the gay activist who organised the March on Washington at which King made his 'I Have a Dream' speech, gets five; W. E. B. Du Bois, a pioneer of Pan-Africanism who died in Ghana while publishing an *Encyclopedia Africana*, is also, according to the authors, a five-star Uncle Tom.

Colin Powell (five stars) becomes 'an official, government issue Uncle Tom', Maya Angelou (two stars) is 'the much glorified but innocuous negro emissary of ebony culture', and Oprah Winfrey (four stars) is 'the best unambiguously black ambassador of plantation placidity since Hattie McDaniel gushed over Scarlett in *Gone with the Wind*'. You do not have to like these people to find these assessments obnoxious. Like the insults 'coconut', 'Bounty bar' and their American equivalent 'Oreo' – all of which mean black on the outside and white on the inside – the racial determinism on which these insults are hinged is in the very worst tradition of identity politics.

The book promises not only constant vigilance – 'More will be nominated. More will be exposed. More will be certified' – but also redemption: 'Only by refashioning his mind and recasting his role in black affairs can the Uncle Tom declare himself to be a friend of his own black race.' In so doing it presents race not as a starting point from which to understand the world from your own experience but as the sole prism through which the world should be viewed and understood. It emphasises not what you do but who you are. As such, it is, effectively, a de-blacking – an attempt to deny racial legitimacy as well as the possibility of genuine debate and disagreement among Black people.

If US Supreme Court justice Clarence Thomas keeps voting against the interests of African Americans, then say that. If you think that, in the UK, *The Voice*'s editor, Mike Best, has with his comments over stop and search contributed to a culture that could lead to more widespread harassment of Black youth, then say that, too. Blame them for being overly ambitious, right-wing, misled, misguided, bankrupt or washed-up. Blame those who back them for being patronising, cynical, opportunistic, manipulative or disingenuous. Call them what you want.

Blame them for what they have done, not who they are. But whatever you do, don't blame Uncle Tom. He has suffered enough.

Riots are a class act – and often they're the only alternative

Violent protest forced France to accept the need for social justice. No petition, peaceful march or letter to an MP could have achieved this.

Guardian, 14 November 2005, New York

'If there is no struggle, there is no progress,' said the African American abolitionist Frederick Douglass. 'Those who profess to favour freedom and yet depreciate agitation are men who want crops without ploughing up the ground; they want rain without thunder and lightning. They want the ocean without the awful roar of its many waters . . . Power concedes nothing without a demand. It never did and it never will.'

By the end of last week, it looked as though the fortnight of struggle between minority French youth and the police might actually have yielded some progress. Condemning the rioters is easy. They shot at the police, killed an innocent man, trashed businesses, rammed a car into a retirement home and torched countless vehicles (given that four hundred cars are burned on an average New Year's Eve in France, this was not quite as remarkable as some made out).

But shield your ears from the awful roaring waters for a moment and take a look at the ocean. Those who wondered what French youth had to gain by taking to the streets should ask what they had to lose. Unemployed, socially excluded, harassed by the police and condemned to poor housing, they live on estates that are essentially open prisons. Statistically invisible (it is against the law and republican principle to collect data based on race or ethnicity) and politically unrepresented (mainland France does not have a single non-white MP), their aim has been simply to get their plight acknowledged. And they succeeded.

Even as the French politicians talked tough, the state was suing for peace with the offer of greater social justice. The government unrolled

Dispatches from the Diaspora

a package of measures that would give career guidance and work place-
ments to all unemployed people under twenty-five living in some of
the poorest suburbs; there would be tax breaks for companies who set
up on sink estates; a €1,000 (£675) lump sum for jobless people who
returned to work, as well as €150 a month for a year; five thousand
extra teachers and educational assistants; ten thousand scholarships
to encourage academic achievers to stay at school; and ten boarding
schools for those who want to leave their estates to study.

'We need to respond strongly and quickly to the undeniable problems facing many inhabitants of the deprived neighbourhoods,' said
President Chirac. From the man who once said that immigrants had
breached the 'threshold of tolerance' and were sending French workers 'mad' with their 'noise and smell', this was progress indeed.

'The impossible becomes probable through struggle,' said the
African American academic Manning Marable. 'And the probable
becomes reality.' And the reality is that none of this would have happened without riots. There was no petition these young people could
have signed, no peaceful march they could have held, no letter they
could have written to their MPs that would have produced these
results.

Amid the charred chassis and broken glass there is a vital point
of principle to salvage: in certain conditions rioting is not just justified but may also be necessary, and effective. From the poll tax
demonstrations to Soweto, history is littered with such cases; what
were the French and American revolutions but riots endowed by
Enlightenment principles and then blessed by history?

When all non-violent, democratic means of achieving a just end
are unavailable, redundant or exhausted, rioting is justifiable. When
state agencies charged with protecting communities fail to do so or
actually attack them, it may be necessary in self-defence.

After the 1967 riots in American cities, President Johnson set up
the Kerner Commission. It concluded: 'What white Americans have
never fully understood – but what the Negro can never forget – is that

white society is deeply implicated in the ghetto. White institutions created it, white institutions maintain it, and white society condones it.' How else was such a damning indictment of racial discrimination in the US ever going to land on the president's desk?

Following the inner-city riots across Britain in 1981, Lord Scarman argued that 'urgent action' was needed to prevent racial disadvantage becoming an 'endemic, ineradicable disease threatening the very survival of our society'. His conclusions weren't perfect. But the kernel of a message Black Britons had been trying to hammer home for decades suddenly took centre stage. A few years later, Michael Heseltine wrote a report into the disturbances in Toxteth entitled 'It Took a Riot'.

Rioting should be neither celebrated nor fetishised, because ultimately it is a sign of not strength but weakness. Like a strike, it is often the last and most desperate weapon available to those with the least power. Rioting is a class act. Wealthy people don't do it because either they have the levers of democracy at their disposal or they can rely on the state or private security firms to do their violent work for them, if need be.

The issue of when and how rioting is effective is more problematic. Riots raise awareness of a situation, but they cannot solve it. For that you need democratic engagement and meaningful negotiation. Most powerful when they stem from a movement, all too often riots are instead the spontaneous, leaderless expression of pent-up frustration, devoid of an agenda or clear demands. Many of these French youths may have had a ball last week, but what they really need is a party – a political organisation that will articulate their aspirations.

If Kerner and Scarman are anything to go by, the rioters will not be invited to help write the documents that could shape racial discourse for a generation. Nor are they likely to be the primary beneficiaries.

'During the 1980s, everyone was desperate to have a Black face in their organisation to show the race relations industry that they were allowing Black people to get on,' says the editor of *Race & Class*, Ambalavaner Sivanandan. 'So the people who made this mobility

possible were those who took to the streets. But they did not benefit.'
The same is true of the Black American working class that produced
Kerner.

Given these uncertain outcomes, riots carry great risk. The border between political violence and criminality becomes blurred, and
legitimate protest risks degrading into impotent displays of hyper-
masculinity. Violence at that point becomes not the means to even a
vague aspiration but the end in itself, and half the story gets missed.
We heard little from young minority French women last week, even
though they have been the primary target of the state's secular dogma
over the hijab.

Finally, violence polarises. The big winner of the last two weeks
may yet prove to be Nicolas Sarkozy. The presidential hopeful courted
the far right with his calculated criticisms of the rioters; if he wins, he
could reverse any gains that may arise. Jean-Marie Le Pen also lurks
in the wings.

The riots in France run all these risks and yet have still managed to
yield a precarious kind of progress. They demand our qualified and
critical support.

Power has made its concessions. But how many, for how long and
to whom depends on whether those who made the demands take
their struggle from the margins to the mainstream: from the street to
the corridors of power.

White history 101

White people also deserve a sense of history that is accurate, honest, anti-racist and inclusive. So what would White History Month look like?
The Nation, 21 February 2007, New York

Whatever happened to James Blake? He is probably the most famous bus driver ever. And yet when he died aged eighty-nine in March 2002, the few papers that bothered to note his passing in an obituary ran just a few hundred words of wire copy and moved on. Given that February is Black History Month in the US, it is worth taking a moment to ask how such a crucial figure could be so cruelly forgotten.

Blake was the Montgomery driver who told a row of Black passengers: 'Y'all better make it light on yourselves and let me have those seats.' Rosa Parks was one of those passengers. She made her stand and kept her seat. The rest, as they say, is history.

Well, Black history anyway. We know how African Americans boycotted the city's transit system for thirteen months until the segregationists caved in. We know how the boycott launched the career of a previously unheard-of preacher called Martin Luther King Jr and made Parks an icon. In schools, bookstores and on TV there is an awful lot of talk about them every February, when the US celebrates Black History Month. But nary a word about Mr Blake. That's because so much of Black History Month takes place in the passive voice. Leaders 'get assassinated', patrons 'are refused' service, women 'are ejected' from public transport. So the objects of racism are many, but the subjects few. In removing the instigators, the historians remove the agency and, in the final reckoning, the historical responsibility.

There is no month when we get to talk about Blake; no opportunity to learn the fates of J. W. Milam and Roy Bryant, who murdered

Emmett Till; no time set aside to keep track of Victoria Price and Ruby Bates, whose false accusations of rape against the Scottsboro boys sent five innocent young Black men to jail.

Wouldn't everyone – particularly white people – benefit from becoming better acquainted with these histories? What we need, in short, is a White History Month.

For some, this would be one racially themed history month too many. Criticisms of Black History Month by cynics, racists and purists are about as predictable as the arrival of February itself. But for all its obvious shortcomings, Black History Month helps clear a space in which we can relate the truth about the past so we might better understand the present and navigate the future. Setting aside twenty-eight days for African American history is insufficient, problematic and deserves our support for the same reason that affirmative action is insufficient, problematic and deserves our support. As one means to redress an entrenched imbalance, it gives us the chance to hear narratives that have been forgotten, hidden, distorted or mislaid. Like that of Claudette Colvin, the Black Montgomery teenage activist who also refused to give up her seat, nine months before Rosa Parks, but was abandoned by the local civil rights establishment because she became pregnant and came from the wrong side of town (see p. 201).

The very notion of Black and white history is both a theoretical nonsense and a practical necessity. There is no scientific or biological basis for race. It is a construct to explain the gruesome reality that racism built. But, logic suggests, you cannot have Black history without white history. Of course, the trouble is not that we do not hear enough about white history but that what masquerades as history is more akin to mythology. The contradictions of how a 'free world' could be founded on genocide or how the battle for democracy during the Second World War could coincide with Japanese internment and segregation, for example, are rarely addressed.

'I am born with a past and to try to cut myself off from that past is to deform my present relationships,' writes Alasdair MacIntyre in his book *After Virtue*. 'The possession of an historical identity and the possession of a social identity coincide.'

The purpose here is not to explore individual guilt – there are therapists for that – but collective responsibility. When it comes to excelling at military conflict, everyone lays claim to their national identity; people will say, '*We* won the Second World War.' By contrast, those who say 'we' raped Black slaves, massacred Indians or excluded Jews from higher education are hard to come by. You cannot, it appears, hold anyone responsible for what their ancestors did that was bad or the privileges they enjoy as a result. Whoever it was, it definitely wasn't 'us'. This is one more version of white flight – a dash from the inconveniences bequeathed by inequality.

So we do not need more white history; we need it better told. Settlement, slavery and segregation – propelled by economic expansion and justified by white supremacy – inform much of what the US is today. The wealth they created helped bankroll its superpower status. The poverty they engendered persists. But white history does not mean racist history any more than Black history means victims' history. Alongside Blake, Milam and Bryant, any decent White History Month would star insurrectionist John Brown; the Vanilla Ice of the Harlem Renaissance, Carl Van Vechten; civil rights workers Michael Schwerner and Andrew Goodman, murdered near Philadelphia, Mississippi, during the Freedom Summer of 1964; and Viola Liuzzo, murdered during the Selma to Montgomery march. It would explain why Ronald Reagan kicked off his presidential campaign in Philadelphia, Mississippi; why George W. Bush chose Bob Jones University to revive his presidential hopes. It would tell the story of how Ruby Bates recanted her rape accusation in a bid to save the Scottsboro boys from the noose and how the Blakes never did reconcile themselves to the event that brought them infamy. 'None of that mess they said was true,' said James's wife, Edna. 'Everybody loved him. He was a good, true man and a churchgoer.'

It would offer white people options and role models, and all of us inspiration, while relieving the burden on African Americans to recast the US's entire racial history in the shortest month of the year. White people, like Black people, need access to a history that is accurate, honest and inclusive. Maybe then it would be easier for them, and the rest of us, to make history that is progressive, anti-racist and inclusive.

The misremembering of 'I Have a Dream'

*Martin Luther King's most famous speech is, like his own political
legacy, widely and wilfully misunderstood.*

The Nation, 14 August 2013, Chicago

When Dr Martin Luther King Jr took the podium on 28 August
1963, the Department of Justice was watching. Fearing that someone
might hijack the microphone to make inflammatory statements, it
came up with a plan to silence the speaker, just in case. A DOJ official
was seated next to the sound system, holding a recording of Mahalia
Jackson singing 'He's Got the Whole World in His Hands', which he
would play to placate the crowd in such an eventuality.

Half a century after the March on Washington and the famous 'I
Have a Dream' speech, the event has been neatly folded into America's
patriotic mythology. Relatively few people know or recall that the
Kennedy administration tried to get organisers to call it off; that the
FBI tried to dissuade people from coming; that racist senators tried to
discredit the leaders; that twice as many Americans had an unfavourable view of the march as a favourable one. Instead, it is hailed not as
a dramatic moment of mass, multiracial dissidence but as a jamboree
in Benetton Technicolor, exemplifying the nation's unrelenting progress towards its founding ideals.

Central to that repackaging of history is the misremembering of
King's speech. It has been cast not as a searing indictment of American
racism that still exists but as an eloquent period piece articulating the
travails of a bygone era. So, on the fiftieth anniversary of 'I Have a
Dream', 'Has King's dream been realised?' is one of the two most
common and, to my mind, least interesting questions asked of the
speech; the other is 'Does President Obama represent the fulfilment
of King's dream?' The short answer to both is a clear 'No', even if

the longer responses are more interesting than the questions deserve. We know that King's dream was not limited to the rhetoric of just one speech. To judge a life as full and complex as his by one sixteen-minute address, some of which was delivered extemporaneously, is neither respectful nor serious.

Regardless, any contemporary discussion about the legacy of 'I Have a Dream' must begin by acknowledging the way we now interpret the themes it raised at the time. Words like 'race', 'equality', 'justice', 'discrimination' and 'segregation' mean something quite different when a historically oppressed minority is explicitly excluded from voting than they do when the president of the US is Black. King used the word 'Negro' fifteen times in the speech; today, the term is finally being retired from the US Census as a racial category.

Perhaps the best way to comprehend how King's speech is understood today is to consider the radical transformation of attitudes towards the man who delivered it. Before his death, King was well on the way to being a pariah. In 1966, twice as many Americans had an unfavourable opinion of him as a favourable one. *Life* magazine branded his anti-Vietnam War speech at Riverside Church 'demagogic slander' and 'a script for Radio Hanoi'.

But in thirty years he went from ignominy to icon. By 1999, a Gallup poll revealed that King was virtually tied with John F. Kennedy and Albert Einstein as one of the most admired public figures of the twentieth century among Americans. He ranked as more popular than Franklin Delano Roosevelt, Pope John Paul II and Winston Churchill; only Mother Teresa was more cherished. In 2011, a memorial to King was unveiled on the National Mall, featuring a thirty-foot-high statue sited on four acres of prime cultural real estate. Ninety-one per cent of Americans (including 89 per cent of whites) approved.

This evolution was not simply a matter of ill feelings and painful memories eroding over time. It was the result of a protracted struggle that sheds light on how the speech for which he is best known is today understood. The bill to establish King's birthday as a federal holiday was introduced just a few days after his death, with few illusions as to its likely success. 'We don't want anyone to believe we hope Congress will do this,' said union leader Cleveland Robinson at a rally with King's widow in 1969. 'We're just sayin', us Black people in America just ain't gonna work on that day any more.'

Congress would pass the bill, but not without a fight. In 1983, the year Ronald Reagan grudgingly signed Martin Luther King Day into law, he was asked if King was a communist sympathiser. 'We'll know in thirty-five years, won't we?' he said, referring to the eventual release of FBI surveillance tapes.

The country's acceptance of King came with its eventual consensus – won through mass marches, civil disobedience and grassroots activism – that codified segregation had to end. 'America was like a dysfunctional drug addict or alcoholic that was addicted, dependent on racial segregation,' says Clarence Jones, who wrote the draft text of King's 'I Have a Dream' speech. 'It had tried other treatments and failed. Then comes along Martin Luther King with his multistep programme – recovery, non-violence, civil disobedience and integration – and forces America to publicly confront its conscience. And that recovery programme enabled America to embark on the greatest political transformation in history.'

By the time white Americans realised that their dislike of King was spent and futile, he had created a world in which admiring him was in their own self-interest. They embraced him because, in short, they had no choice. The only question remaining was what version of King should be honoured. To remember him now as a leader who sought greater government intervention to help the poor, or who branded the US as 'the greatest purveyor of violence in the world today', as he did at Riverside Church in 1967, would sacrifice posterity for accuracy. He did stand for those things. But those issues, particularly at

Dispatches from the Diaspora

a time of war and economic crisis, remain live, divisive and urgent. To associate him with them would not raise him above the fray but insert him into it, leaving him as controversial in death as in life. But remembering him as the man who spoke eloquently and force-fully against codified segregation presents him as an accordant figure whose principled stand rescued the nation in a moment of crisis.

'The speech is profoundly and wilfully misunderstood,' says King's long-time friend Vincent Harding, who drafted the Riverside Church speech. 'People take the parts that require the least enquiry, the least change, the least work. Our country has chosen what they consider to be the easier way to work with King. They are aware that something very powerful was connected to him, and he was connected to it. But they are not ready to really take on the kind of issues he was raising even there.'

Instead, the country has chosen to remember a version of 'I Have a Dream' that not only undermines King's legacy but also tells an inaccurate story about the speech itself. King made explicit reference in his oration to both the limits of legal remedy and the need for economic redress to confront the consequences of centuries of second-class citizenship.

'One hundred years later, the life of the Negro is still sadly crippled by the manacles of segregation *and* the chains of discrimination,' he said (emphasis mine). 'One hundred years later, the Negro lives on a lonely island of poverty in the midst of a vast ocean of material prosperity.'

'We refuse to believe', he said later in the speech, 'that there are insufficient funds in the great vaults of opportunity of this nation.'

No reasonable reading of this can limit King's vision to just doing away with Jim Crow. Only by wilfully conflating codified segrega-tion with racism, and ignoring not just what King had said elsewhere but also the ample contrary evidence in the speech, could one claim he was arguing that the answer to America's racial problems lay in merely changing the law.

*

When it comes to assessing the political content of the speech, the distinction between segregation and racism is crucial. To the extent that King's words were about bringing an end to codified, legal segregation, then the dream has been realised. 'Whites Only' signs have been taken down; the laws have been struck. Since 1979, Birmingham, Alabama, has had only Black mayors. If simply being Black – as opposed to the historical legacy of racism – was ever the sole barrier to economic, social or political advancement, that obstacle has been officially removed.

But to the extent that the speech was about ending racism, one can say with equal confidence that its realisation is not even close. Black unemployment is almost double that of whites; the percentage of Black children living in poverty is almost triple that of whites; Black male life expectancy in Washington, DC, is lower than in the Gaza Strip; one in three Black boys born in 2001 stands a lifetime risk of going to prison; more Black men were disenfranchised in 2004 because they were felons than had been disenfranchised in 1870, the year the Fifteenth Amendment ostensibly secured their right to vote.

Many of the images King evoked in his dream refrain were simple – 'little Black boys and Black girls [joining] hands with little white boys and white girls' – even if descriptions of how we might reach that promised land were intermittent and vague ('Go back to Georgia, go back to Louisiana . . . knowing that somehow this situation can and will be changed'). But the speech was clearly more about wider racism than just segregation. By fudging the distinction between the two – or by actively misinterpreting them – it is possible to cast racism as an aberration of the past, as the Supreme Court effectively did when it gutted the Voting Rights Act this past spring. Only then can the vast, enduring differences in the material position of Blacks and whites be understood as the failings of individuals rather than the consequences of ongoing institutional, economic and political exclusion. Only then does the emphasis on a single line of the speech – in which King aspired to see new generations who would 'not be judged by the colour of their skin but by the content of their character' – make any sense.

This particular misreading is most glaring today in discussions of affirmative action. King was a strong proponent of taking race and ethnicity into account when making appointments for jobs and for college admissions, in order to redress historical imbalances. 'It is impossible to create a formula for the future', he wrote, 'which does not take into account that our society has been doing something special *against* the Negro for hundreds of years.'

Yet the right has come to rely on the 'content of their character' line to use King as anti-racist cover for its opposition to affirmative action. In 1986, Reagan said: 'We are committed to a society in which all men and women have equal opportunities to succeed, and so we oppose the use of quotas. We want a colour-blind society. A society that, in the words of Dr King, judges people not by "the colour of their skin but by the content of their character".'

Such distortions in turn explain the ambivalence voiced by those like Harding and a significant element of the Black intelligentsia when discussing 'I Have a Dream'. It's not the speech itself about which they are reticent, but rather the way King has been co-opted and his message corrupted. King's elevation to a patriotic mascot praising America's relentless and inevitable progress to better days often rankles.

So when it comes to divining the meaning of King's speech, there is substantial disagreement. Ironically, given its theme of racial unity, those differences are most pronounced in terms of race.

In a Gallup poll taken in August 2011, the month the King memorial was opened, a majority of Blacks said they believed both that the government has a major role to play 'in trying to improve the social and economic position of blacks and other minority groups' and that 'new civil rights laws are needed to reduce discrimination against blacks'. The figures for whites were 19 per cent and 15 per cent respectively. Conversely, over half of whites believed that civil rights for Blacks had 'greatly improved' in their lifetime, compared with just 29 per cent of Blacks. Whites were almost six times more likely than Blacks to believe that Obama's policies would 'go too far . . . in promoting efforts to aid the black community', while Blacks were twice as likely as whites to believe they wouldn't go far enough. Other polls show that whites are four times as likely as Blacks to believe that America has achieved racial equality. In short, as the racially polarised responses to George Zimmerman's acquittal revealed, Black and white Americans have very different lived experiences. While the *de jure* enforcement of segregation has been banned, the de facto experience of it remains prevalent. Any journey through a US city, where widely recognised geographical boundaries separate the races, will bear this out. Blacks and whites are less likely to see the same problems, more likely to disagree on their root causes and unlikely to agree on a remedy.

'For those who concentrate so much on that one line about "the colour of their skin" and "the content of their character",' says Harding, 'I wonder how, with the resegregation of our schools and communities, do you get to know the content of anyone's character if you're not willing to engage in life together with them?'

There is pretty much only one question on which the views of Black and white Americans *do* coincide, and that is whether they believe King's dream has been realised. Whenever this question has been asked by major pollsters over the past seven years, the discrepancy between Blacks and whites has rarely topped 10 per cent. If they agree about the extent to which the problems King invoked have been solved, but disagree on what those problems are, the inevitable conclusion is that even as they listen to the same speech, Blacks and whites hear very different things.

*

It is implausible to imagine that, were King to be raised from the dead, he would look at America's jails, unemployment lines, soup kitchens or inner-city schools and think his life's work had been accomplished. Whether one believes that these inequalities are caused by individuals making bad choices or by institutional discrimination, it would be absurd to claim that such a world bears any resemblance to the one King set out to create.

Nor is there anything to suggest that that view would have been much altered by the presence of a Black man in the White House. The claim that Obama's election has a connection to King's legacy has some substance. As Obama himself has often conceded, his election would not have been possible without the civil rights movement, which created the conditions that allowed for the arrival of a new generation of Black politicians. But the aim of the civil rights movement was equality for all, not the elevation of one.

There's no questioning the symbolic value of electing a Black president. Yet the fact remains that African Americans are no better off materially as a result, even if they may have been worse off had he lost, and that the economic gap between Blacks and whites has grown under his presidency. The ascent of America's first Black president has coincided with the descent of Black Americans' standard of living. Reasonable people may disagree on the extent to which Obama is responsible for that. But the fact is undeniable.

The presence of under-represented people in leadership positions only has any significantly positive meaning if it challenges whatever obstacles created the conditions for that under-representation. To believe otherwise is to trade equal opportunities for photo opportunities, whereby a system looks different but acts the same.

In the final analysis, to ask whether King's dream has been realised is to misunderstand both his overall politics and the specific ambition of his speech. King was not the kind of activist who pursued a merely finite agenda. The speech in general, and the dream sequence in particular, are utopian. Standing in the midst of a nightmare, King dreamed of a better world where historical wrongs had been righted and good prevailed. That is why the speech means so much to me, and why I believe that, overall, it has stood the test of time.

I was raised in Britain during the Thatcher years, at a time when idealism was mocked and 'realism' became an excuse for capitulation to the 'inevitability' of unbridled market forces and military aggression. To oppose that agenda was regarded, by some on the left as well as the right, as impractical and unrealistic. Realism has no time for dreamers.

True, we can't live on dreams alone. But the absence of utopian ideas leaves us without a clear ideological and moral centre and therefore facing a void in which politics is deprived of any liberatory potential and reduced to only what is feasible at any given moment.

In the summer of 1963, with a civil rights bill pending and the white population skittish, King could have limited his address to what was immediately achievable and pragmatic. He might have spelled out a ten-point plan, laid out his case for tougher legislation or made the case for fresh campaigns of civil disobedience in the North. He could have reduced himself to an appeal for what was possible at a time when what was possible and pragmatic was neither satisfactory nor sustainable.

Instead, he swung for the bleachers. Not knowing whether building the world he was describing was a Sisyphean task or merely a Herculean one, he called out in the political wilderness, hoping his voice would someday be heard by those with the power to act on it. In so doing, he showed it is not naive to believe that what is not possible in the foreseeable future may nonetheless be necessary, worth fighting for and worth articulating. The idealism that underpins his dream is the rock on which our modern rights are built and the flesh on which pragmatic parasites feed. If nobody dreamed of a better world, what would there be to wake up to?

Boris Johnson's white privilege

Imagine he was a Black woman . . .

Guardian, 2 March 2018, London

To the outside world, Boris Johnson has become a faithful representation of Britain's current foreign policy. Chaotic, implausible, blustering and incompetent, he is an honest reflection of the government's strategic vision of Britain's place in the world at this moment. At home, he is an exemplar of an altogether different dysfunction.

That he was made the nation's chief diplomat – a fact greeted with a mixture of mirth and disbelief by allies and foes alike – and remains in the job clearly illustrates how the privileges of gender, race and class, consciously accrued, fiercely protected and gratefully inherited, can promote incompetence, elevate arrogance and exclude alternatives. His trajectory illustrates the way that wealth, connections and cultural complicity conspire, in ways both clear and concealed, to ensure that to those who are already born with a great deal even more will be given.

If there are any doubts on that score, just imagine, for a moment, that Johnson had been born Black and female.

If Johnson were a Black woman, he would not have gone to Eton. Eton doesn't allow women. But even if it did, since Black women are far more likely to be working class than most, they would be far less likely to go to Eton than most. And if Johnson had not gone to Eton but an inner-city state school, which is where most Black women are educated, he would have been far, far less likely to go to the University of Oxford. Nearly one in three Oxford colleges failed to admit a single Black British A-level student in 2015. For a Black British woman to get a place in 1983, when Johnson started at Oxford, she would have had to have been extraordinary. (There are more former presidents of the Oxford Union, Johnson included, in the cabinet than there are minorities.) And even if Johnson had been that extraordinary, when he got to Oxford he would not have been able to join the Bullingdon Club – the dining club, notorious for its vandalism, where lifelong connections to sustain his political career were made – because it was male-only.

If Johnson were a Black woman, he would not have got an internship at *The Times* thanks to a family connection because, as a Black woman, he'd almost certainly have no family connection at *The Times* (or any national newspaper) who could have made that happen in the late 1980s.

And after Johnson was fired from that internship for making up quotes, he would not have been given a job with the *Telegraph*'s leader-writing team. First of all, because Black women are not generally indulged with second chances like that. Their successes are understood individually ('She's one of a kind'), but their failures are misunderstood collectively ('They're just not up to it'). A transgression of that nature would be followed by much hand-wringing about affirmative action and 'politically correct appointments'.

But secondly, because it's unlikely there's ever been a Black woman on the *Telegraph* leader-writing team. Similarly, he would not have been able to write a column for the *Telegraph* because there isn't a Black political columnist, male or female, on the *Telegraph* newspaper, and to my knowledge, there never has been. (The *Telegraph* did not respond to enquiries.)

And if, as a Black woman, Johnson did occupy such a space, he would not be able to use it to write about men in the way he has written about women. In 1996, Johnson went to the Labour Party conference to rank the 'hot totty' on his 'Tottymeter'. Some years later, when quitting editorship of *The Spectator*, he advised his successor to 'pat [the magazine's publisher] on the bottom and send her on her way' if she came up with any circulation-boosting suggestions.

Nor would a Black woman have been able to write about white people in the way Johnson has written about Black people. In a *Telegraph* column in 2002, he claimed the Queen enjoyed being greeted on Commonwealth tours by 'flag-waving piccaninnies' and 'watermelon smiles'. Only when he was running for London mayor, six years later, did he apologise. Black women do not get to denigrate men or white people in this way while advancing through the political ranks.

If Johnson were a Black woman, he would not have become popularly known as the boisterous panellist on the current affairs comedy quiz *Have I Got News for You*, because over the past fifteen years you could count the number of Black women who appeared on the show on one hand. (I know of Diane Abbott and Moira Stuart, but beyond that the BBC, like the *Telegraph* on its leader writers, did not have available figures.)

If Johnson were a Black woman, the complications in his personal life (three affairs and one love child, and on his second marriage) would not be considered a personal matter, as they should be. (Johnson was dismissed as shadow arts spokesman in 2004 after revelations about one affair, but that was because he allegedly misled the Tory leader Michael Howard about it. Three years later, he was back, as the Tory candidate for London mayor.) Female politicians at this level do not get to ride out infidelity. And given the stereotypes about Black female sexuality, they would automatically be career-ending.

If Johnson were a Black woman, the mop-haired, bumbling-oafish, roguish shtick he has curated over the years would not be an option. Black women do not get to make light of their gaffe-making, impulsive remarks or off-colour comments. They do not get to have bad days. Anything short of exemplary personal behaviour from a senior Black woman would result in public retribution and humiliation. Johnson would not simply be an object of ridicule but the target for violent and bigoted attacks. He would receive more online abuse than any other white MP, male or female.

We have no control over who we are; as such, Johnson does not have to apologise for who he is. But as a public figure he does have to answer for what he does.

He cannot help that he was born rich, white and male. But being a rich white man has certainly helped him. He has been afforded every privilege that his race, sex and class could provide. He has been given chances to come back from failure, which others would not be granted. All of this would be important, but incidental, if he were any good at his job. But he's not.

If he were a Black woman, he would not be insulting the people of Myanmar with a Rudyard Kipling poem, the Italians over prosecco exports or the Irish over the border, because he'd never have got the job.

If Johnson were a Black woman, he'd have to be totally beyond reproach or he'd long since be finished. And since he cannot be better, we should finish with him.

What Black America means to Europe

When the Black Lives Matter protests pollinated this side of the Atlantic, some saw it as an excuse to feel superior to the US. They shouldn't have.
New York Review of Books, 7 June 2020, London

In September 1963, in Llansteffan, Wales, a stained-glass artist named John Petts was listening to the radio when he heard the news that four Black girls had been murdered in a bombing while at Sunday school at the 16th Street Baptist Church in Birmingham, Alabama.

The news moved Petts, who was white and British, deeply. 'Naturally, as a father, I was horrified by the death of the children,' said Petts, in a recording archived by London's Imperial War Museum. 'As a craftsman in a meticulous craft, I was horrified by the smashing of all those [stained-glass] windows. And I thought to myself, "My word, what can we do about this?"'

Petts decided to employ his skills as an artist in an act of solidarity. 'An idea doesn't exist unless you do something about it,' he said. 'Thought has no real living meaning unless it's followed by action of some kind.'

With the help of the editor of Wales's leading newspaper, the *Western Mail*, he launched an appeal for funds to replace the Alabama church's stained-glass window. 'I'm going to ask no one to give more than half a crown,' the editor told Petts. 'We don't want some rich man as a gesture paying for the whole window. We want it to be given by the people of Wales.'

Two years later, the church installed Petts's window, flecked with shades of blue, featuring a Black Christ, his head bowed and arms splayed above him as though on a crucifix, suspended over the words 'You do it to me' (inspired by Matthew 25:40: 'Truly, I say to you, as you did it to one of the least of these my brothers, you did it to me').

Europe's identification with Black America, particularly during times of crisis, resistance and trauma, has a long and complex history. It is fuelled in no small part by traditions of internationalism and anti-racism on the European left, where the likes of Paul Robeson, Richard Wright and Audre Lorde would find an ideological – and, at times, literal – home.

'From a very early age, my family had supported Martin Luther King and civil rights,' the Northern Irish Catholic author and screenwriter Ronan Bennett, who was wrongfully imprisoned by the British in the infamous Long Kesh prison in Northern Ireland in the early 1970s, told me. 'We had this instinctive sympathy with Black Americans. A lot of the iconography, and even the anthems, like "We Shall Overcome", were taken from Black America. By about 1971 or '72, I was more interested in Bobby Seale and Eldridge Cleaver [of the Black Panthers] than Martin Luther King.'

But this tradition of political identification with Black America also leaves significant space for the European continent's inferiority complex, as it seeks to shroud its relative military and economic weakness in relation to America with a moral confidence that conveniently ignores both its colonial past and its own racist present.

In 1998, a public inquiry into the racist murder of British teenager Stephen Lawrence was taking place, when news reached Britain of the plight of James Byrd, a forty-nine-year-old African American man who had been picked up by three men in Jasper, Texas. They assaulted him, urinated on him, chained him to their pickup truck by his ankles and dragged him more than a mile until his head came off. During an editorial meeting at the *Guardian*, where I was then working, one of my colleagues remarked of Byrd's killing: 'Well, at least we don't do that here.'

In the years since then, the number of Europeans of colour – particularly in the cities of Britain, the Netherlands, France, Belgium, Portugal and Italy – has grown considerably. They are either the descendants of former colonies ('We are here because you were there') or the more recent immigrants, who may be asylum seekers, refugees or economic migrants. These communities, too, seek to pollinate their own, local struggles for racial justice with the more visible interventions taking place in the US.

'The American Negro has no conception of the hundreds of millions of other non-whites' concern for him,' Malcolm X observed in his autobiography. 'He has no conception of their feeling of brotherhood for and with him.'

Over the past week, huge crowds have gathered across Europe to express their solidarity with the rebellions against police brutality sparked by the murder of George Floyd. (A woman's plight is less likely to make it across the Atlantic. The name of Breonna Taylor, prominent in the US protests, is less in evidence here.) The air in central Paris was heavy with smoke and tear gas as thousands of protesters took a knee and raised a fist. In Ghent, a statue of Leopold II, the Belgian king who pillaged and looted the Congo, was covered with a hood bearing the caption 'I Can't Breathe' and splashed with red paint. In Copenhagen, they chanted, 'No justice, no peace.' There were scuffles in Stockholm; Labour-controlled councils in municipalities across Britain were lit purple in solidarity; US embassies and consulates from Milan (where there was a flash mob) to Krakow (where they lit candles) were a focus of protest; while tens of thousands of marchers, from London's Trafalgar Square to The Hague, from Dublin to Berlin's Brandenburg Gate, violated social-distancing orders to make their voices heard.

While not new, these transnational protests have become more frequent now because of social media. Images and videos of police brutality, and the mass demonstrations in response, distributed through diasporas and beyond, can energise and galvanise large numbers quickly. The pace at which these connections can be made and amplified has been boosted, just as the extent of their appeal has broadened. Trayvon Martin was a household name in Europe in a way that Emmett Till never has been.

Some of this is simply a reflection of American power. Political developments in the US have a significant impact on the rest of the world – economically, environmentally and militarily. Culturally, the US has a heft unlike any other nation's, and that influence extends to African Americans. Well into my thirties, I was far more knowledgeable about the literature and history of Black America than I was about that of Black Britain, where I was born and raised, or indeed of the Caribbean, where my parents are from. Black America has a hegemonic authority in the Black diaspora because, marginalised though it has been within the US, it has a reach that no other Black minority can match.

And so, across Europe, we know the names of Trayvon Martin, Michael Brown and George Floyd, whereas Jerry Masslo, who escaped apartheid South Africa only to be murdered by racists near Naples in 1989, prompting the first major law in Italy legalising the status of immigrants, is barely known outside that country. Likewise, the story of Benjamin Hermansen, the fifteen-year-old Norwegian–Ghanaian boy who was murdered by neo-Nazis in Oslo in 2001, setting off huge demonstrations and a national anti-racism prize, is rarely told beyond Norway. (Although, through a quirk of acquaintance, Michael Jackson dedicated his 2001 album *Invincible* to Benjamin, but I doubt even his most devoted fans would get the reference.)

The interest is not mutual. While the comparison between Stephen Lawrence and James Byrd at that *Guardian* conference was awkward, at least it was possible; it is unlikely that anyone in most American newsrooms would have heard of Lawrence. This is not the product of callous indifference but the power of empire. The closer you are to the centre, the less you need know about the periphery, and vice versa.

From the vantage point of a continent that both resents and covets American power, and is in no position to do anything about it, African Americans represent to many Europeans a redemptive force: living proof that the US is not all it claims to be, and that it could be so much greater than it is. That theme gives the lie to the lazy, conservative slur that the European left is fundamentally anti-American. The same liberals who reviled George W. Bush went on to love Barack Obama; the same leftists who excoriated Richard Nixon embraced Muhammad Ali, Malcolm X and Martin Luther King Jr. Even as the French decried the 'Coca-Colonisation' of cultural imperialism that began with the Marshall Plan, they welcomed James Baldwin and Richard Wright. In other words, the rejection of US foreign policy and power – at times reflexive and crude, but rarely completely unjustified – never entailed a wholescale repudiation of American culture or potential.

And in times when the US valued its soft power, it cared about how it was perceived elsewhere. '[The] issue of race relations deeply affects the conduct of our foreign policy relations,' said secretary of state Dean Rusk in 1963. 'I am speaking of the problem of discrimination . . . Our voice is muted, our friends are embarrassed, our enemies are gleeful . . . We are running this race with one of our legs in a cast.'

Now is not one of those times. George Floyd's killing comes at a moment when the US's standing in Europe has never been lower. With his bigotry, misogyny, xenophobia, ignorance, vanity, venality, bullishness and bluster, Donald Trump epitomises everything most Europeans loathe about the worst aspects of American power. The day after Trump's inauguration, there were women's marches in eighty-four countries; and today, his arrival in most European capitals provokes huge protests. By his behaviour at international meetings and his resolve to pull out of the World Health Organization in the middle of a pandemic, he has made his contempt for the rest of the world clear. And, for the most part, it is warmly reciprocated.

Although police killings are a constant, gruesome feature of American life, to many Europeans this particular murder stands as confirmation of the injustices of this broader political period. It illustrates a resurgence of white, nativist violence blessed with the power of the state and emboldened from the highest office. It exemplifies a democracy in crisis, with security forces running amok and terrorising their own citizens. The killing of George Floyd stands not just as a murder but as a metaphor.

Those pathologies did not come from nowhere. 'No African came in freedom to the shores of the New World,' wrote the nineteenth-century French intellectual Alexis de Tocqueville. 'The Negro transmits to his descendants at birth the external mark of his ignominy. The law can abolish servitude, but only God can obliterate its traces.' That 'mark' serves as a ticket to a world that seeks to understand Black America as from, but not entirely of, the US – simultaneously central to a version of its culture and absolved from consequences of its power.

This perception of Black America was often patronising or infantilising. 'If I were an elderly Negro,' wrote the fledgling Soviet Union's most celebrated poet, Vladimir Mayakovsky, in his 1927 poem 'To Our Youth', 'I would learn Russian, / without being despondent or lazy, just because Lenin spoke it.' Europe's exoticisation of Josephine Baker in the *Revue nègre* was no one-off, even if Baker herself was unique. In the late 1960s, the West German media described the activist Angela Davis as 'the militant Madonna with the Afro-look' and 'the black woman with the "bush hairdo"'. In East Germany, they referred to her as 'The beautiful, dark-skinned woman [who] captured the attention of the Berliners with her wide, curly hairstyle in the Afrika-Look.'

But for all that it was flawed, the admiration in the connection was nonetheless genuine. There has always been a strong internationalist current of anti-racism, alongside anti-fascism, in the European left tradition, which provided fertile ground for the struggles of African Americans. Back in the 1860s, Lancashire mill workers, despite being impoverished themselves by the blockade on the Confederacy that caused the supply of cotton to dry up, resisted calls to end the boycott of Southern goods. In the early 1970s, the Free Angela Davis campaign told the *New York Times* that it had received 100,000 letters of support from East Germany alone – too many even to open.

If Europe has a proven talent for anti-racist solidarity with Black America, one that has once again come to the fore with the uprisings in the US, it also has a history of exporting racism around the world. De Tocqueville was right to point out that 'No African came in freedom to the shores of the New World,' but he neglected to make clear that it was primarily the 'Old World' that brought those Africans there. Europe has every bit as vile a history of racism as the Americas – indeed, the histories are entwined. The most pertinent difference between Europe and the US in this regard is simply that Europe practised its most egregious forms of anti-Black racism – slavery, colonialism, segregation – outside its borders. America internalised those things.

In the time that elapsed between Petts hearing about the Birmingham bombing and the stained-glass window being installed in Alabama, six African countries liberated themselves from British rule (and there would be more to come), while Portugal hung on to its foreign possessions for another nine years. If Petts had been in search of a heart-rending story thousands of miles from home in the previous years, he could have looked to Kenya, where his own government was torturing and murdering thousands in response to a revolt for freedom.

One of the central distinctions between the racial histories of Europe and the US is that until relatively recently, the European repression and resistance took place primarily abroad. Our civil rights movement was in Jamaica, Ghana, India and so on. In the post-colonial era, this offshoring of responsibility has left significant room for denial, distortion, ignorance and sophistry when it comes to understanding that history.

'It is quite true that the English are hypocritical about their Empire,' wrote George Orwell in 'England Your England'. 'In the working class this hypocrisy takes the form of not knowing that the

Empire exists.' In 1951, a decade after that essay was published, the UK government's social survey revealed that nearly three-fifths of respondents could not name a single British colony.

Such selective amnesia about their own imperial legacy leads ineluctably to a false sense of superiority around racism among many white Europeans towards the US. Worse is the toxic nostalgia that to this day taints their misunderstanding of that history. One in two Dutch people, one in three Britons, one in four French and Belgians and one in five Italians believe that their country's former empire is something to be proud of, according to a YouGov poll from March of this year. Conversely, only one in twenty Dutch, one in seven French, one in five Britons and one in four Belgians and Italians regard their former empires as something to be ashamed of. These are all nations that saw large demonstrations in solidarity with the George Floyd protests in the US.

Their indignation all too often bears insufficient self-awareness to see what most of the rest of the world has seen. They wonder, in all sincerity, how the US could have arrived at such a brutal place – with no recognition or regret that they have travelled a similar path themselves. The level of understanding about race and racism among white Europeans, even those who would consider themselves sympathetic, cultured and informed, is woefully low.

The late Maya Angelou recognised this gulf between what her own relationship to France was compared with France's relationship to others who looked like her. That realisation was what made her decide, while on tour with *Porgy and Bess* in 1954, not to follow the familiar path of Black artists and musicians who had settled there.

'Paris was not the place for me or my son,' she concluded in *Singin' and Swingin' and Gettin' Merry Like Christmas*, the third volume of her autobiography. 'The French could entertain the idea of me because they were not immersed in guilt about a mutual history – just as white Americans found it easier to accept Africans, Cubans or South American blacks than the blacks who had lived with them foot to neck for 200 years. I saw no benefit in exchanging one kind of prejudice for another.'

And that brings us to the other problem with Europe's credibility on this score: namely, the prevalence of racism in Europe today. Fascism is once again a mainstream ideology on the continent, with openly racist parties a central feature of the landscape, framing policy and debate even when they are not in power. There are no viral videos of refugees in their last desperate moments, struggling for breath before plunging into the Mediterranean (possibly headed to a country, Italy, that levies fines on anyone who does rescue them). Only when, in 2015, a three-year-old Syrian boy, Alan Kurdi, was washed up dead on a Turkish beach did we see in Europe an effect like that of the American videos of police shootings – painful proof of the inhumanity in which our political cultures are similarly complicit.

Levels of incarceration, unemployment, deprivation and poverty are all higher for Black Europeans. Perhaps only because the continent is not blighted by the gun culture of the US, racism here is less lethal. But it is just as prevalent in other ways. Racial disparities in Covid-19 mortality in Britain, for example, are comparable to those in the US. Between 2005 and 2015, there were race-related riots or rebellions in Britain, Italy, Belgium, France and Bulgaria. The precariousness of Black life in late capitalism is not unique to the US, even if it is most often and most glaringly laid bare there. To that extent, Black Lives Matter exists as a floating signifier that can find a home in most European cities and beyond.

So, given all of that, with what authority do Europeans get to challenge the US over racism? This is a question that Black European activists constantly seek to triangulate, using the attention focused on the situation in the US to force a reckoning with the racism in their own countries. There is no reason, of course, why the existence of racism in one place should deny one the right to talk about racism in another. (If that were the case, the anti-apartheid movement would never have got off the ground in the West.) But it does mean having to be mindful about how one does it. I have seen many instances of Black activists here trying to turn Europe's wider cultural obsession with the US's bigger canvas to their advantage and educate their own political establishments about the racism on their doorstep. Answering the laments for George Floyd in the US this week, Parisians chanted the name of Adama Traoré, a citizen of Malian descent who died in police custody in 2016.

But it can be a thankless task. In my experience, drawing connections, continuities and contrasts between the racisms on either side of the Atlantic invites something between rebuke and confusion from many white European liberals. Few will deny the existence of racism in their own countries, but they insist on trying to force an admission that it 'is better "here than there"' – as though we should be happy with the racism we have.

When I left the US in 2015, after twelve years as a correspondent living in Chicago and New York, I was constantly asked whether I was leaving because of the racism. 'Racism operates differently in Britain and America,' I'd reply. 'If I was trying to escape racism, why would I go back to Hackney?'

But racism is worse in America than here, they'd insist.

'Racism's bad everywhere,' has always been my retort. 'There really is no "better" kind.'

Why every single statue should come down

Monuments of historical figures are lazy, ugly and distort history. From Cecil Rhodes to Rosa Parks, let's get rid of them all.
Guardian, 1 June 2021, London

Having been a Black, left-wing *Guardian* columnist for more than two decades, I have always understood that I would be regarded as fair game for the kinds of moral panics that might make headlines in right-wing tabloids. It's not like I haven't given them the raw material. In the course of my career I've written pieces with headlines such as 'Riots Are a Class Act', 'Let's Have an Open and Honest Conversation About White People' and 'End All Immigration Controls'. I might as well have drawn a target on my back. But the only time I have ever been caught in the tabloids' crosshairs it was not because of my denunciations of capitalism or racism, but because of a statue – or, to be more precise, the absence of one.

The story starts in the mid-nineteenth century, when the designers of Trafalgar Square decided that there would be one huge column for Horatio Nelson and four smaller plinths for statues surrounding it. They managed to put statues on three of the plinths, before running out of money, leaving the fourth one bare. A government advisory group, convened in 1999, decided that this fourth plinth should host a rotating exhibition of contemporary sculpture. Responsibility for the site went to the new mayor of London, Ken Livingstone.

Livingstone, whom I did not know, asked me if I would be on the committee, which I joined in 2002. It met every six weeks, working out the most engaged, popular way to include the public in the process. I was asked if I would chair the meetings, because they wanted someone outside the arts, and I agreed. What could possibly go wrong?

Well, the Queen Mother died. That had nothing to do with me. Given that she was 101, her passing was a much-anticipated, if very sad, event. Less anticipated was the suggestion by Simon Hughes, a Liberal Democrat MP and potential candidate for the London mayoralty, that the Queen Mother's likeness be placed on the vacant fourth plinth. Worlds collided.

The next day, the *Daily Mail* ran a front-page headline: 'Carve Her Name in Pride: Join our campaign for a statue of the Queen Mother to be erected in Trafalgar Square (whatever the panjandrums of political correctness say!)' Inside, an editorial asked whether our committee 'would really respond to the national mood and agree to a memorial in Trafalgar Square'.

Never mind that a committee, convened by parliament, had already decided how the plinth should be filled. Never mind that it was supposed to be an equestrian statue and that the Queen Mother will not be remembered for riding horses. Never mind that no one from the royal family nor any elected official had approached us.

The day after that came a double-page spread headlined 'Are They Taking the Plinth?', alongside excerpts of articles I had written several years ago, taken out of context, under the headline 'The Thoughts of Chairman Gary'. Once again, the editorial writers were upon us: 'The saga of the empty plinth is another example of the yawning gap between the metropolitan elite hijacking this country and the majority of ordinary people who simply want to reclaim Britain as their own.'

The *Mail*'s comments were truer than it dared imagine. It called on people to write in, but precious few did. No one was interested in having the Queen Mother in Trafalgar Square, and the campaign died a sad and pathetic death. Luckily for me, it turned out that if there was a gap between anyone and the ordinary people of the country on this issue, then the *Daily Mail* was on the wrong side of it.

This, however, was simply the most insistent attempt to find a human occupant for the plinth. Over the years there have been requests to put David Beckham, Bill Morris, Mary Seacole, Benny Hill and Paul Gascoigne up there. None of these figures are particularly known for riding horses either. But with each request I got, I would make the petitioner an offer: if you can name those who occupy the other three plinths, then the fourth is yours. Of course, the plinth was not actually in my gift, but that didn't matter because I knew I would never have to deliver. I knew the answers because I had made it my business to know them: the other three are Major General Sir Henry Havelock, who distinguished himself during what is now known as the Indian Rebellion of 1857, when an uprising of thousands of Indians ended in slaughter; General Sir Charles Napier, who crushed a rebellion in Ireland and conquered the Sindh province, in what is now Pakistan; and King George IV, an alcoholic, debtor and womaniser.

The petitioners generally had no idea who any of them were. And when they finally conceded that point, I would ask them: 'So why would you want to put someone else up there so we can forget them? I understand that you want to preserve their memory. But you've just shown that this is not a particularly effective way to remember people.'

In Britain, we seem to have a peculiar fixation with statues, as we seek to petrify historical discourse, lather it in cement, hoist it high and insist on it as a permanent statement of fact, culture, truth and tradition that can never be questioned, touched, removed or recast. This statue obsession mistakes adulation for history, history for heritage and heritage for memory. It attempts to detach the past from the present, the present from morality, and morality from responsibility. In short, it attempts to set our understanding of what has happened in stone, beyond interpretation, investigation or critique.

But history is not set in stone. It is a living discipline, subject to excavation, evolution and maturation. Our understanding of the past shifts. Our views on sexuality, medicine, education, child-rearing and masculinity are not the same as they were fifty years ago, and will be different again in another fifty years. But while our sense of who we are, what is acceptable and what is possible changes with time, statues don't. They stand, indifferent to the play of events, impervious to the tides of thought that might wash over them and the winds of change that swirl around them – or at least they do until we decide to take them down.

In recent months, I have been part of a team at the University of Manchester's Centre on the Dynamics of Ethnicity (Code) studying the impact of the Black Lives Matter movement on statues and memorials in Britain, the US, South Africa, Martinique and Belgium. Last summer's uprisings, sparked by the police murder of George Floyd in Minneapolis, spread across the globe. One of the focal points, in many countries, was statues. Belgium, Brazil, Ireland, Portugal, the Netherlands and Greenland were just a few of the places that saw statues challenged. On the French island of Martinique, the statue of Joséphine de Beauharnais, who was born to a wealthy colonial family on the island and later became Napoleon's first wife and empress, was torn down by a crowd using clubs and ropes. It had already been decapitated thirty years ago.

Across the US, Confederate generals fell, were toppled or voted down. In the small town of Lake Charles, Louisiana, nature presented the local parish police jury with a challenge. In mid-August last year, the jury voted ten to four to keep a memorial monument to the soldiers who died defending the Confederacy in the civil war. Two weeks later, Hurricane Laura blew it down. Now the jury has to decide not whether to take it down, but whether to put it back up again.

And then, of course, in Britain there was the statue of Edward Colston, a Bristol slave trader, which ended up in the drink. Britain's major cities, including Manchester, Glasgow, Birmingham and Leeds, are undertaking reviews of their statues.

Many spurious arguments have been made about these actions, and I will come to them in a minute. But the debate around public art and memorialisation, as it pertains to statues, should be engaged with, not ducked. One response I have heard is that we should even out the score by erecting statues of prominent Black, abolitionist, female and other figures who are under-represented. I understand the motivations: to give a fuller account of the range of experiences, voices, hues and ideologies that have made us what we are; to make sure that public art is rooted in the lives of the public as a whole, not just a part of it, and that we all might see ourselves in the figures that are represented.

But while I can understand it, I do not agree with it. The problem isn't that we have too few statues, but too many. I think it is a good thing that so many of these statues of pillagers, plunderers, bigots and thieves have been taken down. I think they are offensive. But I don't think they should be taken down because they are offensive. I think they should be taken down because I think all statues should be taken down.

Here, to be clear, I am talking about statues of people, not other works of public memorial, such as the Vietnam Veterans Memorial in Washington DC, the Holocaust Memorial in Berlin or the Famine Memorial in Dublin. I think works like these serve the important function of public memorialisation, and many have the added benefit of being beautiful.

The same cannot be said of statues of people. I think they are poor as works of public art and poor as efforts at memorialisation. Put more succinctly, they are lazy and ugly. So, yes, take down the slave traders, imperial conquerors, colonial murderers, warmongers and genocidal exploiters. But while you're at it, take down the freedom fighters, trade unionists, human rights champions and revolutionaries. Yes, remove Columbus, Leopold II, Colston and Rhodes. But take down Mandela, Gandhi, Seacole and Tubman, too.

I don't think those two groups are moral equals. I place great value on those who fought for equality and inclusion and against bigotry and privilege. But their value to me need not be set in stone and raised on a pedestal. My sense of self-worth is not contingent on see-ing those who represent my viewpoints, history and moral compass forced on the broader public. In the words of Nye Bevan, 'That is my truth, you tell me yours.' Just be aware that if you tell me your truth is more important than mine, and therefore deserves to be foisted on me in the high street or public park, then I may not listen for very long.

For me, the issue starts with the very purpose of a statue. They are among the most fundamentally conservative – with a small 'c' – expressions of public art possible. They are erected with eternity in mind – a fixed point on the landscape. Never to be moved, removed, adapted or engaged with beyond popular reverence. Whatever values they represent are the preserve of the establishment. To put up a statue you must own the land on which it stands and have the authority and means to do so. As such they represent the value sys-tem of the establishment at any given time, which is then projected into the forever.

That is unsustainable. It is also arrogant. Societies evolve; norms change; attitudes progress. Take the mining magnate, imperialist and unabashed white supremacist Cecil Rhodes. He donated significant amounts of money to institutions and trusts, with the express desire that he be remembered for four thousand years. We're only 120 years in, but his wish may well be granted. The trouble is, his intention was that he would be remembered fondly. And you can't buy that kind of love, no matter how much bronze you lather it in. So in both South Africa and Britain we have been saddled with these monuments to Rhodes.

The problem is that they are not his only legacy. The systems of racial subjugation in southern Africa, of which he was a principal architect, are still with us. The income and wealth disparities in that part of the world did not come about through bad luck or hard work.

Dispatches from the Diaspora

They were created by design. Rhodes's design. This is the man who said: 'The native is to be treated as a child and denied franchise. We must adopt a system of despotism, such as works in India, in our relations with the barbarism of South Africa.' So we should not be surprised if the descendants of those so-called natives, the majority in their own land, do not remember him fondly.

A similar story can be told in the southern states of the US. In his book *Standing Soldiers, Kneeling Slaves*, the American historian Kirk Savage writes of the thirty-year period after the civil war: 'Public monuments were meant to yield resolution and consensus, not to prolong conflict . . . Even now to commemorate is to seek historical closure, to draw together the various strands of meaning in an historical event or personage and condense its significance.'

Clearly, these statues – of Confederate soldiers in the South, or of Rhodes in South Africa and Oxford – do not represent a consensus now. If they did, they would not be challenged. Nobody is seriously questioning the statue of the suffragist Millicent Fawcett in Parliament Square, because nobody seriously challenges the notion of women's suffrage. Nor is anyone seeking historical closure via the removal of a statue. The questions that some of these monuments raise – of racial inequality, white supremacy, imperialism, colonialism and slavery – are still very much with us. There is a reason why these particular statues – and not, say, that of Robert Raikes, who founded Sunday schools, which stands in Victoria Embankment Gardens in London – were targeted during the Black Lives Matter protests.

But these statues never represented a consensus, even when they were erected. Take the statues of Confederate figures in Richmond, Virginia, that were the focus of protests last summer. Given that they represented men on the losing side of the civil war, they certainly didn't represent a consensus in the country as a whole. The northern states wouldn't have appreciated them. But, closer to home, they didn't even represent the general will of Richmond at the time. The substantial African American population of the city would hardly have been pleased to see them up there. And nor were many whites, either. When a labour party took control of Richmond city council in the late 1880s, a coalition of Blacks and working-class whites refused to vote for an unveiling parade for the monument because it would 'benefit only a certain class of people'.

Calls for the removal of statues have also raised the charge that long-standing works of public art are at the mercy of political whim. 'Is nothing sacred?' they cry. 'Who next?' they ask, clutching their pearls and pointing to Churchill. But our research showed that these statues were not removed as a fad or in a feverish moment of insubordination. People had been calling for them to be removed for half a century. And the issue was never confined to the statue itself. It was always about what the statue represented, the prevailing and persistent issues that remained, and the legacy of whatever the statue was erected to symbolise.

One of the greatest distractions when it comes to removing statues is the argument that to remove a statue is to erase history; that to change something about a statue is to tamper with history. This is such arrant nonsense that it is difficult to know where to begin, so I guess it would make sense to begin at the beginning.

Statues are not history; they represent historical figures. They may have been set up to mark a person's historical contribution, but they are not themselves history. If you take down Nelson Mandela's bust on London's South Bank, you do not erase the history of the anti-apartheid struggle. Statues are symbols of reverence; they are not symbols of history. They elevate an individual from a historical moment and celebrate them.

Nobody thinks that when Iraqis removed statues of Saddam Hussein from around the country, they wanted him to be forgotten. Quite the opposite. They wanted him, and his crimes, to be remembered. They just didn't want him to be revered. Indeed, if the people

Dispatches from the Diaspora

removing a statue are trying to erase history, then they are very bad at it. For if the erection of a statue is a fact of history, then removing it is no less so. It can also do far more to raise awareness of history. More people know about Colston and what he did as a result of his statue being taken down than ever did as a result of it being put up. Indeed, the very people campaigning to take down the symbols of colonialism and slavery are the same ones who want schools to teach children more about colonialism and slavery. The ones who want to keep them up are generally the ones who would prefer that we didn't study what these people actually did.

But to claim that statues represent history does not merely misrepresent their role; it misunderstands history and their place in it. Let's go back to the Confederate statues for a moment. The American civil war ended in 1865. The South lost. Much of its economy and infrastructure were laid to waste. Almost one in six white southern men aged thirteen to forty-three died; even more were wounded; more again were captured.

Southerners had to forget the reality of the civil war before they could celebrate it. They did not want to remember the civil war as an episode that brought devastation and humiliation. Very few statues went up in the decades immediately after the war. According to the Southern Poverty Law Center, almost five hundred monuments to the Confederate cause went up between 1885 and 1915. More than half were built within one seven-year period, between 1905 and 1912.

The timing was no coincidence. It was long enough since the horrors of the civil war that it could be misremembered as a noble defence of racialised regional culture rather than just slavery. As such, it represented a sanitised, partial and selective version of history, based less in fact than in toxic nostalgia and melancholia. It's not history that these statues' protectors are defending; it's mythology.

Colston, an official in the Royal African Company, which reportedly sold as many as a hundred thousand west Africans into slavery, died in 1721. His statue didn't go up until 1895. This was no coincidence, either. According to historian Peter Hill, half of the monuments contested in the first ten days of the Black Lives Matter protests were erected between 1889 and 1919. This was partly an aesthetic trend of the late Victorian era. But it should probably come as little surprise that the statues that anti-racist protesters wanted to be taken down were those erected when Jim Crow segregation was firmly installed in the US, and at the apogee of colonial expansion.

Statues always tell us more about the values of the period when they were put up than the story of the person depicted. Two years before Martin Luther King's death, a poll showed that the majority of Americans viewed him unfavourably. Four decades later, when Barack Obama unveiled a memorial to King in Washington DC, 91 per cent of Americans approved of it. Rather than teaching us about the past, his statue distorts history. As I wrote in my book *The Speech: The Story Behind Dr Martin Luther King Jr's Dream*, 'White America came to embrace King in the same way that white South Africans came to embrace Nelson Mandela: grudgingly and gratefully, retrospectively, selectively, without grace or guile. Because by the time they realised their hatred of him was spent and futile, he had created a world in which loving him was in their own self-interest. Because, in short, they had no choice.'

One claim for not bringing down certain statues of those who committed egregious acts is that we should not judge people of another time by today's standards. I call this the 'But that was before racism was bad' argument or, as others have termed it, the 'Jimmy Savile defence'. Firstly, this strikes me as a very good argument for not erecting statues at all, since there is no guarantee that any consensus will persist. Just because there may be a sense of closure now doesn't mean those issues won't one day be reopened. But beyond that, by the time many of these statues went up there was already

Dispatches from the Diaspora

considerable opposition to the deeds that had made these men (and they are nearly all men) rich and famous. In Britain, slavery had been abolished more than sixty years before Colston's statue went up. The civil war had been over for thirty years before most statues of Confederate generals were erected. Cecil Rhodes and King Leopold II of Belgium were both criticised for their vile racist acts and views by their contemporaries. In other words, not only was what they did wrong, but it was widely known to be wrong at the time they did it. By the time they were set in stone, there were significant movements, if not legislation, condemning the very things that had made them rich and famous.

A more honest appraisal of why the removal of these particular statues rankles with so many is that they do not actually want to engage with the history they represent. Power, and the wealth that comes with it, has many parents. But the brutality it takes to acquire it is all too often an orphan. According to a YouGov poll last year, only one in twenty Dutch, one in seven French, one in five Brits and one in four Belgians and Italians believe their former empire is something to be ashamed of. If these statues are supposed to tell our story, then why, after more than a century, do so few people actually know it?

This brings me to my final point. Statues do not just fail to teach us about the past, or give a misleading idea about particular people or particular historical events; they also skew how we understand history itself. For when you put up a statue to honour a historical moment, you reduce that moment to a single person. Individuals play an important role in history, but they don't make history by themselves. There are always many other people involved. And so what is known as the Great Man theory of history distorts how, why and by whom history is forged.

Consider the statue of Rosa Parks that stands in the US Capitol. Parks was a great woman, whose refusal to give up her seat for a white woman on a bus in Montgomery, Alabama, challenged local segregation laws and sparked the civil rights movement. When Parks died in 2005, her funeral was attended by thousands, and her contribution to the civil rights struggle was eulogised around the world.

But the reality is more complex. Parks was not the first to plead not guilty after resisting Montgomery's segregation laws on its buses. Before Parks, there was a fifteen-year-old girl named Claudette Colvin. Colvin was all set to be the icon of the civil rights movement, until she fell pregnant. Because she was an unmarried teenager, she was dropped by the conservative elders of the local church, who were key leaders of the movement. When I interviewed her twenty years ago (see p. 201), she was just getting by as a nurses' aide and living in the Bronx, all but forgotten.

And while what Parks did was a catalyst for resistance, the event that forced the segregationists to climb down wasn't the work of one individual in a single moment but the year-long collective efforts of African Americans in Montgomery who boycotted the buses: maids and gardeners who walked miles in the sun and rain, despite intimidation; those who carpooled to get people where they needed to go; those who sacrificed their time and effort for the cause. The unknown soldiers of civil rights. These are the people who made it happen. Where is their statue? Where is their place in history? How easily and wilfully the main actors can be relegated to faceless extras.

I once interviewed the Uruguayan writer Eduardo Galeano, who confessed that his greatest fear was 'that we are all suffering from amnesia'. Who, I asked, is responsible for this forgetfulness? 'It's not a person,' he explained. 'It's a system of power that is always deciding in the name of humanity who deserves to be remembered and who deserves to be forgotten . . . We are much more than we are told. We are much more beautiful.'

Statues cast a long shadow over that beauty and shroud the complexity of even the people they honour. Now I love Rosa Parks, not least because the story usually told about her is so far from who she was. She was not just a hapless woman who stumbled into history because she was tired and wanted to sit down. That was not the first time she had been thrown off a bus. 'I had almost a life history of being rebellious against being mistreated against my colour,' she once said. She was also an activist, a feminist and a devotee of Malcolm X, and argued: 'I don't believe in gradualism or that whatever should be done for the better should take for ever to do.'

Of course I want Parks to be remembered. Of course I want her to take her rightful place in history. All the less reason to diminish that memory by casting her in bronze and erecting her beyond memory.

So let us not burden future generations with the weight of our faulty memory and the lies of our partial mythology. Let us not put up the people we ostensibly cherish so that they can be forgotten and ignored. Let us elevate them and others – in the curriculum, through scholarships and museums. Let us subject them to the critiques they deserve, which may convert them from inert models of their former selves to the complex, and often flawed, people that they were. Let us fight to embed the values of those we admire in our politics and our culture. Let's cover their anniversaries in the media and set them in tests. But the last thing we should do is cover their images in concrete and set them in stone.

Additional reporting by Meghan Tinsley, Ruth Ramsden-Karelse, Chloe Peacock and Sadia Habib.

Black like me? *Bridgerton* and the fantasy of a non-racist past

There's a lucrative market for the depiction of racial difference in the absence of racial inequality. That's the kind of diversity we can do without, even when it does come with lots of bonking in stately homes.

The Nation, 4 April 2022, London

There were moments during my twelve years as the US correspondent for the *Guardian* when being a Black man with a British accent could be a challenge, particularly when reporting from Republican events. Englishness, an American journalist had once made clear to me, carried cultural cachet; Blackness did not. The two arriving in the same body could mess with some people's heads. When I introduced myself as a British journalist, I was occasionally subjected to an interrogation of my credentials. 'Were you born there?' they'd ask. 'I don't hear an accent.' (I sound like Ricky Gervais, with nary a hint of a transatlantic twang.)

But my point here is not partisan. Republicans could be, as it happens, ruder than most. But despite Oscar-winning director Steve McQueen, acclaimed author Zadie Smith and actors Idris Elba, David Oyelowo and Thandie Newton – to name but a few – the general American image of Britain (particularly outside the big cities) remains ossified in a time before the large-scale migration of Black people to Britain following the Second World War. (My parents came from Barbados in the early 1960s.) When I wrote an article for the *Washington Post* about being Black and British in the US, it ran alongside a picture of a Black man in a bowler hat carrying an umbrella in one hand and a cup of tea in the other.

So I can imagine that *Bridgerton*, the Netflix period drama set in 1813, which portrays a multiracial British elite, complete with a Black queen, duke and dowager aunt, as well as debutantes and suitors of virtually every hue, might test credulity in the US and beyond. (Growing up in Britain, where I was born, people would frequently ask me where I was really from, too.) Whatever issues people may have had with this clearly didn't stop them from watching the show: its first season was the second-most-watched Netflix original series of all time.

Bridgerton's appeal is not difficult to fathom. Set in some of Britain's grandest stately homes, with elaborate costumes, flamboyant coiffures (Queen Charlotte's wigs deserve a series all to themselves), quaint rituals and plenty of sex, it promises a great deal. (It didn't hurt that it was released in December 2020, during what was then the deadliest month of the pandemic, when we had little else to do but watch TV.) To the undiscerning eye, it's basically *Downton Abbey* with a bigger budget, better locations, more bonking and a diverse cast.

While the series is named after the Bridgerton family, it might better be named 'Lady Whistledown'. That is the nom de plume of the anonymous scandalmonger whose newsletter spreads well-informed word of the nineteenth-century *haut monde*'s romantic entanglements – as well as tart commentary on their consequences. Each new edition provides fresh gossip, revealing secrets, exposing trysts and assessing the progress of the (debutante) season in all its lustful, scheming glory. We learn at the end of the first season that Lady Whistledown is Penelope Featherington, the youngest daughter of a family struggling to escape ruin.

Season 1 is set, appropriately enough, at the beginning of the 'social season' of 1813, when debutantes and eligible bachelors are presented to high society in what is essentially a marriage market. Male suitors call on young ladies for a delicate courtship dance, in which status is key. The Bridgertons are a family of eight children (named, in alphabetical order, Anthony, Benedict, Colin, Daphne, Eloise, Francesca, Gregory and Hyacinth, and headed by Violet, a widowed viscountess). Queen Charlotte crowns Daphne, the eldest daughter, the season's 'diamond', making her the most sought-after maiden of the moment. Along with welcome attention, this gives her the onerous responsibility of making a match worthy of both the queen's favour and her own affections.

Sex is as key to the spectacle as it is incidental to the storyline. Virtually all the main characters are at it like undergrads on spring break in Cancún. There is almost nowhere they won't do it: against a tree, on the stairs, on a ladder, on a desk, beneath the stands or in the immaculately tended gardens. From time to time they even use a bed. There is oral sex, masturbation, a threesome, sex education (even as Daphne seeks a husband, it transpires she does not know about the birds and the bees), sexual assault and an attempted abortion.

Season 1 charts Daphne's fraught romance with the Duke of Hastings. Though they profess to despise each other, a fissile courtship ensues after they concoct a mutually beneficial pact to hoodwink high society. Daphne calculates that encouraging the belief that she's already being pursued is her best hope of buying time to find the right match. Hastings – a gorgeous, brooding, Byronic figure – has no interest in marriage, but the prestigious title attached to such an Adonis makes the debutantes swoon. He believes that his only hope of avoiding the besotted hordes is if they think he is already attached. So the pair decide to pretend – including with their closest relatives – they are embroiled in a serious but yet-to-be-sealed courtship. Only the ruse works a little too well, and they fall in love with each other.

Season 2 starts with the beginning of the next year's 'marriage market' events. Daphne's eldest brother, Anthony, the season's most eligible bachelor, decides that this is the year he will take a bride. But a romantic connection couldn't be further from his considerations, as he sets about interviewing the candidates for future Bridgerton matriarch with clinical rigour.

'Love is the last thing I desire,' he declares at a ball, describing his future wife in language a horse breeder might use to refer to a prize mare. 'But if my children are to be of good stock, then their mother must be of impeccable quality. A pleasing face, an acceptable wit, genteel manners enough to credit a viscountess. It should not be so hard to find. And yet, the debutantes of London fall short at every turn.'

The rest of the season essentially tests this proposition, as Anthony is torn between his duty to marry a woman with the appropriate attributes and his barely repressed desire to give himself to a woman on whom he has developed a monumental crush. Unfortunately for him, those two women are related.

The Sharma sisters, Kate and Edwina, have arrived from India and, along with their mother, Lady Mary Sharma, are guests of Lady Danbury, the dowager godmother to Hastings from Season 1. Kate effectively acts as Edwina's governess and has come only to secure her sister the marriage she deserves. Headstrong, sharp-tongued and quick-witted, she insists she has no interest in finding a husband for herself – many consider her too old at twenty-six anyway.

Demure, accomplished and intelligent, Edwina ticks all of Anthony's boxes. He courts her determinedly, and she falls in love with him. Everyone up to Queen Charlotte herself agrees it's a great match. There is only one dissenter: Kate, who overheard Anthony's comments at the ball and was not impressed. 'I take issue with any man who views women merely as chattels and breeding stock,' she tells him. 'When you manage to find this paragon of virtue, whatever makes you think she will accept your suit?'

But Kate's loyalties are divided: not only does she believe Anthony is too arrogant, she also fancies the breeches off him. Anthony feels similarly, though it takes both a while to admit it to themselves, let alone each other. Several times – too often to be plausible – they are caught in romantic near misses, with fingers touching, eyes locked, breathing into each other's mouth, only to be interrupted or rein themselves in. At one point Kate clasps his hand to her breast and holds it there to prove she has not been stung by a bee – which, unless things have changed radically in terms of courtship in the last couple of centuries, is a pretty unambiguous play for a straight man's attention.

Elsewhere, Queen Charlotte becomes obsessed with discovering the identity of Lady Whistledown, whose commentaries she finds increasingly impertinent, while Penelope tries to remain anonymous and her family, the Featheringtons, still struggle for money and respectability. The only really standout actor is Adjoa Andoh, who plays Lady Danbury – an omniscient elder and friend of the queen whose mixture of tough love, hard truths, strategic ploys and playful manner are made credible by Andoh's consistently robust performance.

That the Duke of Hastings, Queen Charlotte and Lady Danbury are Black and the Sharma sisters South Asian are facts that do not intrude into the storyline. Their presence is not entirely fanciful. Some Black people did make it into British high society at the time. It has been argued that the real Queen Charlotte, the wife of George III, had some African ancestry, through a branch of the Portuguese royal family, who supposedly mixed with the Moors in the thirteenth century. After six centuries the phenotypic evidence would have been negligible. But according to the historian Mario de Valdes y Cocom – who has done more than any other to extol Charlotte's African heritage – the royal physician described Charlotte as having 'a true mulatto face', while one prime minister wrote of the queen that 'her nose is too wide and her lips too thick'.

Of course, there have been Black people in Britain since Roman times – even if they began arriving in significant numbers only in the 1950s. Initially, their presence usually centred around the ports of Cardiff (home of Shirley Bassey), Bristol (home of the slave importer Edward Colston, whose statue was torn down during the Black Lives Matter protests) and Liverpool (home to the country's oldest Black community), as well as London. They numbered in the hundreds during the sixteenth century, rising to 20,000 as the Atlantic slave trade took off, only to subside with abolition itself. Across Europe throughout this time, a handful of Black people made their way, through one fashion or another, into the elites. There was Juan Latino, of Ethiopian descent, embedded in the Spanish court in the sixteenth century; Joseph Boulogne, made a member of King Louis XV's Royal Guard in the eighteenth century; and Abram Petrovich Gannibal, brought to Russia (probably from Cameroon) as a gift for Peter the Great in the late eighteenth century, eventually rising to become a military engineer, a nobleman – and the great-grandfather of Alexander Pushkin.

Few made it that far in Britain, but in literary classics set only slightly later, Black characters are scattered among the beau monde, usually coming from the colonies. Charlotte Brontë's *Jane Eyre* (1847) includes the character Bertha Mason, a Creole from Jamaica described as having 'dark' hair and a 'discoloured', 'blackened' face – whose parents approved of her marriage to Edward Rochester because he was 'of a good race'. Bertha, portrayed in bestial terms, is hidden from view as she rages with mental illness in the attic before throwing herself from a burning building. In William Thackeray's *Vanity Fair* (1848), there is Rhoda Swartz, the 'rich, woolly-haired mulatto' heiress from St Kitts whom Mr Osborne tries to force his son George to marry. George refuses: 'I don't like the colour, sir,' he says. 'Ask the black that sweeps opposite Fleet Market, sir. I'm not going to marry a Hottentot Venus.'

Britain's colonial relationship with India also produced a significant, if relatively small, Indian community in Britain, long before the arrival of the post-Second World War migrants. With a broader range of classes, including seafarers, scholars and diplomats, there was less need for white patrons (although Queen Victoria's favoured attendant, Abdul Karim, became famous after a film about him, starring Ali Fazal and Judi Dench, was made in 2017). Indian maharajas even funded the sinking of wells in a range of British towns during the early nineteenth century. Their presence in high society is thus more plausible, if only as visitors.

But such Black characters did not – indeed, could not – exist in the number and rank suggested in *Bridgerton*, set less than a decade after the abolition of the slave trade. The creation of a diverse world in which race is not an issue is both one of executive producer Shonda Rhimes's commercial superpowers and narrative kryptonite. There is a lucrative market, particularly on-screen, for the depiction of racial difference in the absence of racial inequality, which one can only assume will grow with the proliferation of global media platforms, like Netflix, that want to sell shows all over the world in which different peoples can see themselves represented. *Sex Education*, another Netflix original, which focuses on the sexual habits and anxieties in a high school located in the fictional rural English town of Moordale, has a notably multiracial cast. The show deals with issues of class, disability, sexual assault, transphobia, homophobia, sexism and body shaming – pretty much everything, in fact, apart from race.

Rhimes's other hit shows – *Grey's Anatomy, Scandal, How to Get Away with Murder* – have for the most part followed the same logic. '*Grey's Anatomy* has differentiated itself by creating a diverse world of doctors – almost half the cast are men and women of color – and then never acknowledging it,' wrote the *New York Times* critic Matthew Fogel in 2005.

This omission, Rhimes explained to *Broadcasting and Cable* a year later, was deliberate. 'I don't think anybody is color-blind in this world. I think I'm a product of being a post-feminist, post-civil-rights baby born in an era after that happened, where race isn't the only thing discussed. And I just felt like there's something interesting about having a show in which your characters could just be your characters.'

This is problematic. It suggests that your characters live in a void in which a key determinant of their life chances is irrelevant; that they can either be themselves or have a racial identity – but not both. It reminds me of the crowd of Barack Obama supporters in South Carolina chanting 'Race doesn't matter!' after he beat Hillary Clinton in the primary there. It didn't make sense, not only because they were in the only state that, at the time, still flew the Confederate flag from its capitol, but because if it really didn't matter, then why shout about it in the first place? By the time Obama's tenure was over, it was pretty clear that race did matter, not least because nine African Americans had been shot dead in a church in that very state by a young white supremacist. Race matters.

'The success of [*Grey's Anatomy*] and of Rhimes as a producer', argues Kristen J. Warner, an assistant professor at the University of Alabama, in a 2015 paper, 'is tethered to the use of racialized bodies as signifiers of historical progress in the struggle of televisual racial representation, as well as undermining the diversity of those bodies through a laundering or whitewashing of social and cultural specificity.'

There is an important debate to be had that goes beyond popular television to the kind of diversity we'd like to have: one where the world looks different, or one where the society actually operates differently. But since this is fiction and not a documentary, it should also be stressed that Rhimes can create whatever world she pleases and is not bound by the constraints of social realism.

The world she creates in *Bridgerton* is not post-racial – after four years of Trump, a place where race no longer matters and people can just be themselves seems not hopeful but deluded. But, at first sight at least, it does pose as pre-racial: a society in which race was never an issue and people wouldn't know any other way to be. The fact that slavery has only just been abolished and colonialism is in full throttle – meaning race was very much an issue – is a point for pedants and killjoys. A world where people are this handsome and life is this plush, and which has not been contaminated by 'race', is too good to pass up. However, what Rhimes can't plausibly do is create a world in which racial difference has no meaning – only to then subject her creation to a racial critique. This is precisely what she does, twice, in Season 1, rendering the entire premise untenable.

First comes a conversation between Lady Danbury and Hastings, in which she tries to convince him that romantic love has made 'a new day begin to dawn in this society'. 'Look at our queen. Look at our king,' she says, referring to Charlotte and George III, as though Charlotte were Nelson Mandela and Meghan Markle all rolled into one. 'Look at their marriage . . . everything it is doing for us. Allowing us to become. We were two separate societies divided by colour, until a king fell in love with one of us. Love, your grace, conquers all.'

Hastings is not convinced. 'He may have chosen his queen,' he replies, 'and elevated us from novelties in their eyes to now dukes and royalty. But with that same whim he may just as easily change his mind. A mind that is hanging on by one very loose and tenuous thread.'

These 'separate societies' are never mentioned again in the series – and we see no evidence of them. In the absence of any reference to or sign of an old day, this 'new day' remains a peculiar abstraction.

The second time is when Baron Featherington attempts to persuade the Black boxer Will Mondrich to take a dive. 'I know you have a fighting spirit, passed down by your father, no doubt: a soldier [who] managed to flee the colonies after serving in Dunmore's regiment. Do you think he sought his freedom all for his future son to become some exhausted fighter, stumbling into the ring to put food on the table for his family?' Without any other mention of colonialism or racism, the reference simply does not make sense.

When it comes to gender, we are presented with the opposite narrative contradiction. Rhimes creates a world in which antiquated gender norms not only govern society but drive the story. Men pursue women, who literally drop their handkerchiefs and feign fainting so that they might be assisted or literally caught mid-swoon. For a woman, merely to be alone with a man, without a chaperone, is to risk disgrace. At one point, the brother of a fallen soldier who impregnated his girlfriend before going to war marries the girlfriend to preserve her honour. 'You have no idea what it is to be a woman,' Daphne tells Anthony at another point. 'What it might feel like to have one's entire life reduced to a single moment. This is all I have been raised for. This is all I am. I have no other value. If I am unable to find a husband, I shall be worthless.'

But when the rules of such a society have not only been laid down but form the basis for the ensuing drama, you cannot then have a man tell a woman how to masturbate (possibly the worst case of mansplaining ever). Nor does it make sense, at the very end, to have Hastings in the room holding Daphne's hand as she is giving birth – a practice still frowned upon in the BBC show *Call the Midwife*, set 150 years later. The problem here, once again, is not one of accuracy but of dramatic consistency. It is difficult to take their buttoned-up courtship seriously when Hastings has told Daphne, just a few episodes earlier, 'When you are alone, you can touch yourself . . . anywhere on your body, anywhere that gives you pleasure . . . But especially between your legs.'

The second season avoids such jarring commentaries and contradictions – and pretty much all of the sex. But it doesn't replace them with much. Anthony is fond of Edwina and thinks she'll make a good wife, while she is enamoured with him. Given the prevailing culture, that's as close to a love match as most are likely to get. Anthony and Kate, on the other hand, have barely had a civil conversation and have spent most of the time sparring. The downsides of consummating their infatuation grow with each episode. In a culture that sets so much store by propriety, pursuing their relationship is as impulsive and reckless a scenario as you're likely to get. Since they are neither impulsive nor reckless, their mutual obsession is unsustainable.

The general issues of status, love, class, marriage and gender – masculine arrogance and restraint pitted against feminine emotion and comportment – provide the essential ingredients of both seasons, as they do in almost every nineteenth-century literary classic, many of which have been made into TV dramas.

That's also part of the problem. We have seen this show before, many times, only better. Indeed, the key elements of *Bridgerton* can be reduced to the single scene in the BBC's *Pride and Prejudice* where

Mr Darcy (Colin Firth) emerges dripping wet from Lyme Park lake in body-clinging linens and riding boots and bumps into a flushed Elizabeth Bennet (Jennifer Ehle) en route to Pemberley. (There is a moment in Season 2 where Anthony Bridgerton falls into a lake, only to be eye-humped by Kate and Edwina as he comes out. The sheer lack of subtlety in the scene nicely illustrates the point.)

Repression is a central element of the drama in both *Pride and Prejudice* and *Jane Eyre*. Seduction in these novels is a subtle, socially distanced affair. There may be cads and mistresses, damaged reputations, falls from grace and dishonourable conduct, but all matters of direct sexual engagement are barely alluded to, let alone explicitly depicted. Britches remain firmly buckled; bodices remain securely bound. Happily for the novelist, the suggestion of, prelude to and promise of sex is often more sensual than the act itself.

Besides explicit sex, what *Bridgerton* adds to the aesthetic is racial repression. Rhimes creates a world in which the historical crime of racism has been resolved, through a royal love match, and non-white people are fully integrated into the dominant classes. We find its modern iteration in the royal wedding between Meghan Markle and Prince Harry, which some commentators claimed illustrated just how far Britain had come racially – and which took place even as the *Windrush* scandal, in which thousands of elderly Caribbean citizens were deported or deprived of their citizenship, was unfolding. *Bridgerton* suggests that the only thing wrong with racial inequality is that non-white people are not allowed to share in the spoils – as though adding points to my IQ for having an English accent would be okay, so long as they didn't take them away for being Black.

It offers viewers a society in which colour is segregated from race – so that things look different but remain the same. 'There's a model of diversity', Angela Davis once told me, 'as the difference that brings no difference and the change that brings no change.' For all the frock coats and corsets, bonking and balls, that's precisely the kind of diversity we can do without.

Dispatches from the Diaspora

4

EXPRESS YOURSELF

Throughout my career I've had the
honour to meet some truly amazing people
and ask them about their life and work

She would not be moved

Months before Rosa Parks's arrest on a bus in Montgomery, Alabama, a fifteen-year-old girl was charged with the same 'crime'. So why wasn't Claudette Colvin granted her rightful place in history?
Guardian, 16 December 2000, New York

This much we know. On Thursday 1 December 1955, Rosa Parks, a forty-two-year-old Black seamstress, boarded a bus in Montgomery, Alabama, after a hard day's work, took a seat and headed for home. The bus went three stops before several white passengers got on. The driver, James Blake, turned around and ordered the Black passengers to go to the back of the bus, so that the whites could take their places. 'Move, y'all, I want those two seats,' he yelled.

The bus froze. Blake persisted. 'Y'all better make it light on yourselves and let me have those seats,' he said.

The three Black passengers sitting alongside Parks rose reluctantly. Parks stayed put. Blake approached her. 'Are you going to stand up?' he asked.

'No,' said Parks.

'Well, I'm going to have you arrested,' he replied.

'You may do that,' said Parks, who is now eighty-seven and lives in Detroit.

It was an exchange later credited with changing the racial landscape of America. Parks's arrest sparked a chain reaction that started the bus boycott that launched the civil rights movement that transformed the apartheid of America's Southern states from a local idiosyncrasy to an international scandal. It was her individual courage that triggered the collective display of defiance that turned a previously unknown twenty-six-year-old preacher, Martin Luther King, into a household name.

It was a journey not only into history but also mythology. 'She was a victim of both the forces of history and the forces of destiny,' said King, in a quote now displayed in the civil rights museum in Atlanta. 'She had been tracked down by the zeitgeist – the spirit of the times.' And, from there, the short distance to sanctity: they called her 'Saint Rosa', 'an angel walking', 'a heaven-sent messenger'. 'She gave me the feeling that I was the Moses that God had sent to Pharaoh,' said Fred Gray, the lawyer who went on to represent her.

But somewhere en route they mislaid the truth. Rosa Parks was neither a victim nor a saint, but a long-standing political activist and feminist. Moreover, she was not the first person to take a stand by keeping her seat and challenging the system. Nine months before Parks's arrest, a fifteen-year-old girl, Claudette Colvin, was thrown off a bus in the same town and in almost identical circumstances.

As with Parks, she, too, pleaded not guilty to breaking the law. And, as with Parks, the local Black establishment started to rally support nationwide for her cause. But, unlike Parks, Colvin never made it into the civil rights hall of fame. Just as her case was beginning to catch the nation's imagination, she became pregnant. To the exclusively male and predominantly middle-class, church-dominated, local Black leadership in Montgomery, she was a fallen woman. She fell out of history altogether.

King Hill, Montgomery, is the sepia South. In this small, elevated patch of town, Black people sit out on wooden porches and watch an impoverished world go by. Broken-down cars sit outside tumble-down houses. The pace of life is so slow and the mood so mellow that local residents look as if they have been wading through molasses in a half-hearted attempt to catch up with the past fifty years.

'Middle-class Blacks looked down on King Hill,' says Colvin today. 'We had unpaved streets and outside toilets. We used to have a lot of juke joints up there, and maybe men would drink too much and get into a fight. It wasn't a bad area, but it had a reputation.' It is here, at 658 Dixie Drive, that Colvin, sixty-one, was raised by a great-aunt, who was a maid, and great-uncle, who was a 'yard boy', whom she grew up calling her parents.

Today, she sits in a diner in the Bronx, her pudding-basin haircut framing a soft face with a distant smile. Her voice is soft and high, almost shrill. The urban bustle surrounding her could not seem further away from King Hill. She now works as a nurses' aide at an old people's home in downtown Manhattan. She turns, watches, wipes, feeds and washes the elderly patients and offers them a gentle, consoling word when they become disoriented.

'I make up stories to convince them to stay in bed.' Her rhythm is simple, her lifestyle frugal. She works the night shift and sleeps 'when the sleep falls on her' during the day. She shops with her workmates and watches action movies on video. Until recently, none of her workmates knew anything of her pioneering role in the civil rights movement.

But go to King Hill and mention her name, and the first thing they will tell you is that she was the first. They remember her as a confident, studious young girl with a streak that was rebellious without being boisterous. 'She was a bookworm,' says Gloria Hardin, who went to school with Colvin and still lives in King Hill. 'Always studying and using long words.'

'She was an A student, quiet, well-mannered, neat, clean, intelligent, pretty, and deeply religious,' writes Jo Ann Robinson in her authoritative book, *The Montgomery Bus Boycott and the Women Who Started It*.

Colvin was also very dark-skinned, which put her at the bottom of the social pile within the Black community. In the pigmentocracy of the South at the time, and even today, while whites discriminated against Blacks on grounds of skin colour, the Black community discriminated against each other in terms of skin shade. The lighter you were, it was generally thought, the better; the closer your skin tone was to caramel, the closer to whatever power structure prevailed you were perceived to be, and the more likely you were to attract suspicion from those of a darker hue.

From 'high-yellas' to 'coal-coloureds', it is a tension steeped not only in language but in the arts, from Harlem Renaissance novelist Nella Larsen's book *Passing* to Spike Lee's film *School Daze*. 'The light-skinned girls always thought they were better-looking,' says Colvin. 'So did the teachers, too. That meant most of the dark complexion ones didn't like themselves.'

Not so Colvin. They had threatened to throw her out of the Booker T. Washington school for wearing her hair in plaits. As well as the predictable teenage fantasy of 'marrying a baseball player', she also had strong political convictions. When Ms Nesbitt, her tenth-grade teacher, asked the class to write down what they wanted to be, she unfolded a piece of paper with Colvin's handwriting on it that said 'President of the United States'.

'I wanted to go north and liberate my people,' explains Colvin. 'They did think I was nutty and crazy.'

One incident in particular preoccupied her at the time: the plight of her schoolmate Jeremiah Reeves. Reeves was a teenage grocery delivery boy who was found having sex with a white woman. The woman alleged rape; Reeves insisted it was consensual. Either way, he had violated the South's deeply ingrained taboo on interracial sex – Alabama voted to legalise interracial marriage only last month (the state held a referendum at the same time as the ballot for the US presidency), and then only by 60 per cent to 40 per cent. 'When I was in the ninth grade, all the police cars came to get Jeremiah,' says Colvin. 'They put him on death row.' Four years later, they executed him.

It was this dark, clever, angry young woman who boarded the Highland Avenue bus on Friday 2 March 1955, opposite Martin Luther King's church on Dexter Avenue, Montgomery. Colvin took her seat near the emergency door next to one Black girl; two others sat across the aisle from her. The law at the time designated seats for Black passengers at the back and for whites at the front, but left the middle as a murky no-man's-land. Black people were allowed to

Dispatches from the Diaspora

occupy those seats so long as white people didn't need them. If one white person wanted to sit down there, then all the Black people on that row were supposed to get up and either stand or move further to the back.

As more white passengers got on, the driver asked Black people to give up their seats. The three other girls got up; Colvin stayed put. 'If it had been for an old lady, I would have got up, but it wasn't. I was sitting on the last seat that they said you could sit in. I didn't get up, because I didn't feel like I was breaking the law.'

To complicate matters, a pregnant Black woman, Mrs Hamilton, got on and sat next to Colvin. The driver caught a glimpse of them through his mirror. 'He asked us both to get up. [Mrs Hamilton] said she was not going to get up and that she had paid her fare and that she didn't feel like standing,' recalls Colvin. 'So I told him I was not going to get up, either. So he said, "If you are not going to get up, I will get a policeman."'

The atmosphere on the bus became very tense. 'We just sat there and waited for it all to happen,' says Gloria Hardin, who was on the bus, too. 'We didn't know what was going to happen, but we knew something would happen.'

Almost fifty years on, Colvin still talks about the incident with a mixture of shock and indignation – as though she still cannot believe that this could have happened to her. She says she expected some abuse from the driver, but nothing more. 'I thought he would stop and shout and then drive on. That's what they usually did.'

But while the driver went to get a policeman, it was the white students who started to make noise. 'You got to get up,' they shouted.

'She ain't got to do nothing but stay Black and die,' retorted a Black passenger.

The policeman arrived, displaying two of the characteristics for which white Southern men had become renowned: gentility and racism. He could not bring himself to chide Mrs Hamilton in her condition, but he could not allow her to stay where she was and flout the law as he understood it, either. So he turned on the Black men sitting behind her. 'If any of you are not gentlemen enough to give a lady a seat, you should be put in jail yourself,' he said.

A sanitation worker, Mr Harris, got up, gave her his seat and got off the bus. That left Colvin. 'Aren't you going to get up?' asked the policeman.

'No,' said Colvin.

He asked again.

'No, sir,' she said.

'Oh God,' wailed a Black woman at the back. One white woman defended Colvin to the policeman; another said that if she got away with this, 'they will take over'.

'I will take you off,' said the policeman, then he kicked her. Two more kicks soon followed.

For all her bravado, Colvin was shocked by the extremity of what happened next. 'It took on the form of harassment. I was very hurt, because I didn't know that white people would act like that and I . . . I was crying,' she says. The policeman grabbed her and took her to a patrolman's car, in which his colleagues were waiting. 'What's going on with these niggers?' asked one. Another cracked a joke about her bra size.

'I was really afraid, because you just didn't know what white people might do at that time,' says Colvin. In August that year, a fourteen-year-old boy called Emmett Till would say 'Bye, baby' to a woman at a store in nearby Mississippi and was later found in a nearby river, brutally murdered. 'I didn't know if they were crazy, if they were going to take me to a Klan meeting. I started protecting my crotch. I was afraid they might rape me.'

They took her to City Hall, where she was charged with misconduct, resisting arrest and violating the city's segregation laws. The full enormity of what she had done was only just beginning to dawn on her. 'I went bipolar. I knew what was happening, but I just kept trying to shut it out.'

She concentrated her mind on things she had been learning at school. 'I recited Edgar Allan Poe, Annabel Lee, the characters in *Midsummer Night's Dream*, the Lord's Prayer and the 23rd Psalm.' Anything to detach herself from the horror of reality. Her pastor was called and came to pick her up. By the time she got home, her parents already knew. Everybody knew.

'The news travelled fast,' wrote Robinson. 'In a few hours, every Negro youngster on the streets discussed Colvin's arrest. Telephones rang. Clubs called special meetings and discussed the event with some degree of alarm. Mothers expressed concern about permitting their children on the buses. Men instructed their wives to walk or to share rides in neighbours' autos.'

It was going to be a long night on Dixie Drive. 'Nobody slept at home because we thought there would be some retaliation,' says Colvin. An ad hoc committee headed by the most prominent local Black activist, E. D. Nixon, was set up to discuss the possibility of making Colvin's arrest a test case. They sent a delegation to see the commissioner, and after a few meetings they appeared to have reached an understanding that the harassment would stop and Colvin would be allowed to clear her name.

When the trial was held, Colvin pleaded innocent but was found guilty and released on indefinite probation in her parents' care. 'She had remained calm all during the days of her waiting period and during the trial,' wrote Robinson. 'But when she was found guilty, her agonised sobs penetrated the atmosphere of the courthouse.'

Nonetheless, the shock waves of her defiance had reverberated throughout Montgomery and beyond. Letters of support came from as far afield as Oregon and California. She still has one – a handwritten note from William Harris in Sacramento. It reads: 'The wonderful thing which you have just done makes me feel like a craven coward. How encouraging it would be if more adults had your courage, self-respect and integrity. Respectfully and faithfully yours.'

But even as she inspired awe throughout the country, elders within Montgomery's Black community began to doubt her suitability as a standard-bearer of the movement. 'I told Mrs Parks, as I had told other leaders in Montgomery, that I thought the Claudette Colvin arrest was a good test case to end segregation on the buses,' says Fred Gray, Parks's lawyer. 'However, the Black leadership in Montgomery at the time thought that we should wait.'

Some in Montgomery, particularly in King Hill, think the decision was informed by snobbery. 'It was partly because of her colour and because she was from the working poor,' says Gwen Patton, who has been involved in civil rights work in Montgomery since the early 1960s. 'She lived in a little shack. It was a case of "bourgey" Blacks looking down on the working-class Blacks.'

'They never thought much of us, so there was no way they were going to run with us,' says Hardin. Others say it is because she was a foul-mouthed tearaway. 'It bothered some that there was an unruly, tomboy quality to Colvin, including a propensity for curse words and immature outbursts,' writes Douglas Brinkly, who recently completed a biography of Parks. But people in King Hill do not remember Colvin as that type of girl, and the accusation irritates Colvin to this day. 'I never swore when I was young,' she says. 'Never.'

Everyone, including Colvin, agreed that it was news of her pregnancy that ultimately persuaded the local Black hierarchy to abandon her as a cause célèbre. For Colvin, the entire episode was traumatic. 'Nowadays, you'd call it statutory rape, but back then it was just the kind of thing that happened,' she says, describing the conditions under which she conceived. She refused to name the father or have anything to do with him. 'When I told my mother I was pregnant, I thought she was going to have a heart attack. If I had told my father who did it, he would have killed him.'

A personal tragedy for her was seen as a political liability by the town's civil rights leaders. In his Pulitzer Prize-winning account of the civil rights years, *Parting the Waters*, Taylor Branch wrote: 'Even

Dispatches from the Diaspora

if Montgomery Negroes were willing to rally behind an unwed, pregnant teenager – which they were not – her circumstances would make her an extremely vulnerable standard bearer.'

'If the white press got ahold of that information, they would have [had] a field day,' said Rosa Parks. 'They'd call her a bad girl, and her case wouldn't have a chance.'

Montgomery's Black establishment leaders decided they would have to wait for the right person. And that person, it transpired, would be Rosa Parks. 'Mrs Parks was a married woman,' said E. D. Nixon. 'She was morally clean, and she had a fairly good academic training . . . If there was ever a person we would've been able to [use to] break the situation that existed on the Montgomery city line, Rosa L. Parks was the woman to use . . . I probably would've examined a dozen more before I got there if Rosa Parks hadn't come along before I found the right one.'

'Facts speak only when the historian calls on them,' wrote the historian E. H. Carr in his landmark work, *What Is History?* 'It is he who decides which facts to give the floor and in what order or context. It is the historian who has decided for his own reasons that Caesar's crossing of that petty stream, the Rubicon, is a fact of history, whereas the crossing of the Rubicon by millions of other people before or since interests nobody at all.'

Montgomery was not home to the first bus boycott any more than Colvin was the first person to challenge segregation. Two years earlier, in Baton Rouge, Louisiana, African Americans launched an effective bus boycott after drivers refused to honour an integrated seating policy, which was settled in an unsatisfactory fudge. And, like the pregnant Mrs Hamilton, many African Americans refused to tolerate the indignity of the South's racist laws in silence.

Nor was Colvin the last to be passed over. In the nine months between her arrest and that of Parks, another young Black woman, Mary Louise Smith, suffered a similar fate. Smith was arrested in October 1955, but was also not considered an appropriate candidate for a broader campaign: E. D. Nixon claimed that her father was a drunkard; Smith insists he was teetotal.

But there were two things about Colvin's stand on that March day that made it significant. First, it came less than a year after the US Supreme Court had outlawed the 'separate but equal' policy that had provided the legal basis for racial segregation – what had been the custom and practice in the South for generations was now against federal law and could be challenged in the courts.

Second, she was the first person, in Montgomery at least, to take up the challenge. 'She was not the first person to be arrested for violation of the bus seating ordinance,' said J. Mills Thornton, an author and academic. 'But according to [the commissioner], she was the first person ever to enter a plea of not guilty to such a charge.'

It is a rare, and poor, civil rights book that covers the Montgomery bus boycott and does not mention Claudette Colvin. But it is also a rare and excellent one that gives her more than a passing, dismissive mention. However, not one author has bothered to interview her. Most Americans, even in Montgomery, have never heard of her. She has literally become a footnote in history.

For we like our history neat – an easy-to-follow, self-contained narrative, with dates, characters and landmarks that allow us to weave together otherwise unrelated events into one apparently seamless length of fabric held together by sequence and consequence. Complexity, with all its nuances and shaded realities, is a messy business. So we choose the facts to fit the narrative we want to hear.

While this does not happen by conspiracy, it is often facilitated by collusion. In this respect, the civil rights movement in Montgomery moved fast. Rosa Parks was thrown off the bus on a Thursday; by Friday, activists were distributing leaflets that highlighted her arrest as one of many, including those of Colvin and Mary Louise Smith: 'Another Negro woman has been arrested and thrown in jail because she refused to get up out of her seat on the bus for a white person to sit down,' they read. 'It is the second time since the Claudette

Colvin case that a Negro woman has been arrested for the same thing.'

By Monday, the day the boycott began, Colvin had already been airbrushed from the official version of events. Meanwhile, Parks had been transformed from a politically conscious activist into an upstanding, unfortunate Everywoman. 'And since it had to happen, I'm happy it happened to a person like Mrs Parks,' said Martin Luther King from the pulpit of the Holt Street Baptist Church. 'For nobody can doubt the boundless outreach of her integrity. Nobody can doubt the height of her character, nobody can doubt the depth of her Christian commitment and devotion to the teachings of Jesus.' Though he didn't say it, nobody was going to say that about the then heavily pregnant Colvin.

But Colvin was not the only casualty of this distortion. Parks was, too. Her casting as the prim, ageing, guileless seamstress with her hair in a bun who just happened to be in the wrong place at the right time denied her track record of militancy and feminism. She appreciated, but never embraced, King's strategy of non-violent resistance, remains a keen supporter of Malcolm X and was constantly frustrated by sexism in the movement. 'I had almost a life history of being rebellious against being mistreated against my colour,' she said.

But the very spirit and independence of mind that had inspired Parks to challenge segregation started to pose a threat to Montgomery's Black male hierarchy, who had started to believe, and then resent, their own spin. Nixon referred to her as a 'lovely, stupid woman'; ministers would greet her with irony at church functions – 'Well, if it isn't the superstar.' Reverend Ralph Abernathy, who played a key role as King's right-hand man throughout the civil rights years, referred to her as a 'tool' of the movement.

Those who are aware of these distortions in the civil rights story are few. Betty Shabazz, the widow of Malcolm X, was one of them. In a letter published shortly before Shabazz's death, she wrote to Parks with both praise and perspective: '"Standing up" was not even being the first to protest that indignity. Fifteen-year-old Claudette Colvin was the first to be arrested in protest of bus segregation in Montgomery.

'When ED Nixon and the Women's Political Council of Montgomery recognised that you could be that hero, you met the challenge and changed our lives forever. It was not your tired feet, but your strength of character and resolve that inspired us.' It is a letter Colvin knew nothing about.

Colvin is not exactly bitter. But as she recalls her teenage years, after the arrest and the pregnancy, she hovers between resentment, sadness and bewilderment at the way she was treated. 'They just dropped me. None of them spoke to me; they didn't see if I was okay. They never came and discussed it with my parents. They just didn't want to know me.'

She believes that if her pregnancy had been the only issue, they would have found a way to overcome it. 'It would have been different if I hadn't been pregnant, but if I had lived in a different place or been light-skinned, it would have made a difference, too. They would have come and seen my parents and found me someone to marry.'

When the boycott was over and the African American community had emerged victorious, King, Nixon and Parks appeared for the cameras. 'It's interesting that Claudette Colvin was not in the group, and rarely, if ever, rode a bus again in Montgomery,' wrote Frank Sikora, an Alabama-based academic and author. After her arrest and late appearance in the court hearing, she was more or less forgotten. Later, she would tell a reporter that she would sometimes attend the rallies at the churches. 'I would sit in the back and no one would even know I was there.'

The upshot was that Colvin was left in an incredibly vulnerable position – a poor, single, Black, teenage mother who had both taken on the white establishment and fallen foul of the Black one. It is this that incenses Patton. 'I respect my elders, but I don't respect what they did to Colvin,' she says. 'For a while, there was a real distance between me and Mrs Parks over this. Colvin was a kid. She needed support.'

If that were not enough, the son, Raymond, to whom Colvin would give birth in December, emerged light-skinned. 'He came out looking kind of yellow, and then I was ostracised because I wouldn't say who the father was, and they thought it was a white man. He wasn't.' She became quiet and withdrawn. 'I wasn't with it at all. All I could do is cry.'

Robinson recalls: 'She needed encouragement, for since her conviction as a law violator her head was not held so high. She did not look people straight in the eye as before.' She received a scholarship to the local, historically Black university, Alabama State, even though the college authorities were none too keen on having a 'troublemaker' on campus.

The tears kept coming. She dropped out. She could not find work in Montgomery, because as soon as white people found out what she had done, they fired her. 'I just couldn't get a job. I'd change my name so that I could work in a restaurant, and they'd find out who I was and that was it. I ran out of identities.' Even when she did get work, it was humiliating. 'I had this baby of my own, and yet I had to leave him with my mother so I could babysit for white people who hated me.'

In the space of a few years, a confident A-grade student had passed through the eye of a political storm and emerged a bedraggled outcast. 'It changed my life,' she says. 'I became aware of how the world is and how the white establishment plays Black people against each other.'

She believes, however, that they were right to choose someone such as Rosa Parks as a standard-bearer. 'They picked the right person. They needed someone who could bring together all the classes. They wouldn't have followed me. They wanted someone who would shake hands and go to banquets. They wanted someone they could control, and they knew, as a teenager, they couldn't control me.'

But she also believes that they were wrong not to support her in her time of need. 'They weren't there for me when I tried to make a comeback. I thought maybe they would help me get a degree or talk to someone about getting me work. I thought they could get me together with Rosa Parks, and we could go out together and talk to children.'

Similarly, Patton believes that the pragmatic decision not to put Colvin in the spotlight at first was probably correct, but that it does not excuse a wilful negligence to acknowledge her contribution afterwards. 'I have no problem with them not lifting up Colvin in 1955. I have a problem with them not lifting her up in 1970. Rosa Parks could have said many times [in the intervening years], "And there were others."'

Colvin's life after Montgomery is a metaphor for post-war Black America. As the struggle moved from civil rights to economic rights, Colvin followed the route of the great migration and went north to a low-paid job and urban deprivation. She left Montgomery for New York in 1958 to work as a live-in domestic and soon became accustomed to the differences and similarities between the North and the South. While the power relationship between maid and madam was the same, she encountered less petty racism and institutionalised indignity in the North. In the South, a live-in domestic would never dream of washing her own clothes with those of her employers. So when she came down one day to find her employer's laundry dumped on top of hers, with a polite request to wash them at the same time, she was shocked. 'That's when I knew I was out of the South. That could just never have happened there.'

At the start, she occasionally travelled back to Montgomery by bus with baby Raymond to see her parents and look for work in a place where her family could lend support, but no one would employ her. A year later, she fell pregnant again, and in 1960 gave birth to Randy. With two infants and no family, the pressure of making ends meet in the urban North became too much, so, in what was a common arrangement at the time, she left Raymond and Randy with her mother in Montgomery as she sought work in the North. Things got tough. A couple of times she even considered going into prostitution. 'The only thing that kept me out of it was the other things that go with it. Stealing, drugging people. I figured that after the first time the physical thing wouldn't matter so much, but I couldn't get involved in all the other stuff.'

At one and the same time, she had become both more independent and more vulnerable, looking in vain for some evidence for the gains of the civil rights era in her own life. 'What we got from that time was what was on the books anyhow. Working-class people were the foot soldiers, but where are they now? They haven't seen any progress. It was the middle classes who were able to take advantage of the laws.'

Her two boys took wildly divergent paths. Like many African American men, Raymond, the unborn child she was carrying during the heady days of 1955, joined the US army. Like all too many, he later became involved in drugs and died of an overdose in her apartment. Like many others, Randy became successful and moved back down south, to Atlanta, where he now works as an accountant. Colvin has five grandchildren.

Earlier this month, on the forty-fifth anniversary of Park's protest, Troy State University opened a Rosa Parks Museum in Montgomery to honour the small town's place in civil rights history. Roy White, who was responsible for much of what went into the museum, called Colvin to ask if she would appear in a video to tell her story. She refused. 'They've already called it the Rosa Parks Museum, so they've already made up their minds what the story is.'

He suggested that maybe she would achieve some closure by participating. 'What closure can there be for me?' she asks with exasperation. 'There is no closure. This does not belong in a museum, because this struggle is not over. We still don't have all that we should have. And, personally, there can be no closure. They took away my life. If they want closure, they should give it to my grandchildren.'

No surrender

I was supposed to spend forty-five minutes with the author and poet Maya Angelou. But eighteen hours, one lunch, one performance, several whiskies and a huge Los Angeles traffic jam later, she was still out-drinking me in the back of her limo.

Guardian, 25 May 2002, Los Angeles

Maya Angelou does not like to fly. So she made it to the West Coast from her home in North Carolina by bus. It is 2,152 miles as the crow flies. But she more than trebled the distance, coming via Toronto and the Rockies, while on her five-week book and lecture tour. It's not a Greyhound, she quickly explains, but a serious tour bus, complete with a double bed, spare rooms, shower, cooking facilities and satellite television.

The first one she had, which she rented from Prince, had a washer–dryer, too. She herself designed the interior for the next one, which will be delivered before the end of the year, decked out in *kente* cloth. Over the thousands of miles that she has travelled around the country in this bus, she has bumped into Lauryn Hill and passed B. B. King.

Angelou gave up flying, unless it is really vital, about three years ago. Not because she was afraid, but because she was fed up with the hassle of celebrity. One of the last times she flew, her feet had not made it to the kerbside at the airport before an excitable woman started shouting her name. 'It's Maya Angelou, Maya Angelou,' she screamed incessantly.

Angelou looked around her and asked the woman, 'Are you with someone?'

'No,' the stranger replied, and continued shouting.

'So who are you calling to?' asked Angelou.

'People over there who maybe haven't seen you yet,' said the woman.

'Well, that was a non sequitur,' recalls Angelou. 'So I just kept walking.'

Heading down an escalator a few minutes later, she was met by a woman who thrust a baby into her arms, while the stranger rummaged in her bag for a pen and something for Angelou to sign. On the plane, a flight attendant crouched beside the author and confessed her intimate woes. Angelou listened politely until the plane took off. With her seat belt still buckled, sitting at forty-five degrees to the Earth, climbing at great speed, the pilot came out to pay his respects. Angelou almost choked. 'Who's minding the store?' she spluttered.

Angelou often gets treated as public property. People think they know her. Not surprising, given that she has told them so much about herself. For, probably more than almost any other writer alive, Angelou's life literally is her work.

She has just released the sixth and final tranche of her autobiography, *A Song Flung Up to Heaven*. It is the culmination of more than thirty years' work, which started with her bestselling debut *I Know Why the Caged Bird Sings* – a title taken from the first line of Harlem Renaissance poet Paul Laurence Dunbar's poem 'Sympathy'.

The first book tells how her father sent her and her elder brother, Bailey, to live with their paternal grandmother in the tiny Southern town of Stamps, Arkansas, after her parents divorced. Aged three and four, the two children arrived at the station wearing wrist tags reading 'To Whom It May Concern'. At eight, she was raped by her mother's boyfriend. Soon after she had identified him as the rapist, he was found murdered – the police said he appeared to have been kicked to death. For the next five years, the young Angelou went mute, thinking that her voice itself had killed him and that if she spoke again she might kill someone else. Later, she would move to California and, while still a teenager, give birth to her only son, Guy.

The huge array of experiences that she managed to pack into her first sixteen years presages a life of ceaseless, albeit occasionally calamitous, adventure. In later years and subsequent autobiographical works, she became a waitress, madam, prostitute, singer, actress and activist, a dancer in Paris, an editor in Egypt and a lecturer in Ghana. She will not say how many times she has been married for fear of sounding frivolous, but it is at least three.

A Song Flung Up to Heaven takes its title from the last line in the same Dunbar poem. It starts with her returning to America to work for Malcolm X, who had just changed his name to Malcolm Malik-Shabazz and his politics from Black nationalism to a socialist version of Pan-Africanism. It ends with her beginning to write her first memoir.

Gliding down the freeway in a stretch limousine, Angelou asks for a whisky.

'Do you want ice and stuff?' asks her assistant, Ms Stuckey.

'I want some ice, but mostly I want stuff,' says Angelou with a smile, and invites me to join her.

We are heading to a packed house of 2,800 in Pasadena. The night before, she performed to 3,000 in Redondo Beach. It is a peculiar kind of stardom for a poet, writer and lecturer. It is difficult to think of a contemporary of hers who commands the same popular appeal. When I call 1-800 FLOWERS the next day to send her a bouquet to say thank you, the young woman taking my order says she is in awe that I have even met her. 'She's a great philosopher,' she says. 'That's what I like about her, because I like philosophy. I like thinking, really.'

Angelou, like her good friend Oprah Winfrey, is in the inspiration business. While the medium may vary, from proverb, poetry, metaphor to mantra, the message is the same. You have only one life, so live it to the full. Be angry, but never bitter. Take risks, love, laugh, acknowledge defeat, but do not succumb to it. And while humility is part of the vocabulary, guile is most certainly not. As she points out in one of her most famous poems, 'Still I Rise', she walks as though she has oil wells pumping in her living room.

Alongside and intertwined with her call for emotional uplift is a simple, humanist, anti-racist message: 'We are more alike than we are unalike.'

'I could fall in love with a sumo wrestler if he told stories and made me laugh,' she says. 'Obviously, it would be easier if someone was African American and lived next door and went to the same church. Because then I wouldn't have to translate. But if I make the effort to learn the language and respect the mores, then I should be able to get along anywhere and with any kind of people. I think I belong wherever human beings are.'

As we pull up and make our way through the artists' entrance, a member of the audience shouts that she's driven two hundred miles to see her. We leave Angelou in the green room, alone with her thoughts and the nibbles.

Inside, the audience is gathering. As Angelou predicted, they are mostly white. 'Maybe 5 per cent Black professional, 5 per cent street.' With the exception of the very few Hispanic faces, it roughly reflects the racial composition of the city itself. It is about three-quarters female. And while more than half appear to be in their sixties or over, many of those have come with either their granddaughters or much younger friends. Whatever city she is in, Angelou insists on doing a signing in an African American-owned bookshop as well. Those, too, are usually packed. In a nation where segregation still defines everything, from where you worship to what television show you watch, this level of crossover appeal is rare.

That breadth, which spans across age groups, too, brought her to the attention of Hallmark cards, who approached her to add both her words and her name to a new range. Angelou was interested at first, but sceptical. One of her friends tried to talk her out of it. But what some saw as crass commercialisation, Angelou viewed as an opportunity.

'My friend said, "Oh no, please. You're the people's poet. Don't trivialise yourself by writing greetings cards." I thought, "You're right," and I hung up the phone. Then I thought about it. I thought, "Suppose I really am the people's poet? Then the people ought to be able to have my work in their hands. People who will never buy a book will buy a card." So I thought, "Oh yes." I called my friend back and said, "Thank you so much. Now I'm going to do it."'

So now her name appears on everything, from bookends to pillows and mugs to wall-hangings. Expansive in range and expensive in price, her Life Mosaic Collection offers a 'Glorious Banquet Bowl', with the message: 'Life is a glorious banquet, a limitless and delicious buffet.' Her work and, given the nature of her work, also her life have effectively been branded. The pain of her early years, and the wisdom she has derived from it, have been commodified. It seems a long way from Malcolm X.

Angelou is unapologetic. 'I agree with Balzac and nineteenth-century writers, Black and white, who say, "I write for money,"' she laughs. 'Yes, I think everybody should be paid handsomely. I insist on it and I pay people who work for me, or with me, handsomely.'

The joint venture with Hallmark, she says, is a literary challenge. 'It's exciting because it means I have to take two or three pages of work and reduce it to two lines. It's haiku, it's an epigram. So there's this woman I know who's in an abusive relationship – not physically, I don't think, but psychologically – and she accepts it. At work she's a boss to the people under her and is much disliked, so I wrote all of that out and then reduced it to these two lines: "A wise woman wishes to be no one's enemy, a wise woman refuses to be anyone's victim." Now it took me a good two days to get that, and it's delicious. It's just great.'

The politics of commercialisation aside, both Angelou's work and her outlook on the world do lend themselves to the epigram. She was raised on dictums, riddles and rhymes with reason. Once, while directing a film in Sweden, she was having trouble with the actors and the crew. She called for her mother, who arrived in Sweden with the words, 'Baby, mother came to Stockholm to tell you one thing – cow needs a tail for more than one season.' Growing up, her more devout and somewhat prudish grandmother told her: 'Wash up as far as possible, and then wash possible.'

When she began this current tour in North Carolina, the county commissioner was part of the official welcoming committee. When Angelou noticed he had tried to get her to sign his books ahead of others in the queue, she told the crowd: 'In West Africa, in times of famine, in times of drought, the chief tightens his belt first. I ask those of you who are leaders to wait.' The commissioner was sent scurrying to find someone in the line to take his books for him.

This didacticism is a form, both literary and oratory, that is prevalent in African American life, from politics to publishing, thanks to the dominance of the church. It's a style developed at the pulpit, when the church was the only organisation independent of white supremacy, and combines charismatic delivery with a mixture of truism and teaching, parable and polemic.

This is her language. And this, in Pasadena, is her audience. Witnessing Angelou on stage is like watching stand-up comedy, a university lecture and a poetry recital all in one. With stories, quips and poems – her own and those of African American poets both dead and living – she has them laughing, gasping and listening for over an hour.

At seventy-four, she has no intention of retiring. 'I wouldn't know how,' she says. With her skin of cinnamon, cane of silver and earrings of pearl, she has reached this point with grace, good humour and relatively good health. Her breasts, she told Oprah recently, 'are in an incredible race to see which one will touch [her] waist first'. Arthritis, she informs an audience in Pasadena, plays tricks on her knee. She may pause to catch her breath mid-sentence. And her six-foot frame may move hesitantly and with a stoop. But beyond the inconveniences of time and gravity, she is in fine form.

Her voice is slow and rich – so deliberate she seems to be tasting words before she lets them leave her mouth. Her speech is peppered with Southern courtesies. You may introduce yourself with your first name, but she will address you with your second. Everybody, in her presence, becomes Mr, Mrs or Miss – a legacy from a time when

African Americans were denied those basic signifiers of civility by whites, and so demanded it within their own community.

'I insist upon that,' says Angelou. 'I did it and do it still. I do it still to Dr Dorothy Hyde, who is ninety. I'm still the young kid and very respectful.'

Later this year, she'll direct the movie version of Bebe Moore Campbell's novel *Singing in the Comeback Choir*. She teaches a course at Wake Forest University, North Carolina, on the Philosophy of Liberation, is writing a cookbook and will continue to pen poems and essays.

For all her optimism, there have been times, she admits, when she has believed that the political equality and personal happiness she sought during the 1960s might never come. Her latest book spans the four crucial, painful years – 1965 to 1969 – in both her life story and America's racial history, when that pessimism had most firmly taken root. A period when two of Black America's greatest leaders, Martin Luther King and Malcolm X, were both murdered. An era when the focus of Black politics in America shifted from civil rights to economic rights, rural to urban, South to North, and from peaceful protest to violent retribution. It was also a time when she had to cope with the guilt of leaving her then troublesome teenage son, Guy, in Ghana, and the end of a long-term relationship with an African man whom she has never named.

Normally, she submits herself to an eccentric, if apparently effective, work regime: to avoid distraction, she rents a motel room and asks for it to be stripped bare of any decoration; then she fills it with a thesaurus, a dictionary and a bottle of sherry and starts writing longhand. But, for this book, a disciplined routine was not enough. 'I went down to Florida for a different mood, a different atmosphere,' she says. 'It was a very difficult book to write. In all my work, I try to say: you may be given a load of sour lemons, why not try to make a dozen lemon meringue pies? But I didn't see how I could do that with this book, dealing with Malcolm's murder, Martin's murder, the uprising

Dispatches from the Diaspora

in Watts, the end of a love affair–marriage-cum-something. It took me six years to write this book, and it's the slimmest of all the volumes.'

Within a week of her arrival from Africa, Malcolm X had been assassinated. 'After Malcolm was killed, the hope and I were both dashed to the ground,' she says. A few years later, Martin Luther King Jr asked her to help organise the Poor People's March on Washington. Soon afterwards, he, too, was assassinated.

The men had more in common, both politically and personally, than most people recognise, she says. 'They were men of passion, exquisite intelligence, great humour, shattering courage. I don't mean the courage to stand up against the possibility of being assassinated. I mean the courage to stand in front of a hostile world and say, "I was wrong."

'Malcolm X, after having gone to Mecca, said, "I've met some blue-eyed men who I can call brother, so I was wrong. All whites are not blue-eyed devils." Now that was courage. It took courage to say that.'

It is her personal connection to these political events that makes them so evocative. Her own narrative is closely interwoven with Black America's political and cultural fabric. She was there in *Roots*, as Kunta Kinte's grandmother, a role for which she was nominated for an Emmy. Her character is there in the film *Ali*, being introduced to the boxer by Malcolm X while in Ghana. She was there in 1997, at the bedside of X's widow, Betty Shabazz, shortly before she died of multiple burns caused by a fire started deliberately by her grandson.

The year before, she had been instrumental in getting together Coretta Scott King, Shabazz and Myrlie Evers-Williams, three women who had been widowed by the civil rights movement. 'They went to the Doral in Miami. And they asked me to come,' she recalls. 'And I said, "I'm not coming. I'm nobody's widow." I made them laugh. I said, "Not one of you knows how to tell a good story, and only one or two of you will have half a glass of white wine."'

But the following year, when the three women repeated the meeting, she accepted the invitation. 'On Thursday, Betty had called me at my apartment and told me she had wanted me to cook some-thing. And I cooked it and she came, and it was the two of us and it was great.' On the Sunday, the day Angelou was supposed to meet her again in Florida, she got a call from Coretta Scott King to say that Shabazz had been seriously injured in a domestic fire. 'She said, "Sister, our sister."' And then Angelou's gift for story-telling dissolves in pain.

The delinquency of Shabazz's grandson and the tragedy of her death seemed, in a sense, emblematic not so much of how little had changed in Black America, but of how deeply some things had regressed. Just as when civil rights icon Rosa Parks was attacked in her home in Detroit by a Black burglar, here, yet again, we saw the embodiment of political purpose bludgeoned by the arbitrary fallout of social disintegration.

Ask her what she thinks King's or Malcolm X's agenda would be now, and she releases a long, helpless breath. 'I can't,' she says. 'I can't. So many things have happened since they were both assassinated. The world has changed so dramatically.'

But significant progress, insists Angelou, has been made, and must be lauded in order for more progress to be forthcoming. 'I think that as one looks at Watts, one must look at the Academy Awards. As one looks at the drug epidemic, one has also got to look at General Colin Powell and Ms Condoleezza Rice and the mayor of Washington and the mayor of Atlanta. I mean, there are changes. It's not nearly what has to happen . . . One has got to say there are changes, and the rea-son for that is this: if we suggest that there are no changes, then young people must say, "Well, damn, with the lives and deaths of Martin King, Malcolm X, the Kennedys, Medgar Evers . . . you mean all of that, and they weren't able to effect any change, then there's no point in me trying." So we've got to say, "Yes, there have been changes, minimal changes, but there have been some. And you must try."' Yet the successes that she points to are all individual, while the setbacks are collective. What connection is there between those who have got on and those who have been left behind, if the successful do not lift others as they rise? 'Some didn't, some don't, some won't, some forget, some have really short memories. They suggest that "I've got mine – too bad about you. Give me the million-dollar contract for the baseball team or the basketball team. Give them my nothing and I'll take their everything." There is that, yes. But that is not general. Usually, Black people do try to serve the race and try to serve the nation, really.'

With poems entitled 'Phenomenal Woman', 'Poor Girl' and 'A Good Woman Feeling Bad', she has always been outspoken on gender issues. But race provided the prism for her analysis of the women's movement in America. 'The white American man makes the white American woman just a little kind of decoration,' she once said. 'He can send his rockets to the moon, and the little woman can sit at home. Well, the Black American woman has never been able to feel that way. No Black American man at any time in our history has been able to feel that he didn't need that Black woman right against him, shoulder to shoulder – in the cotton field, in the auction block, in the ghetto, wherever. That Black woman is integral, if not a most important part of the family unit.'

This mixture of race pride, rugged individualism and realpolitik has made for unpredictable political standpoints over the past twenty years. Angelou backed the nomination of arch-conservative Clarence Thomas to the Supreme Court in 1991, following allegations of sexual harassment. At the time, she argued in the *New York Times*: 'Because Clarence Thomas has been nearly suffocated by the acrid odour of racial discrimination, is intelligent, well-trained, black and young enough to be won over again, I support him.'

Several negative decisions on affirmative action and a court-assisted election victory for George W. Bush later, does she still believe that?

Angelou laughs. 'It's hard for me to say that. I thought so when I wrote the piece. And I may have been right even then. I said, "Let's co-opt him. Don't let's wait for somebody else to co-opt him. Let

African Americans co-opt him, let's surround him with so much camaraderie and friendship, and don't let him forget. Let us do it rather than fall victim to Machiavelli's dictate, separate and rule, divide and conquer." I still think if we had done that at that time, we might have had him. But people laughed at me, rather than consider what had been suggested.'

She spoke at the Million Man March, supporting Minister Louis Farrakhan, whom nine years earlier she had branded as 'dangerous'.

'I think he has become more and more wise. Sixteen years ago, he may have still have been talking about a state apart. I haven't heard him say that in many years. As he speaks of education and self-respect and self-love and race pride and hard work and loyalty, he speaks of the needs of the people. And he has the following. And if they listen to him and are taught by him, follow those teachings, then it will be a better country and there will be a better future.'

She addressed the nation, and the world, at President Clinton's inauguration in 1993 with a poem full of hope. Does she feel the hope was satisfied?

'No. But fortunately there is that about hope: it is never satisfied. It is met, sometimes, but never satisfied. If it was satisfied, you'd be hopeless.'

So was it met? 'Some of it, yes.'

There are many Americans who supported Clinton, Thomas or Farrakhan. But there are few who supported all three. While she is undeniably liberal, if not radical, on most issues, it is her support for Black people who do not necessarily espouse issues commonly regarded as in the interests of Black people that often places her outside America's traditional liberal/conservative spectrum. This eclectic approach to race, she says, she learned from Malcolm X.

'Malcolm once said to me, "Well, you would be upset if the NAACP [referring to the oldest, most conservative civil rights organisation] had a party at the Waldorf Astoria. You wouldn't go, would you?" I said, "No, I wouldn't go." He said, "Think of racism as a mountain. Now cut it open. Now on all the strata we need people. We need people to support the NAACP. Some of the scholarships they give may be given to the young Malcolm X, the young MLK, the young Septima Clark, so we need people on all the levels."'

What some may view as inconsistency, she regards as intellectual rigour. 'I insist to be myself, wherever I am. I have enough of the language to try to explain myself, to convey what I'm really thinking. I'm not always successful, but I try. I've lived long enough to see some things. I have enough courage to try and say what I see. If I'm taken out of context, then I say I've been taken out of context.'

Only in her response to the 11 September terrorist attacks has this approach eluded her. 'I don't want to be dodgy, but I have to be careful, because if only some of what I say is published, then I might have to go on television and lay it out.' She was in her apartment in New York on the day and saw it unfold. 'When the second one hit, I thought, "Terrorism." My second thought was for the people in the buildings on those floors. My God. And my next thought was retribution.'

She agreed to do only one or two interviews with people she trusted, for fear of being given insufficient time to explain her views. 'We should regard it as a hate crime,' she says, arguing that it should be both comprehended and condemned within the context of all hate crimes, wherever they are committed and whomever they are committed against. 'It has made Americans more American – that is to say, protectors and defenders of the country. It has, I think, made a number of Americans more inquisitive about our foreign policy, too. More concerned about what are we doing in other parts of the world, and how did we come so late and lonely to this place.

'Living in a state of terror was new to many white people in America, but Black people have been living in a state of terror in this country for more than four hundred years.'

As our car leaves Pasadena's civic centre, Angelou rolls down the window and waves, thanking those in the audience who have stopped to cheer her. Back on the freeway, the whisky is out again. 'I don't talk down to whites. I don't talk up to whites. I just talk to them,' she says.

She asks Mr Schaeffer, the chauffeur, to drop me at my hotel. It is one of those aggressively trendy places, where the name on the front is upside down and there is a live model asleep in a cabinet behind reception. When I told her about it earlier, she screwed up her nose in mock disapproval. As the car pulls away, she winds down the window and shouts, 'That's swanky!' and laughs. And then they're off. A white driver and his elderly Black female patron. As though someone had pulled out the negatives from *Driving Miss Daisy*.

'We used to think there was a Black community'

With her towering Afro and radical rhetoric, Angela Davis was one of the iconic faces of Black American politics. We talked about Barack Obama, slavery's legacy, the Black middle class, and how it feels to be remembered as a hairdo.

Guardian, 8 November 2007, Santa Cruz, California

Angela Davis was intrigued to see recently that a significant number of young Black women to whom she was delivering a talk were wearing images of her from the 1970s on their T-shirts. She asked what the image meant to them. 'They said it made them feel powerful and connected to other movements,' she says. 'It was really quite moving. It really had nothing to do with me. They were using this image as an expression of who they would like to be and what they would like to do. I've given up trying to challenge commodification in that respect. It's an unending battle, and you never win any victories.'

For all her many achievements over the past thirty-seven years, Angela Davis remains, for many, a symbol frozen in time. The time was 1970. The focus had shifted from integration to Black power; the influences from Gandhi and the Bible to Mao and Marxism. In 1967, Aretha Franklin called for 'r-e-s-p-e-c-t'; by 1970, the anthem was Edwin Starr's 'War'.

The symbol was resistance. Smart, handsome, eloquent, fearless and stylish, Davis strode the political stage with her fist raised high and her Afro combed even higher. A rebel and a revolutionary. A silhouette for summer wear. Radical and chic like Che – except that she has lived to see her political resistance transfer into popular culture.

A student in her History of Afro-American Women's Studies class at San Francisco State University during the 1980s recalls: 'She wanted to teach and she was a very conscientious teacher, really engaging. But she would make some cogent point about history, and then someone would literally put up their hand and make some comment about her hair. I thought, "They're not letting her be who she wants to be."'

Davis once said: 'It is both humiliating and humbling to discover that a single generation after the events that constructed me as a public personality, I am remembered as a hairdo.'

A few weeks ago, at the Women of Color Resource Center in Oakland, California, Davis presented the Sister of Fire award to a young poet from Queens, New York who could barely contain her excitement at being in her presence. 'I can't believe I'm on the same stage as Angela Davis,' she gushed. 'I read about her in school . . . And she's still alive.' Davis and her contemporaries at the ceremony laughed.

'I have reconciled myself to the existence of this historical figure and its relationship to the work that I'm trying to do today,' she says. This is less difficult than it might seem, since her present work is intricately connected to both the work she has been doing most of her adult life and the incident that made her famous: prisons.

Back in the 1960s, as the American state moved to criminalise radical Black protest, she primarily campaigned on the issue of political prisoners, such as the Black Panther George Jackson. Her political activities had already made her a target for the conservative establishment. In 1969, she was fired from her job as assistant professor at the University of California, Los Angeles, for being a member of the Communist Party, only to see that decision overturned by a Supreme Court judge. Then, on 7 August 1970, her own infamous run-in with the criminal justice system started. On that day, Jonathan Jackson, seventeen, held the Marin county courthouse at gunpoint and sprung three prisoners – James McClain, William Christmas and Ruchell Magee – who were either witnesses or on trial. The men led the judge, Harold Haley, the prosecuting attorney and some jurors to a waiting van and fled. In the ensuing chase, Jackson, Christmas, McClain and Haley were shot dead, while the attorney was paralysed by a police bullet.

Dispatches from the Diaspora

Jonathan was the younger brother of George Jackson, whom Davis had fallen in love with during the campaign for his release. Jonathan's gun was registered in Davis's name. Davis was nowhere near the shoot-out, but a warrant was issued for her arrest, for conspiracy to kidnapping and murder. She went on the run.

Davis's disappearance sparked an intensive public search and propelled her into the FBI's top ten most wanted list, and into international attention. Two months later, she was arrested in a motel in midtown Manhattan. President Richard Nixon branded her a 'terrorist'. Facing the trinity of right-wing hate figures – Nixon, California's then governor Ronald Reagan and FBI director J. Edgar Hoover – Davis became an international cause célèbre. A global campaign called for her release. Aretha Franklin offered to post a quarter of a million dollars in bail. 'I have the money,' she said. 'I got it from Black people and I want to use it in ways that will help our people.'

In January 1971, Davis appeared in Marin county court, unapologetic and defiant, facing charges that could have led to her execution. A year and a half later, an all-white jury acquitted her. As an academic of great renown, she went on to enter the canons of Black and feminist theory with her books *Women, Race and Class* and *Women, Culture and Politics*. She wrote a bestselling autobiography and stood for vice president in 1980 and 1984 on the Communist Party ticket.

Much has changed in her life since the days of her trial, but a great deal has remained the same. Davis still teaches at the University of California – although now at Santa Cruz, where she is professor of the history of consciousness and feminist studies. At sixty-three, she is still recognisable from those iconic 1970s shots, although her hair is now a cascade of corkscrew curls. And her primary focus remains the criminal justice system.

'The prison system bears the imprint of slavery perhaps more than any other institution,' she says. 'It produces a state that is very similar to slavery: the deprivation of rights, civil death and disenfranchisement. Under slavery, Black people became that against which the notion of freedom was defined. White people knew they were free because they could point to the people who weren't free. Now we know we're free because we're not in prison. People continue to suffer civil death even after they leave prison. There is permanent disenfranchisement.'

The US, argues Davis, is still struggling with its refusal to address slavery's legacy. 'There was the negative abolition of slavery – the breaking of chains – but freedom is much more than just the abolition of slavery. What would it have meant to provide economic security to everyone who had been enslaved, to have brought about the participation in governance and politics and access to education? That didn't happen. We are still confronted by the failure of the affirmative side of abolition all these years later.'

Does that not leave Black politics entrenched in a paradigm set almost one hundred and fifty years ago? 'The problem is that we [as a country] haven't moved on,' she says. 'Certainly, it's important to recognise the victories that have been won. Racism is not exactly the same now as it was then. But there were issues that were never addressed and now present themselves in different manifestations today. You only move on if you resolve these issues. It took a hundred years to get the right to vote.'

Born in Birmingham, Alabama, in 1944, Davis was raised in the tight-knit world of the Black middle class, in a small Southern town. It included the families of secretary of state Condoleezza Rice and Alma Johnson, who would later marry former secretary of state Colin Powell.

Davis was seven years younger than Johnson and ten years older than Rice. Their worlds intertwined but never quite collided. Rice's father, John Wesley Rice Jr, worked for Johnson's uncle as a high-school guidance counsellor. Johnson knew Rice as a child; Davis knew Johnson because they attended the same church. Birmingham became notorious during the 1960s as the town that set dogs and hoses on African Americans seeking the vote, and for the bombing of the 16th Street Baptist Church, in which four little girls were killed in 1963 (see p. 165), one of whom was Rice's friend. Its reputation was so bad that Colin Powell's parents considered not going to their son's wedding and joked about the likelihood that they would be lynched when they got there.

Although all three emerged from that time and place to take advantage of the new opportunities available, Davis's perspective on her achievements could not be more different to Rice's. 'In America, with education and hard work it really does not matter where you come from,' Rice told the Republican convention in 2000. 'It matters only where you are going.' She later told the *Washington Post*: 'My parents were very strategic. I was going to be so well prepared, and I was going to do all of these things that were revered in white society so well, that I would be armoured somehow from racism. I would be able to confront white society on its own terms.'

Davis insists this is disingenuous. 'It was never about individuals. I never grew up thinking that the measure of my success was as an individual. There was always a sense that the measure of your success was to a large part one that was linked to community advancement. Most people weren't going to make it as far as she or I did. She never would have had the opportunities she had without the benefit of the struggles that took place in the 1960s. If you can, with conscience, talk about a post-civil rights era, we have to talk about the limitations of civil rights. It produced individual successes but it never produced group successes.'

The advancement of the likes of Powell and Rice within the Bush administration, argues Davis, exemplifies a flawed understanding of what it means to tackle modern-day racism. 'The Republican administration is the most diverse in history. But when the inclusion of Black people into the machine of oppression is designed to make that machine work more efficiently, then it does not represent progress at all. We have more Black people in more visible and powerful positions. But then we have far more Black people who have been pushed down to the bottom of the ladder. When people call for diversity and link it to justice and equality, that's fine. But there's a model of diversity as the difference that makes no difference, the change that brings about no change.'

This, she says, is how the presidential candidacy of Barack Obama is generally understood. 'He is being consumed as the embodiment of colour blindness. It's the notion that we have moved beyond racism by not taking race into account. That's what makes him conceivable as a presidential candidate. He's become the model of diversity in this period, and what's interesting about his campaign is that it has not sought to invoke engagements with race other than those that have already existed.'

Davis's initial response to Obama is one she often gives to questions both specific and general: 'It's complicated,' she says. Her answers are candid but measured. Not measured necessarily to fit prevailing public opinion – she believes prisons should be abolished, for example – but measured in their consistency and precision. She talks slowly and in long, whole sentences, and will often deconstruct the question before replying. Asked about class stratification in the Black community and its implications for Black political leadership, she says: 'It's complicated. We used to think there was a Black community. It was always heterogeneous, but we were always able to imagine ourselves as part of that community. I would go so far as to say that many middle-class Black people have internalised the same racist attitudes to working-class Black people as white people have of the Black criminal. The young Black man with the sagging pants walking down the street is understood as a threat by the Black middle class as well. So I don't think it's possible to mobilise Black communities in the way it was in the past.

'I don't even know that I would even look for Black leadership now. We looked to work with that category because it gave us a sense of hope. But that category assumes a link between race and progressive politics, and as Stuart Hall says, "There aren't any guarantees."

What's more important than the racial identification of the person is how that person thinks about race.'

The confluence of Black and progressive politics in the US has been further diminished, argues Davis, as a result of 9/11, which gave all Americans the option of retreating behind the flag or responding to a world that was reaching out. 'In that sense, 9/11 was a pivotal moment,' she says. 'It was a multicultural moment. Black people aren't immune to the nationalism in this country. That was a moment when global solidarity was pouring in, and instead of people reaching out, they closed down. So this was a moment that clearly involved Black people. But it clearly didn't envelop Arabs.'

Black Americans may not have been immune to the hyper-patriotism of recent years, but they were more resistant to it. Of all racial groups, African Americans have still been the least likely to support the wars in both Afghanistan and Iraq. Nonetheless, explains Davis, 'Enough Black people perceived it as a consolidation in nationalism. They finally felt part of the nation. It didn't matter that one million were in prison. It only mattered that they were part of the nation.'

Davis is, however, encouraged by the youth of all races. 'I'm amazed at the sophistication of a lot of younger people,' she says. 'We didn't have the ability when I was younger to say all the things we wanted to say. We didn't have the conceptual opportunities for that. A lot of this stuff just rolls off their tongues. Whatever they produce won't be an insurgency of the old type, although I do think that engagement with race and racism will be an important part of it. You have to get over the idea that you win something once and for all and that struggles have to look the same.'

The situation they have inherited, however, is 'complicated'. 'I don't envy people trying to give political leadership now,' she says. 'In the past it was easy. There was black and white.'

The secrets of a peacemaker

Desmond Tutu claims that he's shy. But the South African Nobel Peace Prize laureate has spent his life making waves and mischief in his struggle for equality.

Guardian, 23 May 2009, Shelter Island, New York

They call him Father, but as he sits at the breakfast table eating Cheerios with fruit and yogurt, giggling as he teases and is in turn teased, Archbishop Desmond Tutu looks more like a mischievous little boy.

'Are you going to wear that shirt?' asks Lynn Franklin, his literary agent and friend, with whom he is staying on Shelter Island, a holiday retreat in the Hamptons, New York State.

Tutu widens his eyes and opens his mouth in mock indignation. 'What is wrong with this shirt?' he says, looking down at his dark blue T-shirt.

'How about the one I ironed for you?' Franklin says.

'But this one has the logo for the World Cup,' says Tutu, pointing to the small emblem on his chest, before turning to me. 'Tell your photographer not to go below the belt,' he says.

As I struggle to work out what he means by this, he gets up from the table to reveal a pair of little legs poking out of the bottom of a pair of long shorts. The cassock-less figure that makes his way back through the kitchen has an air of Clark Kent about him – posing as a civilian but ready to use his powers for good. Less like a Nobel laureate than, well, your father, only on holiday.

Except it doesn't seem like much of a holiday. Tutu, now seventy-seven, has been saying he plans to wind down and lead a more contemplative life for the best part of a decade, particularly after he was diagnosed with prostate cancer twelve years ago. But here he is, almost eight thousand miles away from his home in Cape Town. He's supposed to be taking a break, but the previous day, and the day before that, he was giving television interviews. Today, he's with us. A week later, he'll cross the ocean to appear at the Hay Festival.

'In many ways, when you're a Nobel peace laureate, you have an obligation to humankind, to society,' Tutu says in his slow, deep, deliberate voice. 'And you are able to say things that people might take more seriously than if you were not a Nobel laureate. And with a world that faces so much conflict and suffering, there seems to be a place for those who just might help us change tack. But I am still deeply longing for a quieter life. And I really mean it when I say it. I'm really going to try. My wife says that she's heard me say that several times. I will try next year and be ruthless. But what do you say when the prime minister of the Solomon Islands writes and says, "Please, could you come and be with us when we launch our truth and reconciliation commission?"? It seems so rude, so hard-hearted in a way, to say no and have them think, "We are a small nation. Perhaps we don't count for a great deal." If you do go, it just might lift their morale.'

Given that the Solomon Islands are also eight thousand miles from Cape Town, he could reasonably say, 'No. I'm over seventy, and you're a long way away, but I wish you luck and my prayers are with you.' Perhaps not doing that is what distinguishes a Nobel peace laureate from the rest of us. Nonetheless, it is a tremendous burden, bordering on conceit, that Tutu might take personal responsibility for global conflict and suffering.

'It would be utterly presumptuous to think, off one's own bat, that one would be able to accomplish something as awesome as that,' he says. 'I certainly know that I would not be able to survive if it were not for the fact that I am being upheld by the prayers of so many people.'

Tutu is indeed up there with the Dalai Lama as one of those figures who had their moral stature minted in one specific context and managed to convert it into an international currency that never seems to lose its value. In Tutu's case, the context was apartheid South Africa, where he was appointed the first Black dean of Johannesburg in the mid-1970s. Given that the deanery was in the white part of town, Tutu would have needed a permit to live there. He decided, instead, to make his home in the township of Soweto. 'I probably would have got permission from the government,' he once said, 'but it would have been as an honorary white, and Leah [his wife] and I decided we were not going to humiliate ourselves in that way. We said to the cathedral that we would live in Soweto. It caused a row in the press.'

Shortly afterwards, he sent a letter to the then prime minister, John Vorster, warning him that something cataclysmic was brewing. Vorster ignored him. Not long after came the Soweto Uprising, when Black youths came out en masse to resist the regime's attempt to force them to learn in Afrikaans – the language of the Boer white minority.

'When a pile of cups is tottering on the edge of the table and you warn that they will crash to the ground,' he once said, 'in South Africa you are blamed when that happens.'

So Tutu, among others, got the blame. And thus began his domestic reputation as a rabble-rouser and troublemaker and, internationally, as a clear, forthright and perspicacious voice against injustice. At a time when the ANC's leadership was either in jail or in exile, there was Tutu – cassock flowing, crucifix swaying front and side, as he strode through the brutality of the townships and the mendacity of apartheid. Delivering blistering attacks on the regime one minute, diving into a crowd to save a suspected 'informer' from being necklaced the next. During the transition, he chaired the Truth and Reconciliation Commission: a moral, spiritual conscience to complement Nelson Mandela's political strategic vision. A feisty individual in his own right, Tutu was also part of a tradition of radical Anglican preachers in South Africa who made a stand against apartheid, among them

Trevor Huddleston, Michael Lapsley, Paul Verryn, Njongonkulu Ndungane and Denis Hurley.

Tutu has claimed that his greatest weakness is that he loves to be loved. 'There are not too many who enjoy being castigated as ogres,' he says, 'as someone others love to hate. I think that most of us would prefer to be popular than unpopular. I know for myself that it has tended to be a weakness – a tendency to enjoy the limelight, a weakness that would make you soften things that are hard but that you need to say. Many people would be surprised that, in fact, I'm quite shy. I know it doesn't look like it.'

I smile. It is a common refrain of extroverts that they are, in fact, instinctively withdrawn and inclined to overcompensate. The late Archbishop of Canterbury, Robert Runcie, a good friend of Tutu's, once described him as 'a bit of a showman'. He has been known to bust out a dance move, whether or not there is a dancefloor in sight. At the very least, he is the most outgoing introvert I have met. Tutu notices my scepticism.

'Look at your smile,' he laughs – a big belly laugh that lies somewhere between Sid James and Santa Claus. 'You're thinking, "Wow," but I'm not quite as ebullient as I seem. One of the weaknesses of wanting to be loved is that you hate being confrontational. There are many situations in which one finds oneself where you have to be confrontational, and that is contrary to my temperament.' More laughing. 'Many would say, "What?! When you can be so strident and acerbic in your attacks on others?" But it's put on.'

It's all just a performance?

'Well, not in the sense that it's histrionics, but I have to get myself into that particular moment. And my inclination would be to keep quiet and not muddy the waters. I depend upon and am sustained so utterly by so many people, and I am fortunate enough to have been trained by a religious community for the priesthood and saw how crucial for them the spiritual life was – so one has sought to emulate them. Without that resource, I would have been done for long ago.'

For all his professed reticence, this man who loves to be loved has an uncanny habit of upsetting all sorts of people. 'If you are neutral in situations of injustice, you have chosen the side of the oppressor,' he once said. 'If an elephant has its foot on the tail of a mouse and you say that you are neutral, the mouse will not appreciate your neutrality.' So there he has been, chiding the elephants and looking out for the mice. During the 1980s, he called Ronald Reagan and his policies 'racist' and said that the West 'can go to hell'. He called former apartheid leader P. W. Botha a liar and suggested he was a Nazi sympathiser. 'I don't know whether that is how Jesus would have handled it,' Tutu told his biographer, John Allen, 'but at that moment I didn't actually quite mind how Jesus would have handled it. I was going to handle it my way.'

His criticisms were not reserved for apartheid South Africa. He has called on Robert Mugabe to resign or be sent to the International Criminal Court in The Hague for 'gross violations'; he has expressed his 'disappointment' in Tony Blair for the 'immoral' invasion of Iraq and his disappointment in the new Pope for being a 'rigid conservative'; and he has drawn parallels between Israel's treatment of the Palestinians and apartheid's treatment of Blacks.

Tutu has also been quite stringent in his criticisms of post-apartheid South Africa. He told Mandela that he was setting a bad example by failing to make 'an honest woman' of his now wife Graça Machel, with whom he had been in a relationship for more than a year before they got married, and he slammed former South African president Thabo Mbeki for surrounding himself with yes-men and for replacing an old white oligarchy with a biracial one.

'He speaks his mind on matters of public morality and has from time to time annoyed many of us who belong to the new order,' Mandela once said of his old friend. 'But such independence of mind, however wrong and unstrategic it may at times be, is vital to a thriving democracy.'

Such is the record of this particular 'shy' man that one wonders who else's feathers Tutu might have ruffled if he had been outgoing.

It is a testament to both his charm and his authority that he has managed to court so much controversy and yet avoid its taint.

Most recently, Tutu's ire has been reserved for the recently elected South African president, Jacob Zuma. When Zuma was lobbying for the leadership of the ANC, Tutu said: 'I pray that someone will be able to counsel him that the most dignified, most selfless thing, the best thing he could do for a land he loves deeply, is to declare his decision not to take further part in the succession race of his party.'

At the time, Zuma had been charged with rape, after sleeping with an HIV-positive woman less than half his age, without using a condom. He was also alleged to have been involved in racketeering and fraud, although the National Prosecuting Authority dropped the charges, citing political interference. He defeated Mbeki in a bitter internal party feud, in which the ANC membership vented their frustration at the slow pace of economic reform and Mbeki's distant and haughty manner. Supporters of Zuma, who was later acquitted of rape, led a smear campaign against the woman who brought the charge.

'I for one would not be able to hold my head high if a person with such supporters were to become my president,' Tutu says. 'Someone who did not think it necessary to apologise for engaging in casual sex without taking proper precautions, in a country that is being devastated by the horrendous HIV/Aids pandemic.'

Zuma won the election with a resounding 66 per cent of the vote and is now Tutu's president. When I read these quotes back to him, he chuckles. How is his head holding up now?

'I said that during his rape trial, when some of his supporters were saying quite unacceptable things against the woman who brought the charges against him,' he says. 'I would have thought that one would have remonstrated with them more forcefully than was the case.'

He fears that the trial, and the way it was resolved, has produced a cloud that will forever follow Zuma. 'I think that many have felt uneasy about the fact that he had these charges hanging over his head.

And it is also the way they were dealt with – not through a court, but administratively. So there will always be this shadow hanging over him. And that's a shame. But he is hugely popular with a large section of our community, so the thing to do is to wait and see – let us give him the chance to prove himself, hoping against hope that what we might have feared will not, in fact, eventuate.'

As he weighs his words even more carefully, the clear-cut moralism for which Tutu is renowned finally gives way to a more measured pragmatism. 'It's water under the bridge. It's the new reality. He's been inaugurated. He's appointed a new cabinet. Let's see what happens. At this stage, I am perhaps neutral . . . I'm sad for my country. I think we could have done a great deal better in the way that we handled the differences . . . But then, politics is politics, and we have to live with these realities as they are.'

The fact that Tutu is hoping against hope does not, ultimately, suggest that he is that optimistic. He is prepared to give Zuma the benefit of the doubt, but the doubts are still very apparent. 'We are facing very serious problems. Like the rest of the world, we are facing the economic downturn, but we also have problems that are peculiar to us. There is a very high incidence of HIV/Aids. We are the epicentre in many ways. We have high levels of crime, levels of poverty that are unacceptable, and then the usual bang shoot of corruption and things of that sort. So they have a very full plate to deal with. One must wish them well for everybody's sake. They have to succeed.'

He thinks some encouraging signs emerged in the handover from one president to another, although he feels that the new Zuma administration has been unnecessarily vindictive towards some of Mbeki's supporters. 'One positive thing is that we are constantly castigating African presidents who want to be presidents for life. And I think the rejection of Thabo Mbeki going for a third time and somehow to ensconce himself as a president in perpetuity is a good thing. There was also a reaction to Mbeki's style. Many experience him as perhaps too English. He didn't carry his heart on his sleeve, as most of our

Dispatches from the Diaspora

people tend to do. He appeared to be aloof. Zuma, on the other hand, is warm and engages people. You can see, when he's dancing on the stage, people warm to him in a way that they didn't to Thabo Mbeki. So all of those factors militated against Thabo.'

If political developments in South Africa have left Tutu somewhat jaded, then the election of Barack Obama in the US has made him very excited. 'It's such a fantastic thing,' he says. 'He's filled Americans with a new pride in their country. Quite justifiably. But he's also filled the world. Everybody assumed that once he came to power, there would be a new style in American politics, where previously they behaved like bullyboys. Everybody said, "No, you shouldn't invade Iraq. Give the UN inspectors more time." And America says, "Go jump in the lake." They didn't sign the Kyoto Protocol. They didn't sign the Rome Statute of the International Criminal Court. Now people believe that we are going to have an America that is a leader of the world, not by being obstreperous, not by being a bully, but by being collaborative. Already you've seen a change in style. Just look at how the Germans turned out for him even before he won. Here, African Americans are walking with a new spring in their step . . . He has such a presence. He is presidential. He's warm. But you won't take any liberties with him. What a gift of oratory.'

Haven't we been here before? Black people with a spring in their step, a nation rehabilitated abroad and, apparently, reconciled with its own racial history at home? For all the huge differences, doesn't the America Tutu is describing in 2009 sound a lot like the South Africa in 1994 with which he is now disenchanted?

'There is always a theoretical possibility of total disillusionment and disappointment,' he says, 'but I think that the indications are in the other direction. He's a very astute person. And I think he has sought to find those next to him, near to him, who are more than competent. He's shown that in things like shutting down Guantánamo Bay and appointing George Mitchell as his special envoy to the Middle East. The signs are propitious . . . But obviously, yes, maybe we could muck ourselves up by being unrealistic in our expectations . . . But it is important that he has filled people of colour with a new sense of who we are, and that is great.'

There are other questions I want to ask. About the Truth and Reconciliation Commission and how it might relate to the US grappling with torture; about the children's book he has just written; and about the global group of Elders he chairs, which aims to apply its wisdom to conflicts in the global village.

But this particular elder is fading. As he leans back in the sofa, his speech slows and his eyelids droop. I ask a few questions anyway, and he answers wearily. A man who has devoted his life to struggle is struggling to finish a sentence and keep his eyes open. The laughs become more muted. As we pack up, Franklin asks if he can spare fifteen minutes tomorrow to do something else. Then Leah, his wife, calls. As I say goodbye, Tutu is on the phone and virtually horizontal. Sustained by prayer, a big cushion and a comfy sofa. Father needs a nap.

'I started to realise what fiction could be. And I thought, "Wow! You can take on the world"'

Andrea Levy found success late in her career. Having retired from striving, she now wants to engage with Britain's slave-owning past.

Guardian, 30 January 2010, London

When *Small Island* was published five years ago, it started out faring much the same as Andrea Levy's first three books: well reviewed but not particularly widely read. 'Give me a basket and I'll go door to door with it,' she joked to the publishers. The book 'wasn't really selling. It certainly wasn't doing anything fantastic.'

It was a mark of the enduring quality of the first three – *Every Light in the House Burnin'*, *Never Far from Nowhere* and *Fruit of the Lemon* – that none had gone out of print. It was perhaps a mark of their limitations that she had not managed to sell a single one abroad. 'Middle-aged and middle list,' she points out. 'It's bloody tough out there in that position. They were giving up.'

But then came the prizes. First there was the Orange. Even then, she says, *Small Island* only got a halfway decent bump in Britain, and no one abroad was interested. Then, in fairly quick succession, came the Whitbread, the Commonwealth and the Orange Best of the Best, as well as it being shortlisted for the National Book Critics Circle award in the US, two National Book awards in this country and Levy's nomination for Romantic Novelist of the Year. The novel – about four Jamaicans who emigrate to Britain during the Second World War – broke through, in a very big way indeed. Translated into twenty-two languages, from Vietnamese to Macedonian, it became a bestseller in both the UK and Canada and was chosen as the Big Read in Hull, Liverpool, Bristol and Glasgow.

'I'm still reeling from the success of it,' she says. 'I'm still wondering what it was all about. It got sanctioned as part of the canon.

Once I won the Whitbread, I could see that it was going beyond what I ever thought was possible. Older white men interested in RAF gunners were buying it and reading it and enjoying it – the kind of people who'd never bought my books before. I wonder whether it was because we'd just gone through this massive period of immigration from Eastern Europe, and maybe there was safety in looking back at that part of our immigration history with some nostalgia.'

Either way, the success gave her the space, time and resources to pursue her literary interests more freely. A couple of years ago, she joked that she was retiring and settled into a rhythm of doing the household chores – paying bills, shopping, etc. – in the morning and then writing in the afternoon.

'Well, my retirement is from striving,' she explains. 'Thanks to *Small Island*, I don't have to pay the mortgage any more. There's not a day goes by that I'm not grateful I'm in that position. This girl who had "shop girl" written right the way through her. "Shop girl,"' she repeats, and acts out writing the words on her forehead. 'Now I can explore what I'm passionate about.'

Small Island signalled a significant shift in scale and scope from her three earlier works, which were strong, engaging novels drawn from her immediate life experience, with a familiar cast of characters. Each was set, for the most part, in north London, with a working-class Black family whose parents had emigrated from Jamaica. Each family had at least one daughter who aspired to higher education and at least one sibling who did not. The parents, meanwhile, were more interested in keeping their heads above water than in issues of race, racism and class inequality.

Levy calls these books her 'baton race'. 'I'm a writer learning my craft and gaining in confidence, or not,' she explains. 'So that was the person who I was. Then you write the next one. Anyone reading my books could say, "Well, she got a dictionary there," and "She got a thesaurus at this point."'

She can tell you, almost to the day, when she was injected with the creative adrenaline that produced *Small Island*: it was 1997, and she was judging the Orange Prize.

'I suddenly understood what fiction was for,' she says. 'I had to read books that I wouldn't have necessarily read. I had to read them well and I had to read them in a short space of time. Back to back. Annie Proulx and Margaret Atwood and Beryl Bainbridge and Anne Michaels – boom, boom, boom. And I started to realise what fiction could be. And I thought, "Wow! You can be ambitious, you can take on the world – you really can."'

Her ambitions took her further and further away in time and place from her own beginnings. *Small Island* roamed from London to the Midlands to Jamaica and was set during the wartime years. Her latest book, *The Long Song*, is set on a Jamaican slave plantation, Amity, in the early nineteenth century, in a period leading up to emancipation. It tells the story of a slave girl, July, and the love, envy, intrigue and spirit of playful insubordination that consume her, as well as the political resistance and personal rivalries that surround her – an everyday tale of ordinary plantation folk a continent and several generations away from where she started out.

While invitations to parties and literary events have been more plentiful in recent years, she has been less likely to accept them. 'Something got put to bed with *Small Island*,' she says. 'Running to stand still, wanting to be part of that literary thing – all that has left me. I could quite happily not have anything to do with that world now.'

Descriptions of her as 'angry' (she once said 'fuckers' in an interview) or 'worthy' are ham-fisted attempts to force racial stereotypes on her that simply do not fit. In person, she is both irreverent and somewhat shy. There's an endearing anxiety about her, and because success came fairly late in her career – she was forty-eight when *Small Island* appeared – she has remained largely unaffected by her recent renown. When she was close to finishing the novel, she woke up one night in a sweat, fearing she might lose it. She already kept three copies in her handbag, as well as the one on her computer and the one hidden in her car in case the house burned down. But what, she fretted, if the house caught fire and a spark took the car with it? The next morning, she made another copy and sent it to a friend.

'If I go away, I send a copy of my work to my agent, asking him not to look at it, but should I not return, please to publish it posthumously,' she says. 'I am forever convinced that I am never going to get to the end of a book or that I'm going to lose it. I am an extremely cautious person.'

When Levy's mother, Amy, was going to marry her father, Winston, in Jamaica, her father's family hired a detective to make sure there was nothing untoward in Amy's family history. Middle-class, light-skinned Jamaicans – Amy was a trained teacher, Winston a book-keeper with Tate & Lyle – they arrived in Britain in the late 1940s to discover that none of the privileges they had inherited counted for much in Britain. Her mother's teaching qualifications were not accepted here, so she took in sewing while she retrained. Her father worked for the post office.

Raised on a predominantly white council estate in Highbury, north London, Levy was inculcated with a sense of class rooted more in cultural behaviour than in resources. 'I thought we were middle class because we had three meals a day,' she says.

Whatever conscious racial identity she had while growing up seems to have been remarkable more in terms of what was to be avoided than what was to be embraced. 'I was not at all curious about Jamaica as a child,' she says. 'We were told, not in so many words, to be ashamed of it.' She only discovered that her father came over on the *Empire Windrush* when it was shown on television and her dad casually mentioned it while he was ironing.

The London she was raised in was not the multicultural city it is now. 'We didn't know that many Black people,' she says. 'There was another Black family at my church. But I just used to feel terribly

Dispatches from the Diaspora

sorry for them because I knew how difficult it was, and we would never have spoken. I'm not proud of who I was then. But I was just dealing with things as they came.'

It was only when she went to art college that she encountered the social confidence and material resources of Britain's middle classes. It would be some time before she started to locate herself within the country's racial hierarchies – during the 1980s, when London prided itself on equal opportunities, and she was working in the voluntary sector. During a racial awareness workshop, her office was asked to divide into Black and white, so she went with the whites.

'And everybody said, "No, no, you should be on the other side," and it was a bloody shock. I thought Black people were doing something somewhere else that I wasn't a part of. I felt embarrassed to go to their side. Not ashamed. I just thought, "I don't know anything about being Black" – I was inauthentic. I was a political person, a left-leaning person. I thought I'd got my politics sussed. And suddenly this thing came along, and I had to learn about it.'

When did she work it out? 'Any day now,' she says, laughing. 'I'm still learning.'

She points to a boxed set of *Who Do You Think You Are?*, the BBC TV show in which well-known Britons trace their ancestry, and says, 'They'd never have me on because I'm not a big enough celebrity, but I love it. People can go back generations, but they've only done about three Black people, and they can only take them back so far and then the door shuts, because all that's there are ledgers. Nothing else – just a big mass of nothing. I know my ancestors were slaves, but what did they do? How did they live? How did they manage to survive it? We know so little, and very little of what we do know comes from them. The only way you can go any further is through fiction.'

This was the curiosity that produced *The Long Song*, in which July tells her story, urged on by her son. Levy says she was inspired to write the book after a young Black woman at a conference on the legacy of slavery rose to ask how she could have pride in her ancestry, when all her ancestors had been slaves. 'I thought, "Wow, how could anyone have any shame or ambivalence at having slave ancestry?"' She wanted to see if she could change this woman's mind and make her proud of her ancestry.

'When you try to imagine slavery in terms of what happened, it's almost unthinkable,' she says. 'But people got through it. Not every day was: "Got up, got whipped thoroughly, saw someone hung from a tree." So I try to give a sense of the daily life – the drinking milk and eating yam of it – as well as the lives of the planter class. I try to give people their humanity.'

But she is acutely aware of how the subject matter itself could overpower her literary efforts. When *Small Island* failed to make the Booker longlist, one of the judges explained that the book was 'worthy', but that the acclaim 'comes from the topic rather than the treatment . . . People feel guilty about not thinking about our colonial past.'

This is not the world that Levy wants to take on in *The Long Song*, and she did not begin with the intention of writing a book set during the time of slavery. She wants her books to be read, she explains, but many people, for different reasons, prefer not to engage with that aspect of their past. She talks about slavery as though it is a live wire in the public imagination. When people touch it, there is a short-circuit; either they think they know all about it, they don't want to know about it or they think that it's not a topic worth knowing about.

'There are a lot of people who are open to talking about it,' she says. 'But there are many who will say that it was a very long time ago, and a lot who just don't want you to mention it because it will make them feel bad. It's painful, both for Black and white people. But it's three hundred years. You can't just ignore it. I don't want people to feel guilty. I don't want them to pick it up and feel like they're taking vitamins.'

The novel was intended to cover a much longer period of time, she says. 'I was intending to get out of there very quick. But you can't avoid slavery. You can't. You have to go to that place. You keep banging into it. I'm not proselytising. It's the book I had to write because of who I am.'

The man who raised a Black power salute at the 1968 Olympic Games

One single act of resistance made John Carlos a global icon but cost him both his livelihood and his marriage. He regrets nothing.

Guardian, 30 March 2012, Palm Springs, California

You're probably not familiar with the name John Carlos. But you almost certainly know his image. It's the Mexico City Olympics, 1968, and the medals are being hung round the necks of Tommie Smith (USA, gold), Peter Norman (Australia, silver) and Carlos (USA, bronze). As 'The Star-Spangled Banner' begins to play, Smith and Carlos, two Black Americans wearing black gloves, raise their fists in the Black power salute. It is a symbol of resistance and defiance, seared into twentieth-century history – one that Carlos feels he was put on Earth to perform.

'In life, there's the beginning and the end,' he says. 'The beginning don't matter. The end don't matter. All that matters is what you do in between – whether you're prepared to do what it takes to make change. There has to be physical and material sacrifice. When all the dust settles and we're getting ready to play down for the ninth inning, the greatest reward is to know that you did your job when you were here on the planet.'

Carlos's beginning was, to say the least, eventful. Raised by two involved, working parents, he learned to hustle with his friends in Harlem and fight his way out of and into trouble. As a teenager, he used to chase Malcolm X down the street after his speeches and fire questions at him. Carlos always knew he was good at sports and originally wanted to be an Olympic swimmer, until his father broke it to him that the training facilities he needed were in private clubs for whites and the wealthy. He used to steal food from freight trains with his friends and then run into Harlem and hand it out to the poor.

When the police gave chase, he was often the only one who never got caught. Running came so naturally, he never thought of it as a skill.

That single moment on the podium cost Carlos dear. More than four decades later, you'll find him at his desk in a spacious portable building behind the basketball courts at Palm Springs High School in California, where he works as a counsellor. Among the family photographs on the wall are the vaguest allusions to his moment in history: pictures of Malcolm X and African American writer Zora Neale Hurston; the pledge of allegiance, which American schoolkids must say to the flag every day; and a small poster saying 'Go for Gold Olympics'.

For all its challenges, Carlos loves his job. 'Being a counsellor, you have to talk to the children as though you're talking to a thousand people,' he says. 'Sometimes you say, "I love you," and they say, "I don't want your love," and you say, "Well, it's out there, so you're going to have to deal with it." And I learn a lot from them, too.'

Bald, tall, with a grey goatee, Carlos has glided into old age with a distinguished air and convivial manner – and more than a passing resemblance to the late activist and intellectual W. E. B. Du Bois.

'The first thing I thought was, the shackles have been broken,' Carlos says, casting his mind back to how he felt in that moment. 'And they won't ever be able to put shackles on John Carlos again. Because what had been done couldn't be taken back. Materially, some of us in the incarceration system are still literally in shackles. The greatest problem is we are afraid to offend our oppressors.

'I had a moral obligation to step up. Morality was a far greater force than the rules and regulations they had. God told the angels that day, "Take a step back – I'm gonna have to do this myself."'

The image certainly captures that sense of momentary rebellion. But what it cannot do is evoke the human sense of emotional turmoil and individual resolve that made it possible, or the collective, global gasp in response to its audacity. In his book *The John Carlos Story*, Carlos writes that in the seconds between mounting the podium and the anthem playing, his mind raced from the personal to the political and back again. Among other things, he reflected on his father's pained explanation for why he couldn't become an Olympic swimmer, the segregation and consequent impoverishment of Harlem, the exhortations of Martin Luther King and Malcolm X to 'be true to yourself even when it hurts', and his family. The final thought before the band started playing was: 'Damn, when this thing is done, it can't be taken back.

'I know that sounds like a lot of thoughts for just a few moments standing on a podium before the start of the national anthem,' he writes, 'but honestly this was all zigzagging through my brain like lightning bolts.'

Anticipating some kind of protest was afoot, the International Olympic Committee (IOC) had sent Jesse Owens to talk them out of it. (Owens's four gold medals at the 1936 Olympics in Berlin themselves held great symbolic significance, given Hitler's belief in Aryan supremacy.) Carlos's mind was made up. When he and Smith struck their pose, Carlos feared the worst. Look at the picture, and you'll see that while Smith's arm is raised long and erect, Carlos has his slightly bent at the elbow. 'I wanted to make sure, in case someone rushed us, I could throw down a hammer punch,' he writes. 'We had just received so many threats leading up to that point, I refused to be defenceless at that moment of truth.'

It was also a moment of silence. 'You could have heard a frog piss on cotton. There's something awful about hearing fifty thousand people go silent, like being in the eye of a hurricane.'

And then came the storm. First boos. Then insults and worse. People throwing things and screaming racist abuse. 'Niggers need to go back to Africa!' and 'I can't believe this is how you niggers treat us after we let you run in our Games.'

'The fire was all around me,' Carlos recalls. The IOC president ordered Smith and Carlos to be suspended from the US team and the Olympic village. *Time* magazine showed the Olympic logo, with the words 'Angrier, Nastier, Uglier' instead of 'Faster, Higher, Stronger'. The *LA Times* accused them of engaging in a 'Nazi-like salute'.

Beyond the establishment, the resonance of the image could not be overstated. It was 1968; the Black power movement had provided a post-civil rights rallying cry, and the anti-Vietnam protests were gaining pace. That year, students throughout Europe, east and west, had been in revolt against war, tyranny and capitalism. Martin Luther King had been assassinated, and the US had plunged into yet another year of race riots in its urban centres. Just a few months earlier, the Democratic Party convention had been disrupted by a huge police riot against Vietnam protesters. A few weeks before the Games, scores of students and activists had been gunned down by the authorities in Mexico City itself.

The sight of two Black athletes in open rebellion on the international stage sent a message to both America and the world. At home, this brazen disdain for the tropes of American patriotism – flag and anthem – shifted dissidence from the periphery of American life to prime-time television in a single gesture, while revealing what Du Bois once termed the 'essential two-ness' of the Black American condition. 'An American, a Negro; two souls, two thoughts, two unreconciled strivings; two warring ideals in one dark body, whose dogged strength alone keeps it from being torn asunder.'

Globally, it was understood as an act of solidarity with all those fighting for greater equality, justice and human rights. Margaret Lambert, a Jewish high-jumper who was forced, for show, to try out for the 1936 German Olympic team, even though she knew she would never be allowed to compete, talked about how delighted it made her feel. 'When I saw those two guys with their fists up on the victory stand, it made my heart jump. It was beautiful.'

As Carlos explains in his book, their gesture was supposed to say, among other things: 'Hey, world, the United States is not like you might think it is for blacks and other people of colour. Just because we have "USA" on our chest does not mean everything is peachy keen and we are living large.'

Carlos understood, before he raised his fist that day, that once done, his act could not be taken back. What he could not have anticipated, at the age of twenty-three, was what it would mean for his future. 'I had no idea the moment on the medal stand would be frozen for all time. I had no idea what we'd face. I didn't know or appreciate, at that precise moment, that the entire trajectory of our young lives had just irrevocably changed.'

During the Jim Crow era, life for even the most famous Black sportsmen who were past their prime was tough. After his celebrated Olympic victory, Owens ran a dry-cleaning business, was a gas pump attendant, raced horses for money and eventually went bankrupt. 'People say it was degrading for an Olympic champion to run against a horse,' he said. 'But what was I supposed to do? I had four gold medals, but you can't eat four gold medals.'

Joe Louis, a world champion boxer on whose shoulders rested national pride when he fought German Max Schmeling shortly before the Second World War, greeted visitors at Caesars Palace in Las Vegas and went on quiz shows. And these were sporting figures who tried to keep in with the establishment. Carlos was still in his prime, but that single act of defiance ensured his marginalisation.

Paradoxically, the next year was the best of his career. In 1969, he equalled the 100-yard world record, won the American Athletics Union 220-yard dash and led San José State to its first National Collegiate Athletic Association championship. The trouble was, in the years before lucrative sponsorship deals, running didn't pay, and few would employ him. In the years immediately following his protest, he worked security at a nightclub and as a janitor. At one point, he had to chop up his furniture so he could heat his house. The pressure started to bear down on his family. 'When there's a lack of money, it brings contempt into the family,' he says. Moreover, his wife was facing constant harassment from the press, and his children were being told at school that their father was a traitor. The marriage collapsed.

He tried American football for a few seasons, starting in Philadelphia, then moving north to Toronto and Montreal. He is keen to emphasise that the one thing that never happened, despite claims to the contrary, was that his medal was confiscated. It's at his mother's house. And while he does not cherish it as you'd expect an Olympian might, he's adamant that this part of the story is set straight. 'The medal didn't mean shit to me. It doesn't mean anything now . . . The medal had no relevance. The one way it had relevance was that I earned it. So they never took my medal away from me. I'd earned it. They can't take it.'

As time passed and the backlash subsided, Carlos was gradually invited back into the fold. He became involved as an outreach co-ordinator in the organising committee for the group bringing the Olympics to Los Angeles in 1984 and worked for the US Olympic Committee.

Did he worry, as the picture for which he was famous started to adorn T-shirts and posters, that his readmission into the Olympic world meant his radicalism was being co-opted and sanitised? 'The image is still there,' he says, proudly. 'It keeps getting wider. If you look at the images of the last century, there's nothing much like it out there. And "the man" wasn't the one that kept this thing afloat for forty-three years. "The man" was the same man whupping my ass. And the Olympics are part of my history. I'm not going to run away from that.'

Carlos remains politically engaged. Late last year, he addressed Occupy Wall Street protesters in New York. 'It's the same fight as it was forty-three years ago. We fought unemployment; for housing, education. It's the same thing as people are fighting for today.'

He defends Barack Obama, whom he believes has not been given a fair shake. 'Mr Obama didn't get us where we are. He's trying to get us out. Someone fabricates shit to get us into wars, then makes ordinary Americans pay for them. Now someone else is trying to make it right. If George W. Bush can have two terms to put this country into this mess, we should give Obama two to get us out of it.'

But unlike during the 1960s, today Carlos sees little hope of resistance emerging through sport, which is awash with too much money and too many drugs. 'There wasn't a whole bunch of money out there back then,' he says, 'so just a few people were ever going to be shakers and bakers. But today, if an athlete doesn't have a view of their history before them, then they have a view of just that big cheque in front of them. It's not the responsibility of the oppressor to educate us. We have to educate ourselves and our own. That's the difference between Muhammad Ali and Michael Jordan. Muhammad Ali will never die. He used his skill to say something about the social ills of society. Of course, he was an excellent boxer, but he got up and spoke on the issues. And because he spoke on the issues, he will never die. There will be someone else at some time who can do what Jordan could do. And then his name will just be pushed down in the mud. But they'll still be talking about Ali.'

Eight years earlier, during a different phase of anti-racist activism in the US, a seventeen-year-old student, Franklin McCain, had gained his place in the history books when he sat at a Woolworth's lunch counter in Greensboro, North Carolina, with three friends and refused to move until they were served. Many years later, McCain was philosophical about how that experience had affected him. 'Nothing has ever come close,' he told me. 'Not the birth of my first son, nor my marriage. And it was a cruel hoax, because people go through their whole lives and they don't get that to happen to them. And here it was being visited upon me as a seventeen-year-old. It was wonderful, and it was sad also, because I know that I will never have that again. I'm just sorry it was when I was seventeen.'

Carlos has no such regrets. He's just glad he could be where he was to do what he felt he had to do. 'I don't have any misgivings about it being frozen in time. It's a beacon for a lot of people around the world. So many people find inspiration in that portrait. That's what I was born for.'

In my diction, in my stance, in my attitude, this is Black British

I met Stormzy, not long after he'd performed at Glastonbury, to talk everything from faith and south London to scholarships and left-wing leadership.

GQ, 5 February 2020, London

Stormzy is twenty-five minutes into his headlining Glastonbury set when he feels something go 'boom' in his in-ear. The pack that pumps studio-quality sound to the singer while he's on stage had gone haywire. 'It was just going, "Eeeeeeee!" I'm talking deafening. Then it blew, and I couldn't hear shit.'

He'd just finished 'Sweet Like Chocolate'. The stage lights had gone down. Stormzy stands there, eyes intense, back straight, standing tall, very tall, black, lean, buff, clad top to toe in lily white. Sweat cascades from his face. He lifts his fingers to his earpiece and stares ahead. Back-up soul singers gather around to cover Kanye West's 'Ultralight Beam'. Fireworks erupt; jets of sparks shoot out beside the stage; search lights strafe the night. 'That was one of the most powerful moments in the show,' he says. 'And I can't hear shit. All I can hear is the festival speakers. And I'm just rapping and just praying to God that I'm on time. And the song just finishes and I'm thinking, "Bruv, you can't hear shit. You're at Glastonbury. And you can't hear shit. This is a shitshow."'

He makes it through 'Ultralight Beam'. The stage goes dark again. Chris Martin comes on with a piano; Stormzy runs off into the wings. 'I take my pack off and I'm close to tears and I'm screaming, "I can't fucking hear nothing!" They're switching my pack, and I'm thinking, "Glastonbury. Chris Martin. What the fuck?"'

Martin stalls, looking over his shoulder, wondering where Stormzy is. Stormzy returns, his pack fixed, and takes his seat next to Martin.

He does one more song. Then the pack blows again and remains out for the rest of the set. 'I'm listening to the festival speakers, which are delayed, so if I go with that I'm going to be off beat. So then I'm just listening to the drums and performing with muscle memory. I'm like, "You're fucked, but just do it." And I'm thinking the whole time that I'm off beat. I know it's delayed, but I'm thinking, "Just spit, just spit, just spit." All that was going through my head was, "Bruv, you have absolutely fucked it." I was thinking of all the people who wanted me to fuck it – "Stormzy? Glasto? That small-timer?" – just watching and thinking, "Look at him. He can't even spit on beat. He's all over the place."'

When he came off stage, he smashed his pack, flew into a rage for five minutes and then collapsed into tears. 'I was just bawling my eyes out. I thought, "You have just absolutely fucked that." I haven't cried like that since primary school. I just broke down.' It was only later, when someone handed him a memory stick so he could see the performance for himself, that he came around to the notion that it had, in fact, gone rather well.

Stormzy – real name Michael Ebenazer Kwadjo Omari Owuo Jr – is sitting on the edge of his sofa at his home in south London, wearing an all-black tracksuit and with the television on mute. His height is not obvious when we're both sitting down (I'm 5ft 6in, he's 6ft 5in; when we take selfies later, he has to stoop low just to get in the shot, as he does when dancing with his mother in the video for 'Know Me From'), but his scale is. He talks like he raps, with his hands, and at times, when he has a point to make, he flings them out wide. The sheer span is impressive. Stormzy has reach.

Hearing about his brush with calamity at Glastonbury, contrasting the confidence and physical energy he exhibited on stage with the frailty of the inner monologue that was torturing him simultaneously, I'm reminded of Ice-T's explanation of why young rappers are so vulnerable to scandal. 'When you're rolling at the speed these cats are rolling at,' he told me in 2001, 'it's hard to keep things straight.'

Stormzy identifies with this immediately. 'You're going from one extreme to another extreme,' he says. 'From poverty, not having anything, violence and street life to glitz and glam, and finally having resources and money at your disposal. And that's a rapid, gear-six change.'

Stormzy has been rolling at quite a speed ever since he came on the scene. It is a steep climb to go from Best Grime Act at the 2014 MOBO Awards to headlining Glastonbury in just five years. Yet despite being a good-looking, outspoken, famous, wealthy guy at the gritty, combative end of his industry, he has managed to keep it straight.

If he appears in the tabloids, it's generally for his music or his politics, not for the women he's sleeping with, the men he's feuding with, the scenes he's caused or the cases he's caught. Even after he split with his long-term girlfriend, the TV and radio presenter Maya Jama, last August, the break-up made headlines because a telegenic celebrity couple were no more. As a twenty-six-year-old grime artist, he has provided less copy for the gossip columns than the Conservative prime minister, who is twice his age.

I assumed this might be due to his belief in God. In the time we talk, he is never more than five minutes away from saying he's been 'blessed', 'God willing' or 'thank God'. He refers to his on-stage challenges at Glastonbury as his 'God-ordained story', and his journey as a 'blessing from God'. It is rare to hear British artists draw on their faith so openly or so often.

'God gets all the glory for everything,' he says. 'I know I'm capable of being a success. But more than all of that, God engineers my whole shit. He's the reason for everything. Even coming from where man comes from. I got so many bredrens who are just as smart as me, or smarter than me, or can make music just as well, and still didn't have that opportunity. So there's something deeper here to it.'

But he says he owes his relative sobriety and self-control to a more earthly experience: the two-year engineering apprenticeship he undertook in Leamington Spa after he was excluded from school. 'Lucky for me I moved out of London when I did,' he says, 'because at that time I was probably going to end up fully submerged with all the street stuff. I left my little place in south London, and I was with seventeen white kids from Yorkshire, Newcastle, Scotland and all over. My bredrens would never know anyone from Scotland. Thank God for me I had an insight into not being a little bad boy Michael. I had to become a project engineer. On those five days of the week there was no street. Nothing. I just had my headphones on, going to college.'

The moment when he realised the things to which he had been accustomed were not necessarily normal came when he took his hat off during a welding course and one of his fellow apprentices asked him how he got the scar on his head. 'I got stabbed,' Stormzy told him.

'And the shock and the looks of horror on their faces was like, "What?" And I'm thinking, "Brother, I've been stabbed a few times." And I'm telling this story, and they're just horrified. And I'm thinking if one of my bredren phoned me now and said they'd got stabbed, I would be upset, but it wouldn't rock my world. It'd be like, "Ahh, fucking hell. I hope you're cool." And that's when I started to realise there was a whole world outside south London.'

For all that, south London and his 'ends' remained, and indeed remain, his central point of reference and his lodestar. He's so London, he's so south.

'There are so many things about me that are so south London, which I wouldn't have learned anywhere else. I wouldn't have had the heart or the character, or my strength and my wits.'

He talks of returning home at the weekends from Leamington Spa as though he's Morpheus coming back to Zion in *The Matrix*. 'When the train started getting to Norbury, I would feel it in my stride. Like, "I'm back." I'd go and see the mandem. It was me learning how to keep one foot in and one foot out.'

In *Prison Notebooks*, Italian Marxist Antonio Gramsci coined the term 'organic intellectual'. Unlike 'traditional intellectuals', who come through academia or think tanks, an organic intellectual emerges from their social class without formal, bookish training but with an ability to articulate the interests and influence the consciousness of that class. They have lived its experiences, are embedded in its culture and speak in its vernacular.

Stormzy's is the voice of a generation raised through war, austerity, capitalist collapse, left-wing realignment and racist revival: socially libertarian and economically statist; idealistic about what is possible, resigned to what is likely, contemptuous of what is happening. The tone of defiance and disdain in his work cuts through.

He doesn't know where he got his politics from. 'I remember when I was [a kid] seeing Tony Blair and thinking, "He's the guy," because he was Labour. Turns out he was one of the worst.'

His first political memory is the terrorist attacks on 11 September. He was eight. 'At the time, I didn't understand. But I remember feeling the weight of it because of teachers crying.'

Was his mother, who raised him and his three siblings alone, a big influence? 'I don't think so,' he says. Then, after a pause, 'But maybe. Seeing how she had to work, what she had to go through. That's obviously going to give me a certain heart and empathy. It was super-tough. My mum worked super-hard. She had to graft her arse off to keep a roof over our heads.'

There was no single moment, person, book or event that shaped his world view. He imbibed it less through his mother's milk than her sweat. Stormzy is a child of crises. He was nine when the Iraq War started; fifteen when the financial crash hit; seventeen when austerity started; eighteen when riots spread through Britain like a bushfire, with young people looting and confronting the police in several English towns. He could not avoid them. His intervention is authentic. This is the story not of a musician who is getting into politics, but of politics coming out of a musician.

His political voice is central to his meaning both as a public figure and a performer. He came on stage in Glastonbury wearing a stab vest emblazoned with the Union Jack, designed by Banksy, which *Guardian* art critic Jonathan Jones described as 'the banner of a divided and frightened nation'. Early in his Glastonbury set, we heard the voice of David Lammy talking about the criminal justice system: 'The system isn't working. If recidivism rates are 46 per cent for Black men, then something isn't working.'

When he sang at Glastonbury in 2017, just a couple of weeks after that year's election, he engaged in a call-and-response with the crowd, chanting, 'Oh, Jeremy Corbyn.' But while there is politics in his lyrics, it isn't central to his music. He's not Billy Bragg or Chuck D. We didn't get to politics until a third of the way through the interview, and I don't know if it would have come up had I not mentioned it. It would be possible to like his music and not even know his politics.

'It was obviously very disappointing,' he says of December's election result. What does he feel it says about Britain? 'We're living in a time where people are scared, anxious or worried about their future and the future of the country, so those higher up are clearly manipulating that and playing on it, and playing on people's fears and insecurities. It's sadly a very divisive time, and there's evidently a long way to go.' That's not to say, of course, that Stormzy's influence was not felt. A few weeks before the election, he signed an open letter, published in the *Guardian*, for Grime4Corbyn, calling for an end to austerity. The day before the voter registration deadline, he posted on Instagram, encouraging his 2.7 million followers to register. 'There were millions of people who thought their one little vote didn't mean shit and now Trump is the president of America and we are leaving the EU,' he wrote. Explaining why he was voting Labour, he described Corbyn as 'the first man in a position of power who is committed to helping those who need a helping hand from the government most'. After that, voter registration spiked 236 per cent compared to the day before. Ultimately, of course, Corbyn failed to harness enough of Stormzy's audience. Nevertheless, the Conservatives were anxious to belittle Stormzy. Michael Gove dismissed him, telling Talk Radio: 'He's a far, far better rapper than he is a political analyst.'

Stormzy's political analysis is sophisticated enough for him to have seen this coming. 'It's easy to target myself and young people,' he tells me, 'and say, "You young people don't know what you're talking about. You don't know about politics. You're just going with the Robin Hood fairy tale story. That's not real politics."'

The problem, he says, isn't that he's oversimplifying the politics, but that his critics are overcomplicating it. 'Maybe man just wants a good person to do the job. People will act like that's such a stupid opinion. Someone who man thinks makes just decisions and is trying to help people and bring people out of poverty, that is a just enough reason for man to support someone. People try to make you feel proper stupid for saying that. But I say, "Bruv, cool. Man doesn't know the fucking economy or whatever. But man knows righteousness. You can't deny righteousness over evil. That's point blank." And people try to make people feel dumb for that. But that is a fair enough political reason to support someone.' Having a bit of common decency? 'Even further than decency,' he insists. 'Every government has let Black people down, let working-class people down. Since when I've been young, whether it's been a Labour government or a Tory government, not much has changed for the people who need it the most.' He shakes his head. 'It might just be how man has grown up, and my heart and my character and all that, but you don't fool man. Man will always rather someone with clean intention do that job.'

A month before the election, some grime artists had expressed regret for supporting Labour in 2017. Skepta said acts sold 'themselves for bullshit', and that four months after the campaign, politicians didn't 'give a fuck about us again'.

'I see it more black and white,' says Stormzy. '[Boris Johnson] is literally not for man. He has made it clear in his vocabulary and in the stances he takes. I always feel, as a country, as a people, that we should always be trying to uplift one another. Give it a chance.'

There are moments when, were it not for the cussing, Stormzy can sound pious. He wants to share, raise up, support and provide. He will talk of God, humility, self-effacement, destiny and how it's really not about him. He means it. In the past couple of years he has set up #Merky Books, a publishing imprint at Penguin Random House, and launched the Stormzy Scholarship, funding the tuition fees and living costs of four Black students studying at Cambridge University.

I assume these are part of a grander plan, but they owe more to a series of impulsive acts of generosity that are neither entirely random nor remotely strategic. He is casting seeds, quite haphazardly, on the soil of Black British culture to see what will grow. 'I'm just trying to do anything and everything and whatever I can that is sick,' he says. 'Whatever it is, I think, "How fucking brilliant would that be? How powerful would that be? Or how funny would that be?" Thank God I've been blessed, so why wouldn't man do sick shit with other people? I want to live out my wildest dreams and realise other people's wildest dreams.' But he's wary of sounding worthy. 'I hate the shine, because it's not hard. There are people who have way less resources than me who dedicate their whole lives to helping other people. For me, it's quite easy. I can just make a phone call.'

He says it's a trait he got from his older sister Rachael, whom he calls his OG. 'She used to proper appreciate when I did something nice to people. It's almost like I've been trained. That's what I used to get ratings for. So now that's what I relate to being a sick thing to do.'

All of these 'sick things' add up to a reputation. Philanthropist, activist, organic intellectual, headlining Glastonbury, guest-editing the *Observer Magazine*, gracing the covers of *GQ* and *Time*, above the headline 'Next Generation Leaders'. The Archbishop of Canterbury listens to 'Blinded by Your Grace' while preparing to officiate at major events. A picture of Stormzy hangs in London's National Portrait

Gallery. 'Stormzy has undoubtedly had a significant influence on British culture today,' the gallery director, Nicholas Cullinan, said.

Stormzy is clearly aware that he risks graduating from left-wing firebrand of a criminalised art form (the grime scene almost collapsed under intense police scrutiny following a high-profile shooting) to the ultimate corruption of co-option: a national treasure. He wears his public persona lightly, but it stalks him constantly, taunting him to play a role he did not seek but does not want to disown entirely. 'I'm a human being and I don't always move correct,' he says. 'So I always think someone might see me in traffic – I get bad road rage – and I'm saying, "You're a fucking idiot, bruv! Fucking manner you're driving!" And they'll think, "Oh God. That's a Next Generation Leader." And I don't want to be judged. I still get angry and chat shit sometimes. I want to say, "Yo, don't be thinking I'm the one. I'm a fucking dumb-ass."'

He doesn't want to sound noble because he doesn't feel noble. 'I'm not fucking Gandhi,' he says. He wants to maintain the right to be the flawed twenty-six-year-old he is. It's not that he doesn't enjoy the limelight, it's just that he attracts more of it than he can meaningfully occupy and he'd rather not be blinded by it. 'What am I going to do with this platform? That's not all for one man. It can't be. I'm good. My family's good. Now maybe other people can be good.'

This was the mindset that framed his Glastonbury show, which included a gospel choir, Black ballet dancers and two other rappers. He wanted to showcase 'Black British excellence' – those achieve-ments and achievers too often eclipsed or submerged by the more powerful cultural economies of White Britain and Black America. Stormzy is passionate about Black Britain. When he talks about the south, he means Croydon, not Mississippi. 'It's super-deliberate,' he says, 'in my pronunciation, in my diction, in my stance, in my dress-ing, in my attitude. This is Black British. I wear it with pride and honour. Man grew up on Skepta, Wiley, Ghetts, Wretch [32]. I didn't grow up listening to Nas and Rakim. I knew about tracksuits and

Channel U and Krept & Konan and Roadside Gs. So I'm super-Black British.

'We should never be under the water. Black British is part of British culture. But they don't always get thrown to the forefront. We're a part of it, but we've been getting left out of the conversation. I make a point of it. There's this whole spectrum. There's me, Malorie Blackman, Dina Asher-Smith, Raheem Sterling, Derek Owusu, there's Ballet Black. And they take one of us, like Idris Elba or Stormzy or Sterling – the one Black guy per mainstream media per two years.'

He saw Glastonbury as an opportunity to widen the public imagination of the breadth, depth, scale and range of Black British culture.

'It was my time to say, "Yes, there's man. But there's bare of us, in bare different ways. You can't keep doing this. Yes, Stormzy's great and that person's great. But it's not an exception. There's bare of us." And I can't just come here and be like, "It's just me." I can't do it.

'That's not trying to be, like, "Kumbaya". It was my truth in every way, shape and form – musically, set design. That was the most genuine, honest moment of us. Because in a way, me doing it is jokes. There are so many people who came before me that had to go through whatever for me to be there, for me to be the first Black British male to headline.'

Watch as the camera pans out to the crowd at his Glastonbury performance, and it becomes painfully clear how few Black people were present for this presentation in their name. For Stormzy, that made it even more important to do it right. 'Loads of Black people tuned in, but I knew this would be a lot of white British people's first proper one-on-one experience with the art we do, our culture, our style. So it can't be the Stormzy show. It's like a whole lesson and presentation and display of everything Black British, south London – grime, rap, soul, R&B, garage. That's what it was: "Hey, England. This is our art. This is it." I knew a lot was riding on it.'

For an older artist to decide to share the spotlight with up-and-coming acts – Dave and Fredo – would be generous. To have only just made it and already be ceding the stage seems eccentric. But to Stormzy it was necessary. 'It's the easiest shit for me to do. Thank God. I'm blessed. I'm good. I'm doing Glasto. At the end of the day, it's my headline slot. I'm good. I have this sick purpose. God said, "Yo, I'm going to bless you. I'm going to anoint you. And with that just fucking lift and shine and elevate. Because man can and man should." And also, in a weird way, I'd feel guilty about going up there and going, "It's all about man," because it's not. Being this black and this dark and from south London, my people have always championed me. So it can never be just about man.'

Something got put to bed with Glastonbury. In the vertiginous climb of Stormzy's brief career, here was a milestone where he could stop and survey the view. 'For the first time in my whole career, and maybe in my life, I was at peace. "Bruv, you done the job, bruv. It was your biggest test and you've done something way bigger than yourself." I patted myself on my back and I spoke to myself nicely about it.'

As the title, *Heavy Is the Head*, suggests, his new album is dominated by themes of uncertainty, defiance, frailty, suspicion, isolation and responsibility, which all come with fame, and shuttles between self-assertion and self-doubt. In 'Lessons' he mourns the end of his relationship with Jama; in 'One Second' he lambasts the *NME* for putting him on the cover of a mental health special without permission.

Pushing himself to this point, at this pace, has evidently taken its toll. 'I'm usually quite hard on myself,' he says. 'I haven't had much peace in the past five years, and that's not even necessarily a bad thing, because life can't always be peaceful. But it was the first time I could sit on this sofa and feel like, "You're good," with no lingering thought of "I've got to do this."'

I tell him about a conversation I had more than twenty years ago with Franklin McCain, who, in 1960, as a nineteen-year-old African American, went with three Black friends to the whites-only counter at Woolworth's in Greensboro, North Carolina, and took a seat (see

p. 258). 'The day I sat at that counter I had the most tremendous feeling of elation and celebration,' McCain told me. 'I felt that in this life nothing else mattered. If there's a heaven, I got there for a few minutes.' McCain said nothing had ever come close to that feeling and he wondered if it was cruel of the universe to offer such an intense state of serenity so early in life. I told him I thought it was kind of the universe to offer it at all, at any stage.

The story seems to chime with Stormzy, who continues enthusiastically: 'Exactly. There's no award that's going to beat my first MOBO. But, of course, God willing, one day I'll get a Grammy. I'm never going to feel like Glasto again. But one day maybe I'll headline Coachella, and then I'll have that. That's the blessing from God. He gave you an indescribable feeling that's so personal to you. And only you can hold it.'

So what does he do now? He can't hold it forever. 'Now I want to do it all over again,' he says, laughing. 'I was standing at the pinnacle of music at twenty-five. It's like winning the World Cup. I wonder how Mbappé feels. You won the World Cup. And it's like, "Wow. I've done it . . . I guess there'll be more World Cups."'

Everything that I'd suppressed came up –
I had to speak up

Lewis Hamilton, who is from my home town, is the most successful driver Formula One has ever seen, and its only Black star. Now he has a new mission: to change the sport that made him.
Guardian, 10 July 2021, London

As Lewis Hamilton rose through the ranks of competitive go-karting, his father, Anthony, told him: 'Always do your talking on the track.' Lewis had a lot to talk about. Bullying and racial taunts were a consistent feature of his childhood in Stevenage, Hertfordshire, a new town thirty miles north of London. His dad taught him the best response was to excel at his sport.

The trouble was, he didn't have many people to talk to about what he was going through off the track. Lewis is mixed race, born to a white mother, Carmen Larbalestier, who raised him until he was twelve, when he went to live with his Grenadian–British father, from whom she had separated. 'My mum was wonderful,' he tells me. 'She was so loving. But she didn't fully understand the impact of the things I was experiencing at school. The bullying and being picked on. And my dad was quite tough, so I didn't tell him too much about those experiences. As a kid, I remember just staying quiet about it because I didn't feel anyone really understood. I just kept it to myself.' Sport offered him an outlet. 'I did boxing because I needed to channel the pain,' he says. 'I did karate because I was being beaten up and I wanted to be able to defend myself.'

I understand where he's coming from: I, too, grew up in Stevenage. Hamilton's mother and I went to the same school – though not at the same time. As close to London as it was, it might as well have been in a different universe. In London, the Black experience appeared authentic; in Stevenage, it felt synthetic. Race in London was something you read about in the papers; race in Stevenage was something you didn't even acknowledge. I was twenty-two before I found my first Black male friend.

Racing was a release for Hamilton, who is now Stevenage's most famous progeny. 'I got in a car and I was the only kid of colour on the track. And I'd be getting pushed around. But then I could always turn their energy against them. I'd out-trick them, outsmart them, outwit them and beat them, and that, for me, was more powerful than any words.'

We meet on Zoom, with Hamilton sitting in front of a huge TV, on a massive sofa, in the otherwise featureless motorhome he uses for European races. Today, it is parked on site at Circuit Paul Ricard, in Le Castellet, ahead of the French Grand Prix. His oval, caramel-complexioned face is framed by well-groomed facial hair, and a hint of his plaits pokes out from the back of his head. He chats in an unguarded, reflective manner, without guile or jargon, gesturing with his hands, but only occasionally cracking a smile.

On the track, Hamilton talks with the greatest authority. At thirty-six, he is the most accomplished Formula One driver of all time, with ninety-eight grand prix wins, a hundred pole positions and 171 podium finishes. The only meaningful record he hasn't broken is the number of drivers' championships won, where he is tied with Michael Schumacher at seven. Put bluntly, he's the best the world has ever seen, and is still at the top of his game.

But in the past year, off the track Hamilton has started to find a voice in terms of his racial identity. He has been taking a knee and raising a clenched fist. Long-dormant concerns about racism and discrimination have been rudely awakened following the Black Lives Matter uprisings. In the process, Hamilton has transformed the way he sees himself: from a compliant go-with-the-flow character to an agent of change who is determined to make waves. He has shaped the way others see him, too, going from an inoffensive, if gaffe-prone, socialite focused only on his sport to a politically aware role model conscious of his wider cultural significance. Now, he is about to take on the sport that brought him fame and fortune, with a commission demanding racial diversity and meaningful outreach to underrepresented groups – as well as more racial equality in general.

It's been a long journey for Hamilton, and there have been bumps along the road. 'I'd be in Newcastle, and people would shout, "Go back to your country,"' he says. 'Or in Spain, in 2008, when people painted themselves black and put on wigs and were really mocking my family. And I remember the sport not saying anything about it.'

Even playful attempts to refer to his race felt perilous. After stewards penalised him for two collisions in Monaco in 2011, he was asked: 'Why are you such a magnet for stewards? You obviously feel you are being targeted.' Lewis replied, laughing: 'Maybe it's because I'm black. That's what Ali G says. I don't know.' The *Telegraph* ran a headline: 'Lewis risks disciplinary action after astonishing outburst'.

'It often felt that maybe I didn't speak about [race] in the right way, or wasn't great at explaining it or maybe educated enough to talk about it,' he says. 'Either way, I got a lot of pushback, and it seemed like more hassle than it was worth. So I reverted to just doing my talking on the track.'

If he had anything to say, he would do so privately. He remembers returning from the British Cadet Karting Championship in 1995, aged ten, while singing Queen's 'We Are the Champions' in the camper van with his dad. 'No one saw it. We didn't do it in people's faces. We had so much against us.'

Last year, that attitude changed. Before the Austrian Grand Prix, just a month after George Floyd's murder, Formula One's only Black driver ever donned a Black Lives Matter T-shirt and took the knee. When some drivers refused to follow his lead, he warned them that 'silence is complicit'. In the end, they all wore 'End Racism' T-shirts, and fourteen drivers joined him in the gesture, while six stood behind.

A week later, after he won the Styrian Grand Prix, also in Austria, he raised his fist in a Black power salute. He also called out his competitors on social media: 'I see those of you who are staying silent, some of you [are] the biggest stars yet you stay silent in the midst of injustice,' he wrote. Then he came for Formula One as a whole. 'It's lacking leadership,' he told the *New York Times*. 'It shouldn't be for me to have to call the teams or call the teams out.' At the same race, Formula One, which controls the cameras broadcasting the event, cut away from the moment some of the drivers took the knee, instead showing Red Bull skydivers dropping from the sky.

It was as though a dam broke. 'This wrath of emotions came up, and I couldn't contain myself,' Hamilton says, recalling this profoundly emotional moment in a matter-of-fact way. 'I was in tears. And this stuff came up that I'd suppressed over all these years. And it was so powerful and sad, and also releasing. And I thought, "I can't stay quiet. I need to speak out because there are people experiencing what I'm experiencing, or ten times worse. Or a hundred times worse. And they need me right now." And so when I did speak out, that was me letting the Black community know: "I hear you and I stand with you."'

I get the impression that however much he may have thought about this, he still hasn't spoken about it much. He is not reciting well-rehearsed lines; his words carry the air of a confession.

That sounds like a lot to take on, I suggest, particularly from a standing start. 'I don't see it as a burden,' he replies. 'It was definitely liberating to be able to be open and speak about things. For people to know that there's much more to me than perhaps they realised from watching me on TV. I feel like I was built for this. There's a reason it was suppressed over all that time. And if it happened any sooner, I wouldn't be ready, wouldn't be strong enough to handle it. I wouldn't be able to do my job as well and do both things at the same time. But now I'm equipped with the tools to do so. I look at my niece and nephew. I look at my little cousins. And I think, "How can I make things better for you guys and your friends?"'

While the outrage and activism that followed Floyd's murder gave Hamilton the confidence to speak up, Black Lives Matter did not create his racial consciousness; it emboldened it. He had in the past cited Nelson Mandela, Martin Luther King and his own father as his role models, and listed Bob Marley, Nas and Marvin Gaye among his favourite musicians. (One doubts that Niki Lauda or James Hunt would ever have come up with a similar list.) He was aware his racial difference had meaning. 'Being Black is not a negative,' he said in 2007. 'It's a positive, if anything, because I'm different. In the future that can open doors to different cultures . . . It will show that not only white people can do it . . . It will be good to mean something.' He just hadn't figured out what that meaning was, what to make of it or what to do about it.

Hamilton had already found himself asking why there were so few people of colour on his team (Mercedes revealed last summer that just 3 per cent of its Formula One staff were from ethnic minorities) and receiving unsatisfactory answers. So, in 2019, he worked with the Royal Academy of Engineering to produce some research, with a view to improving the representation of Black people in motor sport. 'We had no idea the whole George Floyd situation would kick in,' he says. The Black Lives Matter uprisings gave the initiative a sense of urgency and broader relevance.

The resulting Hamilton Commission report will be published on 13 July. It embraces a broad agenda, ranging from school exclusions (Lewis himself was excluded after a fellow pupil was attacked and needed hospital treatment, only to be reinstated when it was determined that he had been wrongly identified and was not involved) and anti-racist curricula to actively promoting STEM subjects (science, technology, engineering and mathematics) to students of colour. It will also look at targeted programmes for graduates and those in post-sixteen education from diverse backgrounds, and expanded motor sport apprenticeships. Its board draws from a broad pool of expertise and disciplines, including a Labour MP and a Tory MP, a Formula One grandee, a trade unionist, professors, engineers and equality campaigners.

But for Hamilton, who has been actively involved in the commission's process, the mission is deeply personal. The quest sounds almost religious. 'Over time, I've been trying to figure out my purpose. There's got to be a reason why I'm not only the only Black driver but the one at the front. And it's not just about winning. I won the world championship last year, and in that year everything became visible and I felt that my purpose was shown to me, and now I'm on that journey.'

Last year, as the Black Lives Matter demonstrations were escalating, Ben Carrington, an associate professor of sociology and journalism at USC Annenberg, was allowed to sit in on an informal online gathering of one of the main F1 teams. He tells me that he asked a senior figure in the team what he thought of Hamilton's stance, and was stunned by the response. 'Well, if Lewis is really so committed to that cause, perhaps he should donate all of his salary to it,' the senior figure said, before going on to claim that his team was so non-racial he didn't know how many Black or Asian employees there were because he doesn't 'see race'.

'He seemed to be insinuating that Hamilton's beliefs were not sincere and his personal wealth somehow undermined his stance,' says Carrington, author of *Race, Sport and Politics: The Sporting Black Diaspora*. 'It was such a tone-deaf and arrogant response that it would almost certainly have got that person fired if they were in the NBA or NFL. But it made me realise, "Wow, this is what Hamilton is up against within F1."'

In a sport that is so exclusive, racial discrimination is invariably linked to class. Hamilton's father had to remortgage his house and spend all his and his second wife's savings to get Lewis through just one year of go-karting. He was the lucky one among his peers. 'We had dear friends who threw everything and the sink at it, and today don't have any money,' Hamilton says.

Young Lewis found an advocate in Ron Dennis, then the owner of the McLaren team. It is said that when he was ten, Hamilton, wearing a borrowed silk suit, approached Dennis and told him he wanted to drive for him. Dennis replied, in Lewis's autograph book: 'Try me in nine years.' By thirteen, Hamilton had joined McLaren's young driver programme, and by twenty-two he had made his Formula One debut as a McLaren driver. He went on to win the world championship in his second season, in 2008. Dennis has reportedly referred to Hamilton as his '*My Fair Lady* project' and told Sky News last year: 'Our relationship was very much positioned as surrogate father and son – and I don't think Anthony would have ever been uncomfortable with that.'

Hamilton has called Formula One a 'billionaire boys' club'. 'There's no way that we would make it now if we started from where we started,' he says. He thinks that's one of the things that has driven his success. 'I know how hard it was for my dad just to have fresh tyres at the weekend. It's impacted me heavily. I can't just think, "I deserve to be here." I can't squander this opportunity. I have to grab it with both hands and really dig deep every single time I'm in the car.'

Others have it far easier. A few days after I speak to Hamilton, he comes second in the French Grand Prix. First is Max Verstappen, whose father is former F1 driver Jos; third is Sergio Pérez, whose dad was a driver and agent, and who was sponsored at an early age by the son of billionaire Carlos Slim, formerly the world's richest man. And fifth is Lando Norris, whose dad has a reported fortune of £200 million. The only other driver in the top five with a regular background is Hamilton's Mercedes teammate Valtteri Bottas, whose dad owns a small cleaning company and whose mum is an undertaker.

But Hamilton is not interested primarily in opportunities for racing drivers. 'There's only twenty seats in the drivers' space. That's not so important to me. But there are over 40,000 jobs across motor sports in the UK, and less than 1 per cent are filled by people from Black backgrounds. So there's a lot of opportunity in so many different categories, not just engineering.'

The Hamilton Commission's recommendations are ambitious and logical. They also include asking F1 teams to implement a diversity charter; increasing the number of Black teachers in STEM subjects; a fund to expose excluded students to STEM and motor sport-related activities; and a scholarship programme to encourage Black STEM graduates into specialist motor sport roles. But the world is not short of commissions providing proposals on how to pursue equality in a range of areas. The challenge is making institutions adopt these plans as their own, prioritising and then enforcing them.

'I want this to be about action. I know there's a lot of commissions that perhaps don't get the backing or manage to continue,' Hamilton says. 'But this one has me. And I don't fail at a lot of things.'

Formula One is not for everyone. Some people are compelled by strategic tyre changes, fast straights and tight corners; others are left indifferent by the sight of cars whizzing around endlessly. But Hamilton's dominance speaks for itself. And British sporting figures rarely, if ever, attain this level of international supremacy. So it is curious that he has never enjoyed the full-throated national acclaim that others, who have achieved far less in their fields, have. A YouGov poll in October last year – the year he equalled Schumacher's championship-winning record – found that only 21 per cent of Britons thought he deserved a knighthood, compared with 46 per cent who believed he didn't (he got one in the 2021 New Year honours). In another YouGov poll ranking the most popular sports personalities of all time, he came thirty-seventh, behind Schumacher (ninth) and the late Stirling Moss, who never won a single championship (fifteenth). Why don't people like Hamilton more? 'I'm not living my life to make everyone happy,' he says. 'You can't make everyone happy. People are always going to have their own opinions.'

He concedes that some of this may be down to his numerous, if mostly minor, gaffes: taking a selfie while riding a Harley-Davidson in New Zealand; any number of reckless driving incidents off the track; and the time he directly sprayed a woman on the podium with champagne. Others have revealed a tin ear, such as when he referred to Stevenage as 'the slums', which he retracted immediately, or made jokes about his nephew's princess dress on social media, telling him: 'Boys don't wear princess dresses.'

In 2010, Hamilton fired his dad as his manager. Compared with other celebrity parent/manager splits, this appeared to be relatively civilised and cordial: the inevitable, if painful, disentanglement of work and family that comes with maturity. But it was framed at the time as a callous act of betrayal. The two have since reconciled, and his father is back on the team.

And then there is the challenge of aligning his lifestyle with his pronouncements. Anti-racist messages are easier to dismiss when they come from a tax haven in Monaco, where he lives; statements about climate change from the world leader of a sport that produces so many carbon emissions can also rankle. Lewis has apologised for most of these missteps, adopted veganism, sold his private jet and insisted that his Tommy Hilfiger clothing line is sustainable. He has become a strident voice for improving environmental standards in Formula One.

But criticisms seem to stick to him in a way that they don't to others. 'I haven't done things in a perfect way,' he accepts. 'I was never media-trained. I was just thrown into a room with people. And at the same time, I'm probably a later bloomer, growing into my adulthood, because I'd been this kid protected by my dad for a long time. And suddenly I'm really in a man's world and I'm being asked all these questions. Everything I say is taken literally; all the mistakes are in plain sight.'

This in part explains his recent support for tennis champion Naomi Osaka, after she pulled out of the French Open following a dispute with organisers about her refusal to speak to journalists. He lauded her bravery. 'It's not that I have an opinion about everything,' he says. 'But I know what it's like to be young in sport. I didn't have strong enough shoulders to do what she has done at her age. So I'm proud of her. I wish my young self had me to say, "You're going to be good." I had my dad. But even for him it was all new.'

But there's more to Hamilton's less-favoured status than that. Beyond Formula One fans, he lacks a solid constituency. He is difficult to place. The political voice of anti-racist protest he is nurturing has a long lineage, from Muhammad Ali to Colin Kaepernick. But the influences on his literal voice are difficult to fathom – his accent is a kind of intercontinental, media-enunciated, Home Counties hybrid that defies categorisation. He's a very wealthy, biracial man from a working-class background in an elite sport, from a town with which few Britons have any cultural association. He has character, but he's not a character. We have never seen or heard his like before. He is what the African American TV super-producer Shonda Rhimes, responsible for *Grey's Anatomy*, *Scandal* and *Bridgerton*, refers to in her autobiography, *Year of Yes*, as an FOD – first, only and different. 'When you are an FOD,' she writes, 'you are saddled with that burden of extra responsibility – whether you want it or not. This wasn't just my shot. It was *ours*.'

Watching him in 2007, when he was in serious contention for the championship during his first season, my sports enthusiast friend Kieron Rablah, who was also raised in Stevenage, told me: 'When I see him on TV, I just can't help cheering. I've not watched a Formula One race for ten years. But all I keep thinking when I see him racing is, "He's a Black kid from Stevenage." It's not just that he's made it to that level, which would be pretty amazing in any sport; it's that he's made it in Formula One. If you come from Stevenage, Formula One might as well be polo.'

Feeling comfortable in your own skin, under those conditions, is easier said than done. 'I remember not being able to be myself,' Hamilton says. 'Of not being able to speak the way I want to speak. That's the point of all this inclusivity: including people and not asking them to change in order to fit. I remember feeling that I had to be

Dispatches from the Diaspora

a different shape. The entry point to my sport was a square, and I was like a hexagon, and I thought, "I'm never going to fit through that bloody thing." So I had to morph my way in in order to fit into that world, and then try to get back into the shape I was before.'

Even as Hamilton competes for a record eighth world championship, his sights are set both on the horizon and in the rear-view mirror at his legacy. 'My dream when I was younger was to get to Formula One. Then I thought I would love to emulate Ayrton [Senna]. And then I reached three world championships [Senna's record before he died]. And then I'm like, "Shoot, now what?"

'My dream now is to be a father like my dad one day, but better. Just as he wanted to be like his dad one day, but a better version of his dad. I want to carry on the Hamilton name and make him proud.'

'Is there something you want to tell me, Lewis?' I joke.

'No, no, no, no,' he laughs, baring a big, gap-toothed smile. 'I'm not there yet.' Currently single, he has been linked to many models and singers over the years, from Rita Ora to Nicole Scherzinger.

But this moment is as much about how he feels about himself as his relationship with others. There is no going back for Hamilton now. As John Carlos, who famously raised his fist while on the podium at the 1968 Olympics in Mexico City (see p. 252), told me, his first thought on doing the Black power salute was: 'The shackles have been broken.' But as political activist Angela Davis also told me (p. 232), there is more to freedom than just the breaking of chains. Isolated in his sport, nurturing his voice in public even as he continues to do his talking on the track, the path forward promises to be as personally fulfilling as it is politically perilous.

'We'll see where we can go,' he says breezily. 'As the years pass, you realise that success is a wonderful thing. But it feels relatively short-lived. And I don't just want to be remembered as a driver, because I care about so many more different things.'

Express Yourself

5

ME,
MYSELF,
I

Personal essays on experiences
that shaped my life and my thinking

Black bloke

The first time I came to the US to work, being Black and British confused everyone – including, at times, myself.
       Washington Post, 6 October 1996, Washington

Before I came to America from England three months ago, I asked an American journalist in London what kind of reaction to expect. 'Well, when they hear an English accent, Americans usually add about twenty points to your IQ. But when they see a Black face, they usually don't,' he said. 'You'll be an anomaly.'

Recalling that the authors of the book *The Bell Curve* had claimed that Black people have an IQ fifteen points lower than whites, I was heartened to think that even in the eyes of the most hardened racist I would still come out at least five points ahead.

After three months here I am left wondering whether 'anomaly' quite covers the mixture of bemusement, amazement and curiosity I have encountered since I arrived. Often people just think I am showing off. This is especially the case with African Americans. All I have to do is open my mouth, and they prime themselves to ask, 'Who are you trying to impress with that accent?' They don't actually say anything. Their thoughts are revealed in the downward trajectory of the eyebrows and the curl of the lip.

Once I say I'm English, the eyebrows go back up and the lips uncurl. Now they are in shock. At times I have had to literally give the people I have met here a couple of minutes to compose themselves. 'I had no idea,' said a white woman near Baton Rouge, Louisiana, in a tone my grandmother might use if I came out.

Then there was the woman in the bank who called her colleagues over to hear my accent. 'Listen to this, listen to this,' she said. 'Go on, say something,' she demanded, as though I was a circus marmoset.

Most people here who have not travelled much abroad seem astounded to learn that Black people exist outside of America and Africa at all. Their image of England is what they see on television (*Fawlty Towers* and *Upstairs, Downstairs*) and what they read in the papers (Lady Di and mad cow disease). Whether that is the image that England wants to sell or the one that America wants to buy is not quite clear – my guess is that it's a mixture of both – but either way, it doesn't leave much room for Black people.

Once I have told someone I am English, they are generally pre-pared to take me at my word, which is more than can be said about people I meet back home, where a typical conversation goes some-thing like this:

'Where are you from?'

'London.'

'Well, where were you born?'

'London.'

'Well, before then?'

'There was no "before then"!'

'Well, where are your parents from?'

'Barbados.'

'Oh, so you're from Barbados.'

'No, I'm from London.'

Although there have been Blacks in Britain for centuries, they only arrived there in sizeable numbers after the Second World War. During the 1950s and 1960s, they came from Africa and the Caribbean – alongside those from the Indian subcontinent – to do the sorts of jobs that the indigenous white population wasn't eager to do.

My parents came to England from Barbados in the early 1960s, and I was born there. Like many immigrants, they planned to stay only for a few years, work hard, earn some money and then return home. But like many immigrants, they ended up staying, starting a family and building a life there. Blacks now make up about 3 per cent of the British population.

Britain's sense of national identity is still trying to catch up. But in the meantime, questions like 'Where are you from?' are often interpreted to mean, 'Please tell me you are not from here.'

Which is why meeting so many Americans with names like Gugliotta, Biskupic and Shapiro is so refreshing. Almost everybody here is originally from somewhere else. Even the white people. And most people lay claim to another identity – Italian American, Irish American, Hungarian American – which qualifies their American identity but does not necessarily undermine it.

The same is true for Black Briton. They are two separate words relating to two very distinct and often conflicting identities. If Black people in Britain define themselves as British at all – I was seventeen before I would admit it publicly – then they will usually put 'Black' in front of it to show that they do not see themselves as fully British and are not always accepted as such.

At the NAACP's annual convention, which I recently attended in Charlotte, North Carolina, there seemed to be only three higher authorities which the speakers called upon: God, the Constitution and the American flag. The NAACP may represent the 'old school' of African American politics, but throughout my time here I have yet to meet an African American who does not place some faith in these common reference points. Britain, in contrast, doesn't have a written constitution, is far less religious, and you wouldn't get a Union Jack within five miles of a political meeting full of Black people, regardless of how moderate the organisation may be.

This may change in time. But for now the difference seems stark. Black Americans who feel aggrieved can, and often do, look to the symbolism of their national flag as a form of redress. Black Britons see their flag not as a possible solution but as part of the problem.

For Americans, this seems to breed a kind of confidence that allows a more open discussion of race issues than in my country. During my interview for the fellowship at the *Washington Post* that brought me here, I was asked what problems I faced as a Black journalist in Britain. An Englishman would never ask that sort of question. It would be considered . . . well, rude.

I was amazed, on a recent day trip to Harpers Ferry, West Virginia, to see an all-white group of cub scouts learning all about the legacy of Frederick Douglass and how John Brown fought alongside Black abolitionists. White kids learning about Black history on a day out during the summer holidays – at the time I felt like I had died and gone to heaven.

Upon reflection, it was much more like purgatory. I know that one of the reasons that Americans discuss race so much is because there is so much to talk about. Both the present – affirmative action, the demise of the inner cities, poverty, church burnings – and the past – civil rights, slavery, segregation – offer no end of subjects that can and should be debated. Nevertheless, in England, which has similar but nowhere near as acute social problems affecting the Black community, race ranks alongside sex, politics and religion as a topic not to be brought up in polite conversation. At my newspaper in London, I was once described to someone as 'the short, stocky guy with an earring', even though I am one of only half a dozen Black journalists in the building.

Here, I look local and sound foreign – an object of intrigue in public places. At home I look foreign and sound local – and everybody tries hard not to notice. To say one is better or worse than the other would be too simplistic. The bottom line is that I will soon return to a racism I understand.

But I will miss those extra twenty IQ points for my accent.

Borders of hate

Travelling through Europe, where fascism had returned as a mainstream ideology, I met virulent racism in a continent I was supposed to claim as my own.

Guardian, 17 June 1998, Nice

It was a clear, sunny day in the Dordogne when Richard came into my room with tears in his eyes and a tent under his arm. We had met in England in the spring, when he had come over on a school exchange. When he was leaving, he invited me back to France to stay with him in the summer. I had been there just three days when he stood at the door, his eyes red and swollen, to say there was a 'big problem'.

His father had told him he could not bear having a Black person in the house. He set out to visit a friend and said he wanted me gone by the time he came back. 'Tell me your thinks,' said Richard, whose proficiency in English was pretty much confined to swear words I had taught him. By this time, I had already started frantically packing my rucksack. I didn't know what to say.

'I think we'd better go,' I said, and we trudged the two miles to the campsite just out of town in pitiful silence and glorious sunshine.

I was fifteen years old, and it was 1984. Wham! were in the charts, the miners were on strike and a little-known party of the French hard right called the Front National had just won 11 per cent of the vote in the European elections. Commentators claimed it was a freak occurrence, but within a few years their success was replicated across the continent. In 1989, Jorg Haider, leader of the right-wing Austrian Freedom Party, was elected provincial governor of Carinthia; in 1993, the Republikaner Party made sweeping gains in Germany, and the largest party in the European city of culture,

Antwerp, was the far-right Vlaams Blok; by 1994, Italy had fascists in the cabinet.

And each time I went back to mainland Europe things seemed to get worse. I was beaten up by the police in a Paris metro in 1991; a year earlier, I had stood with my brother in a hotel reception in Barcelona and watched two white tourists get the room we had just been told was not available; a few years later, I was threatened with being thrown overboard by a Flemish ferry worker for putting my feet on the chairs during an overnight crossing. A range of petty indignities and personal violations that could have happened in Britain – but there is one major difference: Britain does not have fascists sitting in government. Here, the debate on race no longer revolves around repatriation. The battle over Black people's right to stay in this country has largely been won. In many countries on the continent it is still being fought and, in most places, lost.

Today, five countries in the European Union – Austria, Italy, France, Belgium and Denmark – have parties of the hard right which enjoy more than 5 per cent of the popular vote. In three – Austria, Italy and France – they enjoy as much or more of the vote as the Liberal Democrats get in Britain. In many others, like Germany, they make erratic and dramatic appearances at regional level. As we approach the twenty-first century, fascism has reinvented itself as a mainstream ideology in European politics. In the words of the Front National's number two, Bruno Mégret, earlier this year: 'We have brought off a great strategic victory. We are no longer demonised.'

But that is not the only thing that has changed on the continent since 1984. When I was thrown out of Richard's house, I took a black hardback British passport with me. Now my passport is purple, flimsy and says 'European Community' on it. Richard's father is now my fellow citizen in a supranational project extending from Lapland to Lisbon. This is supposed to be my continent as much as his. But like many Britons (albeit for different reasons), I am sceptical.

Dispatches from the Diaspora

The passport controller in the glass box at Marseille airport shares my suspicions. She flicks backwards and forwards through my passport several times before asking me to stand to one side while she goes to have a word with her colleagues.

I fear it may be my picture. Not just the fact that it has a Black face on it, although that is certain to confuse. But because it has been tampered with. When passing through Rome airport a month earlier, I asked an official for directions to my gate. He asked me for my passport, and I handed it to him. He started trying to put his fingers underneath the laminate with my photograph in it. I went to snatch it back and told him to leave it alone. He patted his gun, told me to 'Calm down,' and took it to the police. I only managed to get it back and make it to my flight with the help of an Air Afrique representative. 'They are fifty years behind, these people. I am so sorry,' he said.

Back at Marseille airport, the passport controller comes back and asks me if I have a return ticket.

'Yes,' I say.

'Can I see it?' she asks.

'I don't need a return ticket to come into France,' I say.

She sighs a very weary sigh. Now I am being unreasonable. I have a ticket but I won't show her it. I don't see why I should. But by this time six white European citizens have gone through in another queue. Even two Filipinos in the 'non-EU citizens' queue have beaten me to the baggage carousel. I show her my ticket. She studies it for a moment and then waves me through.

There is a cloying, heavy heat in Provence. This is France's deep south, an area where racial conflict stretches back over generations. There are the *pieds noirs*, French settlers in Algeria who were kicked out during the war of independence; the *militants de FLN*, who fought for the liberation movement the FLN; and the *harkis*, Algerians who fought for the French against their compatriots and are now despised by both sides.

'Some of the older people are still at war here,' says Thierry Curbelie, a local anti-racism campaigner. This is the Front National's heartland. Just a few miles away from the airport is Vitrolles, the small town which elected a Front National mayor – one of four in the area – in February 1997. Since Catherine Mégret, the wife of Bruno, was elected, the town hall has been busy. It gave a 'baby bonus' to 'French parents' to encourage them to outbreed immigrants; only one payment was made before a court ruled the payments illegal, and when the family found out what it was for, they returned the money. It has shut down a local municipal-sponsored youth club because it refused to play 'traditional' French music. And it has changed many of the street names in order to 'reaffirm Vitrolles' Provençal and French identity'.

'[Bruno] Mégret is using Vitrolles as a testing ground,' says Phillipe Lamotte of the anti-fascist organisation Ras l'Front. 'It is like a laboratory for his policies to show how he would run the country.'

Vitrolles is a new town born from an 'industrial zone' that drew the working-class overspill from Marseille and Paris. Soon what was a small village became surrounded by low-cost housing and soulless shopping malls. Thirty years, and a few recessions, later, it has not aged well – a fraying, anodyne, municipal monument to an architectural dark age.

This is the cornerstone of European fascism's newly expanded base. Not the dilapidated housing estates of the major towns with high crime and low employment – though there is significant support for them there, too – nor big cities where there are large numbers of immigrants, but the lower middle classes and small traders on the urban peripheries: people who do not have much and are afraid they might lose it, who don't know any foreigners and don't want to.

Since the Front National came to power, the atmosphere in the town has changed, says Lamotte. 'There is a degree of mistrust now among people. Because most of the time you could be sitting next to someone who voted for the FN and not really know it. And the FN made great play of the crime issue, so now people think they cannot go out in the evening. The thing is, they never did go out in the evening before. But now they are afraid.'

We are sitting in Place de Provence, which was, until recently, Place Mandela. Around the corner is the town hall, where they have pulled down the EU flag and replaced it with one of pre-revolutionary Provence. 'Everything they do is symbolic. But symbols have meanings. They give people the confidence to say things they would have kept to themselves before. They can make the unacceptable commonplace,' says Martine Sintas, a representative of the Human Rights League.

Nowhere is this more clear than in the local *lycée*, where the headteacher received Ms Mégret at a school open day with a pomp previously unheard of for a visiting local dignitary, prompting demonstrations by both staff and students and the headteacher's suspension.

A few months later, the Touzaline family returned to Vitrolles, where they had lived many years before, from rural Provence. Sofia, a bright seventeen-year-old with sparkling wide eyes, went to the school to register for her final year so that she could sit her baccalaureate. It should have been a formality. The school was legally obliged to accept her. 'I went in and told the headmistress's secretary that I wanted to sign up for the final year. She didn't say anything for a while and then she looked up, stared at me for a moment and said, "You think you can go into the final year with a face like that?"

'I didn't move. Then she just carried on doing what she was doing. A few moments later, she looked up and said, "Are you still here?"'

She wouldn't allow Sofia to register and told her to come back in September. Sofia asked what would happen if there were no places left in September. 'That's your problem,' the secretary said. When Sofia's mother, Lila, tried to register Sofia's twin brothers, she had the same problem. Their father took time off work to see the headteacher and was told, 'If that is what my secretary said, then I support her all the way.'

They complained to the local authorities and got nowhere. The matter is now at appeal, but whatever the outcome, it will be too late for Sofia. So the young woman who was born in France, who lives five minutes from her local school, has to commute three hours a day to her old school. Her brothers, who were also refused, travel for two and a half hours. If there are traffic jams or strikes, they miss their classes.

'It was the first time something like that had happened to me so directly,' says Sofia, who wants to study international business. 'When I lived in the country, it was like living in a cocoon. I was the only Arab in my class. There were only three in my school. You got funny looks there, but it stopped at looks. It will be the same thing when I leave school. When they see my name, they will just throw my application in the bin.'

Now the family are trying to move again. 'When we lived here before, it was a nice town. Smaller and more friendly. Now . . . now it's awful, and with the fascists in the town hall it's not going to get any better,' says Lila.

I took the train from Marseille along the rocky facades of the Côte d'Azur, around the thigh-high portion of Italy's boot on the Ligurian Sea, and then inland to Milan.

If Vitrolles provides a blueprint for the kind of town the fascists are taking, then Italy provides the model for how they have come to take them. The country's fascist party, the MSI (Italian Social Movement), has undergone the kind of political makeover that makes New Labour look old-fashioned. In an attempt to cast off the fascist shadows, it merged into a wider coalition of right-wingers that called itself the National Alliance. Its leader, Gianfranco Fini, is in favour of a European currency, believes the country should accept Kurdish asylum seekers and wants to make a pilgrimage of remorse to Israel.

By 1994, he had three seats in the cabinet and was seen as the standard-bearer of the right. Fini started marketing himself as a 'post-fascist'. The MSI MP, and granddaughter of Mussolini, Alessandra Mussolini was not so sure about the 'post-': 'If he had lived today, my grandfather would have done what Fini is doing.' Italy's fascists did make a move to the political centre, but Italian society met them halfway. When it comes to parties championing anti-immigration policies, they have the National Alliance and the Milan-based Northern League, far more vociferous on the race issue, to choose from.

When a Black woman was chosen as Miss Italy two years ago, officials complained that she was 'unrepresentative of Italian beauty', and the press crowned her 'Miss Discord'. When Black British foot-baller Paul Ince ironically applauded a crowd hurling racist insults in Cremona, he was given a yellow card.

The success of Italy's fascists is all the more remarkable, given that it remains a nation of emigrants, exporting more labour to other EU countries than it imports from the rest of the world put together.

The streets of Milan seem almost normal: a few mixed-race couples walk unselfconsciously hand in hand; in the nightclubs they are danc-ing to everything from garage to Motown; and on the corner of Via Georgio and Corso Buenos Aires an Asian man is selling pictures of Bob Marley and Snoop Doggy Dogg, under posters calling on people to vote for the National Alliance.

The most visible sign of non-white life in the town is the army of street sellers offering everything from key rings to fake designer watches. Outside the cathedral, the city's main tourist attraction, a tall, sleek Senegalese man the colour of five past midnight, has an arm full of fake Yves Saint Laurent bags, which arrived on a train from Naples. On a good day he can make £80. On a bad day, nothing. Most days are pretty bad. 'Maybe I sell one or two bags. Not many, but enough to live,' he says.

But his living costs are few. For the past eighteen months he has been staying with three other Senegalese men in one room on the outskirts of town. He often thinks of returning to Senegal but fears he may never have the chance to come back to Europe again. Trouble with the police is an occupational hazard, but otherwise, he says, he has no problems. 'Sometimes people shout things, and I know some friends who had to leave their goods and run when they were chased by Italian men. But generally it is not a problem.' He does not go out at night. He does not know any Italians.

That night, I went in search of food and ended up at a restaurant called Al Graticiello, on Via Pisani. The woman at the door would not let me in. 'We are full,' she said.

She was lying. I have been refused service at far swankier places than the Al Graticiello and I know the drill. When they are booked up, they will scan the diary for a space, ask you to wait for an impossible length of time, make a face and then say sorry. When there is a colour bar, they will just say, 'We are full,' and trust that you will take the hint. I peered around the corner at the empty dining hall. 'It doesn't look very full,' I said.

'We are only serving in the garden,' she said.

'Can I have a look in the garden then?' I asked.

'I told you, we are full,' she said, and testily moved from behind her desk, as if to prevent my entrance.

'I know but I don't believe you,' I said, and walked away.

It took around six hours to get from Milan to Innsbruck, in Austria. The train climbed through the mountains of the South Tyrol, where the houses turn from Romance to Germanic, while blankets of thick cloud descended ever lower over hills of pines and, as we drew closer, turned to rain. Border guards dropped by on the way. I was the only Black person in the carriage and the only person whose passport they were interested in. Two of them, soon to be aided by a third, studied

Dispatches from the Diaspora

it with a mixture of curiosity and disbelief, and then handed it back while I tried to look bored. Between these two countries, both covered by the Schengen accord, these controls should be a thing of the past. But, when it comes to race, a Europe without borders clearly has its limits.

Even in the rain Innsbruck is a town fit for a chocolate box, squeezed between the northern chain of the Alps and the Tuxer mountain range to the south. Quite how Sonny (not his real name), a thirty-four-year-old Ghanaian, got there is a long story that starts in the Libyan desert.

Sonny, who joined the Ghanaian army at the age of twelve, was part of a battalion seconded to the Libyan government to fight the Chadians. He ran away, first to Malta, where he bought a Kenyan passport, then to Yugoslavia and finally to Hungary. There, he paid a local man $200 to smuggle him, along with around fifty Bangladeshis and Pakistanis, over the Austrian border. They were caught by the border police. He ripped up his forged passport so they would have no idea where he came from. Soon afterwards, he escaped. He then claimed, and was granted, political asylum in Austria.

'I couldn't do it now because the rules are too strict, but I couldn't go back to Ghana after I had left the army,' he says. When he first arrived in Austria, things were bad. 'People used to shout at me in the street – "Hey, nigger" . . . "Hey, monkey man" – and there were always problems with the police. They still shout sometimes, and occasionally Austrian men try to start something. But I can't do anything because if there was a fight, I would be blamed, and once you are in trouble with the police, they can expel you. So I only say something when little children shout at me.'

Today, he works on a building site with Turks and Czechs and lives a bachelor's life – a West African version of *Auf Wiedersehen, Pet*, chasing women, drinking beer with his friends from Togo and sending money home to his family. He has been in Austria ten years but can vote only in local elections.

Sonny and his workmates represent both the European right's greatest ammunition and its greatest paradox. He is an economic migrant, ostensibly taking jobs from unemployed Austrians. But few Austrians want the sort of casualised, low-skilled, low-paid work he has. He recognises that the Austrian economy needs him as much as he needs it: 'Austrians wouldn't do my work. It is too dirty and the pay is too bad. It is okay for me because I have no family here, but even when there is unemployment, they wouldn't do it.'

From Innsbruck to Munich is commuting distance, two hours past the mountain tops and into the hilly, green expanses of Bavaria. Ali, who was born in the region, feels about as German as Sonny does Austrian. 'My parents came here in the 1960s, and I've been here all my life. But here, if you are born to immigrants, you will die an immigrant. It doesn't matter if you've read Goethe, wear lederhosen and do a Bavarian dance, they'll still treat you like an immigrant.'

Germany has one of the most prohibitive citizenship laws in Europe, based on the principle that only those with 'German blood' have an automatic right to citizenship. Those born there have faced huge obstacles to gaining their rights. 'Immigration law is one of the biggest problems in the country,' says Dr Chong Suk Kang of Munich's equivalent of the Community Relations Council. 'There is a whole generation of young people who were born here and who have never even been to Turkey or Morocco or wherever but who have no stake in this society.'

The most striking example of the absurdity of this came at the end of April, when the German authorities ordered the deportation of a thirteen-year-old persistent offender in Munich 'back' to Turkey, along with his parents, who had been in Germany for thirty years, even though he was born in Germany. The teenager was said to represent a 'massive risk to public security and order'.

The announcement was made within a week of the Munich-based DVU Party netting the best result for a party of the extreme right since the war – a graphic example of how even when fascists do not win elections they act as arsenic in the water supply of a political culture, polluting everything it touches as established parties seek to establish their 'anti-immigrant' credentials.

During the two days I was in Munich, I was asked twice for my papers while walking through the underground of the main station at night. Both times I said that I was English and did not have my passport, then baffled them by offering an American driver's licence and my union card. Both times they grunted and let me go.

Ali Habba Jaffna was not so lucky. Jaffna, an asylum seeker who escaped from Iraq ten months ago, was on his way to the mosque with a friend a few months ago when they were stopped by two plain-clothes policemen (who did not identify themselves) at gunpoint. They grabbed his arm and thrust it behind his back, and then pushed him against the wall. It was eight-thirty in the morning, in the middle of the street. He asked what he had done. He was told not to move and not to speak.

Two police cars came up, and uniformed policemen took over. They forced the two men into the car, took them to the police station and told them to strip off. Jaffna stripped to his underpants and said that for cultural reasons he could not stand completely naked in front of his friend. After a long argument, the police took him into a separate room and then forced him to bend over so they could search his anus.

'I kept asking why. I kept asking, "What have I done?" But they kept telling me to shut up,' he says.

Sitting in the Burger King in the main station, he describes the incident with a mixture of resignation and disbelief at how he finally bent over so they could search him. I knew how he felt. After more than a week of petty harassment, I was worn out. The defence I had put up in Marseille airport had been whittled down to petulant sighs and irritated compliance. Like Jaffna, I soon learned to bend before I broke.

Jaffna's is the kind of story that doesn't even make the papers here. Like shootings in America or bribery in Nigeria, it is an abnormal fact of life. 'I came here from Iraq to get away from police actions like this. I thought I would be safe in Europe. I thought that here there was democracy and human rights.'

I left Munich and returned to Marseille by train the way I had come. I stopped in Nice en route and met an English football supporter in a bar. The conversation skipped, under his guidance, from England's chances against Tunisia to Arabs in France to Blacks in Britain. 'I live in Southall, and it's sweet. Some of them can be a bit pushy, you know, wanting special favours, bringing over their families and all that, but mostly it's all right,' he said. 'I think the asylum seekers are taking the piss, though . . . I think it's time we looked after ourselves for once.'

I was on my way back to a racism that I at least understood.

Farewell to America

After twelve years as the Guardian*'s US correspondent, I left the US during a period of protracted racial conflict and returned to Britain.*

Guardian, 1 July 2015, Chicago

For the past couple of years the summers, like hurricanes, have had names. Not single names like Katrina or Floyd, but full names like Trayvon Martin or Michael Brown. Like hurricanes, their arrival was both predictable and predicted, and yet somehow, when they landed, the effect was still shocking.

We do not yet know the name that will be attached to this particular season. He is still out there, playing *Call of Duty*, finding a way to feed his family or working to pay off his student loans. He (and it probably will be a he) has no idea that his days are numbered; and we have no idea what the number of those days will be.

The precise alchemy that makes one particular death politically totemic while others go unmourned beyond their families and communities is not quite clear. Video helps, but is not essential. Some footage of cops rolling up like death squads and effectively executing people who posed no real threat has barely pricked the popular imagination. When the authorities fail to heed a community's outrage or substantively investigate, let alone discipline, the police, the situation can become explosive. An underlying, ongoing tension between the authorities and those being policed has been a factor in some cases. So we do not know quite why his death will capture the political imagination in a way that others will not.

But we do know, with gruesome certainty, that his number will come up – that one day he will be slain in cold blood by a policeman (once again, it will probably be a man) who is supposed to protect him and his community. We know this because it is statistically inevitable and has historical precedent. We know this because we have seen it happen again and again. We know this because this is not just how America works; it is how America was built. Like a hurricane, we know it is coming – we just do not know yet where or when or how much damage it will do.

Summer is riot season. It's when Watts, Newark and Detroit erupted in violence in the 1960s, sparked by callous policing. It's when school is out, pool parties are on and domestic life, particularly in urban centres, is turned inside out: from the living room to the stoop, from the couch to the street. It's when tempers get short and resentments bubble up like molten asphalt. It's when, to paraphrase Langston Hughes, deferred dreams explode.

This is not my desire; it is my prediction. You can feel it building with every new Facebook post, viral video and Twitter storm. You can hear it from conversations with strangers in post offices, liquor stores and coffee shops. It is an unpleasant prediction to make because, ultimately, these riots highlight a problem they cannot, in themselves, solve; and it is an easy one to make because, as one bystander in Baltimore put it when disturbances flared there earlier this year: 'You can only put so much into a pressure cooker before it pop.'

This is the summer I will leave America, after twelve years as a foreign correspondent, and return to London. My decision to come back to Britain was prompted by banal, personal factors that have nothing to do with current events; if my aim was to escape aggressive policing and racial disadvantage, I would not be heading to Hackney.

But while the events of the last few years did not prompt the decision to come back, they do make me relieved that the decision had already been made. It is why I have not once had second thoughts. If I had to pick a summer to leave, this would be the one. Another season of Black parents grieving, police chiefs explaining and clueless anchors opining. Another season when America has to be reminded that Black lives matter because Black deaths at the hands of the state have been accepted as routine for so long. A summer ripe for rage.

I arrived in New York just a few months before the Iraq War. Americans seemed either angry at the rest of the world, angry at each other, or both. The top five books on the *New York Times* bestseller list the month I started were *Bush at War* (Bob Woodward's hagiographic account of George W. Bush's post-9/11 White House); *The Right Man* (Bush's former speechwriter relives his first year in the White House); *Portrait of a Killer* (Patricia Cornwell on Jack the Ripper); *The Savage Nation* (a right-wing radio talk-show host saves America from 'the liberal assault on our borders, language and culture'); and *Leadership* (Republican former New York mayor Rudolph Giuliani's post-9/11 victory lap).

There has barely been a quiet moment since. First there was the jingoism of the Iraq War, then the re-election of George W. Bush in 2004, Hurricane Katrina, disillusionment with the Iraq War, the 'Minutemen' anti-immigration vigilantes, the huge, pro-immigrant *¡Sí se puede!* protests, Barack Obama, Sarah Palin, the economic crash, Occupy Wall Street, the Tea Party, Obama's re-election and the current rise in anti-racist activism. Being a foreigner made all these phenomena intriguing. Politically and morally, I picked sides. But when reporting, it was more like anthropology. I saw it as my mission to try and understand the US: why did poor white people vote against their economic interests? How did the descendants of immigrants become xenophobic? Why were people disappointed in Obama, when he had promised so little? The search for the answers was illuminating, even when I never found them or didn't like them.

But the cultural distance I enjoyed as a Briton in a foreign country felt like a blended veneer of invincibility and invisibility. I thought of myself less as a participant than an onlooker. While reporting from rural Mississippi in 2003, I stopped to ask directions at the house of an old white couple, and they threatened to shoot me. I thought this was funny. I got back into my car sharpish and drove off – but I never once thought they would actually shoot me. How crazy would that be? When I got home, I told my wife and brother-in-law, who are African American. Their parents grew up in the South under segregation; even today, my mother-in-law wouldn't stop her car in Mississippi for anything but petrol. They didn't think it was funny at all: what on earth did I think I was doing, stopping to ask old white folk in rural Mississippi for directions?

Yet, somewhere along the way, I became invested. That was partly about time: as I came to know people – rather than just interviewing them – I came to relate to the issues more intimately. When someone close to you struggles with chronic pain because they have no healthcare, has their kitchen window pierced by gunfire or cannot pay a visit to their home country because they are undocumented, your relationship to issues like health reform, gun control or immigration is transformed. Not because your views change but because knowing and understanding something simply do not provide the same intensity as having it in your life.

But my investment was primarily about circumstances. On the weekend in 2007 that Barack Obama declared his presidential candidacy, our son was born. Six years later, we had a daughter. For the most part I have kept my English accent. But my language relating to children is reflexively American: diapers, strollers, pacifiers, recess, candy and long pants. I have only ever been a parent here – a role for which my own upbringing in England provides no real reference point. One summer evening, a couple of years after we moved to Chicago, our daughter was struggling to settle down, and so my wife decided to take a short walk to the local supermarket to bob her to sleep in the carrier. On the way back there was shooting in the street, and she had to seek shelter in a local barbershop. When the snow finally melted this year, one discarded gun was found in the alley behind our local park and another showed up in the alley behind my son's school. My days of being an onlooker were over. I was dealing with day-care, summer camps, schools, doctor's visits, parks and other parents. The day we brought my son home, an article in the *New York Times* pointed out that in America 'a black male who drops out of high school is 60 times more likely to find himself in prison than one with a bachelor's degree'. Previously, I'd have found that interesting and troubling. Now, it was personal. I had skin in the game. Black skin in a game where the odds are stacked against it.

Obama's ascent, I was told by many, and frequently during his campaign, would change these odds. Whenever I asked, 'How?' no one could say exactly. But his very presence, they insisted, would provide a marker for my son and all who look like him. I never believed that. First of all, one person cannot undo centuries of discrimination, no matter how much nominal power they have. Second, given the institutions into which Obama would be embedded – namely the Democratic Party and the presidency – there would only ever be so much he could or would do. He was aspiring to sit atop a system awash with corporate donations, in which congressional seats are openly gerrymandered and 41 per cent of the upper chamber can block almost anything. He was the most progressive viable candidate for the presidency, which says a great deal, given the alternatives, but means very little, given what would be needed to significantly shift the dial on such issues as race and inequality.

Pointing this out amid the hoopla of his candidacy made you sound like Eeyore. I was delighted when he won. But somehow I could never be quite as delighted as some people felt I should have been. When Obama beat Hillary Clinton in the South Carolina Democratic primary – in the first Southern state to secede from the union, which sparked the civil war, where the Confederate flag still flies above the state capitol and a white supremacist recently gunned down nine parishioners at a Black church – the crowds chanted, 'Race doesn't matter.' (An odd rallying cry, since it was precisely because he was a Black candidate that they were shouting it; it's not like Hillary's crowd would have shouted the same thing if she had won.)

The symbolic advantages of Obama's election were clear. For two years I pushed my son around in his stroller; we were surrounded by pictures of a Black man framed by the words 'Hope' and 'Change'. A year or so after Obama took office, my son had a play date with a four-year-old white friend, who looked up from his Thomas the Tank Engine and told my son, 'You're Black.' It was a reasonable thing for a child of that age to point out – he was noticing difference, not race. But when my son looked at me for a cue, I now had a new arrow in my quiver to deflect any potential awkwardness. 'That's right,' I said. 'Just like the president.'

But the substantial benefits were elusive. Obama inherited an economic crisis that hurt African Americans more than any other community. The discrepancy between Black and white employment and wealth grew during his first few years and has barely narrowed since. In 2010, I used this anecdote in a column by way of pointing out the limited symbolic value of having a Black president. 'True, it is something,' I wrote. 'But when Thomas is safely back in the station and the moment is over, it is not very much. Because for all the white noise emanating from the Tea Party movement, it has been black Americans who have suffered most since Obama took office. Over the last 14 months the gap between my son's life chances and his friend's have been widening.'

This last statement was as undeniably true as it was apparently controversial. I had not claimed that my son was likely to do badly, simply that his odds for success were far worse than the kid he was playing with, and that they were further deteriorating. A study in 2014 found that a Black college student has the same chances of getting a job as a white high-school dropout. 'As the recession has dragged on,' the *New York Times* pointed out just a couple of months before my son's play date, the disparity between Black and white unemployment 'has been even more pronounced for those with college degrees, compared with those without. Education, it seems, does not level the playing field – in fact, it appears to have made it more uneven.' But insisting that racism would have a material effect on my son's life ruffled some readers' feathers.

'Nonsense,' wrote one commenter. 'Your middle-class status means his future will have more in common with his white friends than any poor black kid.' Another – a *Guardian* contributor, no less – also chimed in: 'For you to claim shared victimhood on skin colour alone is highly disingenuous. Your son is highly likely to do OK, to say the least. He has most of the advantages in the world.'

Such responses betrayed complete ignorance about the lived experience of race in a country as segregated as the US. Class does makes a big difference, of course – this is America. We have healthcare, jobs, university educations and a car; we live in a community with reasonable schools, supermarkets and restaurants. In short, we have resources, and therefore we have options.

We do not, however, have the option to not be Black. And in this time and this place that is no minor factor. That is not 'claiming shared victimhood'; it is recognising a fact of life. Class offers a range of privileges, but it is not a sealant that protects you from everything else. If it was, rich women would never get raped, and wealthy gay couples could marry all around the world.

To even try to have the kind of gilded Black life to which these detractors alluded, we would have to do far more than just revel in our bank accounts and leverage our cultural capital. We would have to live in an area with few other Black people, since Black neighbourhoods are policed with insufficient respect for life or liberty; send our children to a school with few other Black students, since majority-Black schools are underfunded; tell them not to wear anything that would associate them with Black culture, since doing so would make them more vulnerable to profiling; tell them not to mix with other Black children, since they are likely to live in the very areas and go to the very schools from which we would be trying to escape; and not let the children go out after dark, since being young and Black after sunset makes the police suspect that you have done or are about to do something.

The list could go on. None of this self-loathing behaviour would provide any guarantees, of course. Racism does what it says on the packet: it discriminates against people on the grounds of race. It can be as arbitrary in its choice of victim as it is systemic in its execution. And while it never works alone (but in concert with class, gender and a host of other rogue characters), it can operate independently. No one is going to be checking my bank account or professional status when they are looking at my kids.

Trayvon Martin was walking through a gated community when George Zimmerman pegged him for a thug and shot him dead. Clementa Pinckney, a South Carolina state senator, was in one of Charleston's most impressive churches when Dylann Roof murdered him and eight others.

I have not only never met an African American who thought they could buy themselves the advantages of a white American; I have yet to meet one who thinks they can even buy themselves out of the disadvantages of being Black. All you can do is limit the odds. And when one in three Black boys born in 2001 is destined for the prison system, those odds are pretty bad. Having a Black man in the White House has not changed that.

Most days, the park closest to us looks like *Sesame Street*. White, Black and Vietnamese American kids climbing, swinging and sliding. Occasionally, particularly late on weekday afternoons, teenagers show up. Like adolescents the Western world over, they are bored, broke, horny and lost. They don't want to stay at home but can't afford to be anywhere that costs money, and so they come to the public space most approximate to their needs, where they squeeze into swings that are meant for smaller kids and joke, flirt and banter. Very occasionally they swear and get a little rowdy – but nothing that an

Dispatches from the Diaspora

adult could not deal with by simply asking them to keep the language down because there are little kids around. Oh, and in this park the teenagers are usually Black.

Their presence certainly changes the mood. But the only time it ever really gets tense is when the police come. The better police chat with them; the worse ones interrogate them. Either way, the presence of armed, uniformed people in this children's space is both unsettling and unnecessary. The smaller kids and those new to the park imagine something seriously wrong must have happened for the police to be there; the older ones (by which I mean those aged seven and over) and those who are already familiar with the drill just shrug: 'The cops are in our park again.' It is difficult to tell which response is worse.

Once, when some adolescents were hanging out relatively quietly one afternoon, I struck up a conversation with a white woman. Her son was roughly the same age as mine, we both lived nearby and neither of our kids would have to cross a road to get to the park. We were discussing at what age we thought it would be appropriate to let our boys come by themselves. 'The thing is, you just don't know if it's going to be quiet or if the junior gangbangers are going to be hanging around,' she said, gesturing to the youths on the swings.

I was stunned. Whenever I have written about police killings, at least one reader reminds me that Black people are most likely to be killed by Black people. This is both true and irrelevant. First, because all Americans are overwhelmingly likely to be killed by assailants of their own race, so what some brand 'Black-on-Black crime' should, more accurately, just be called 'crime'. But also because Black people are not, by dint of their melanin content, entrusted to protect and serve the public. The police are. Over the last decade I have reported from many impoverished neighbourhoods where I have felt unsafe, populated by all races. That hasn't made me fear Black people or any other racial group; it has just made me loathe poverty and gun culture in general, since it is that toxic combination that both drives the crime and makes it lethal.

This woman and I were looking at the same kids but seeing quite different things.

'What makes you think they're going to become gangbangers?' I asked. She shrugged. The conversation pretty much dried up after that.

There is a section of white society – a broad section that includes affable mothers who will speak to Black strangers like me in the park – who understand Black kids as an inherent threat. Beyond the segregated ghettos where few white people venture, the presence of Black youth apparently marks not just the potential for trouble but the arrival of it. When George Zimmerman saw Trayvon Martin, he didn't see a seventeen-year-old boy walking home from the store. He saw someone 'real suspicious . . . up to no good', whom he assumed bore some responsibility for recent burglaries.

Indeed, Black children are often not even regarded as children at all. In Goose Creek, South Carolina, police demanded DNA samples from two middle-school students after they were mistaken for a thirty-two-year-old suspect. After the killing of Tamir Rice – the twelve-year-old shot dead by police in Cleveland after someone reported him brandishing what they assumed was a 'probably fake' gun – a police spokesman said it was Tamir's fault. 'Tamir Rice is in the wrong,' he said. 'He's menacing. He's 5ft 7in, 191 pounds. He wasn't that little kid you're seeing in pictures. He's a twelve-year-old in an adult body.' When testifying before the grand jury into the shooting of Michael Brown in Ferguson, Darren Wilson described his assailant more like an animal than an eighteen-year-old: 'He looked up at me and had the most intense, aggressive face. The only way I can describe it, it looks like a demon, that's how angry he looked.' Even after Wilson shot Brown, he continued to depict him as both physically super-human and emotionally subhuman. 'He was almost bulking up to run through the shots, like it was making him mad that I'm shooting him. And the face that he had was looking straight through me, like I wasn't even there, I wasn't even anything in his way.'

The evidence is not merely anecdotal. A study published last year in the American Psychological Association's online *Journal of Personality and Social Psychology* revealed that white Americans overestimated the age of Black boys over ten years old by an average of four and a half years; white respondents also assumed that Black children were more culpable than whites or Latinos, particularly when the boys were matched with serious crimes. 'Children in most societies are considered to be in a distinct group with characteristics such as innocence and the need for protection,' wrote Phillip Atiba Goff of the University of California, Los Angeles. 'Our research found that black boys can be seen as responsible for their actions at an age when white boys still benefit from the assumption that children are essentially innocent.' My son is tall for his age; these are the things you worry about.

It wasn't long before my wife and I began to notice the degree to which some white adults felt entitled to shout at Black children – be it in the street or on school trips – for infractions either minor or imagined.

Last summer, on the afternoon I arrived home from reporting on the disturbances after Michael Brown's death in Ferguson, Missouri, there was a barbecue and music at the local park. I took the kids. The park has a water feature that shoots wet jets from the ground and sprays kids in fountains from all sides as they paddle around. The younger ones peel down to their underwear, while the older ones just pile in in whatever they have on. It was a scorching day, and my son and several other kids were having a water fight – a tame affair with very little collateral damage for those not involved beyond the odd sprinkling. At one stage, while in hot pursuit of his main rival, my son splashed a woman on her leg. She yelled at him as though he'd hit her with a brick.

I'd seen the whole thing and ran over.

'What's the problem?' I said.

'Look. He's covered me in water,' she shouted.

I looked. She was barely wet. But even if he had . . .

'You're standing in a children's park, on a hot day, next to a water feature,' I said. 'Deal with it. Just stop shouting at him.'

'Don't you tell me what to do,' she barked.

'Now you're shouting at me,' I said. 'Just stop it.'

'Who the hell are you?' she yelled.

'I'm his dad, that's who.'

'You're nobody, that's who you are,' she bellowed. 'Nobody.'

One of the first stories I covered on my arrival was the funeral of Mamie Till Mobley, the eighty-one-year-old mother of the late Emmett Till. In 1955, Mamie sent her fourteen-year-old son from Chicago to rural Mississippi to spend his summer holiday with family. She packed him off with a warning: 'If you have to get on your knees and bow when a white person goes past,' she told him, 'do it willingly.'

Emmett didn't follow her advice. While in the small town of Money, in the Delta region, he either said 'Bye, baby' or wolf-whistled at a white woman in a grocery store. Three days later, his body was fished out of the Tallahatchie River with a bullet in his skull, an eye gouged out and his forehead crushed on one side.

Raising a Black child in a racist society poses a very particular set of challenges. On the one hand, you want them to be proud and confident about who they are. On the other, you have to teach them that they are vulnerable precisely because of who they are, in the knowledge that awareness of that vulnerability just might save their life. We are trying to raise self-confident children for long lives, not hashtags for slaughter.

Explaining the complex historical and social forces that make such a dance necessary is not easy at the best of times. Making them comprehensible to a child is nigh impossible without gross simplifications and cutting corners. Once, during our ten-minute walk to day care, my son asked if we could take another route. 'Why?' I asked.

'Because that way they stop all the Black boys,' he said.

He was right. Roughly twice a week we would pass young Black men who were being frisked or arrested, usually on the way home. He was also four, and until that point I was not aware that he had even noticed. I tried to make him feel safe.

'Well, don't worry. You're with me, and they're not going to stop us,' I told him.

'Why not?' he asked.

'Because we haven't done anything,' I said.

'What have they done?' he asked.

He had me. From then on we took another route.

When I interviewed Maya Angelou in 2002, she told me that the 11 September attacks of the previous year were understood differently by African Americans. 'Living in a state of terror was new to many white people in America,' she said. 'But Black people have been living in a state of terror in this country for more than four hundred years.' It is that state of terror that has been laid bare these last few years.

The American polity and media episodically 'discovers' this daily reality, in much the same way that teenagers discover sex – urgently, earnestly, voraciously and carelessly, with great self-indulgence but precious little self-awareness. They have always been aware of it, but somehow, when confronted with it, it nonetheless takes them by surprise.

The week I arrived, in December 2002, the Senate minority leader, Mississippi Republican Trent Lott, resigned from his position after he said in a speech that America would have been a better place had the segregationist Strom Thurmond won the presidency in 1948. The mainstream media saw nothing outrageous in this – as if it was just the kind of thing a conservative Southern senator might say. It took bloggers to make it a story. As I write, some Southern states are debating whether to keep the Confederate flag flying on state grounds in various guises – as though it took nine people dying on their doorstep to understand its racist connotations.

Me, Myself, I

It is as though the centuries-old narrative of racial inequality is too tiresome to acknowledge, except as a footnote – until it appears in dramatic fashion, as it did after Hurricane Katrina or the protests in Ferguson. At that point, the bored become suddenly scandalised. In a nation that prides itself on always moving forward, the notion that they are 'still dealing with this' feels like an affront to the national character. That's why Obama's candidacy had such a simple and uplifting appeal to so many Americans. As the radical academic and 1970s icon Angela Davis explained to me in 2007, it represented 'a model of diversity as the difference that makes no difference, the change that brings about no change'.

This most recent episode of racial awakening has lasted longer than most. For the last couple of years the brutal banality of daily life for some people in this country has become visible and undeniable to those who have no immediate connection to it. But nothing new has happened. There has been no spike in police brutality. What's new is that people are looking. And thanks to new technology (namely, the democratisation of the ability to film and distribute), they have lots to look at. As a result, a significant section of white America is outraged at the sight of what it had previously chosen to ignore, while a dwindling but nonetheless sizeable and vocal few still refuse to believe their eyes.

I've never found it particularly useful to compare racisms – as though one manifestation might be better than another. Every society, regardless of its racial composition, has overlapping and interweaving hierarchies. Insisting on the superiority of one over another suggests there are racisms out there worth having – a race to the bottom with no moral centre.

I have more cousins in the US than in Britain. They are doing fine. At one stage I fully intended to immigrate here. While that plan no longer stands, it still doesn't strike me as insane.

While I have been in America, I have not been shot at, arrested, imprisoned or otherwise seriously inconvenienced by the state. I do not live in the hollowed-out, jobless zones of urban economic despair to which many African Americans have been abandoned. I have been shouted at in a park, taken different routes to school and occasionally dealt with bigoted officials. (While driving through Mississippi to cover Katrina I approached a roadblock that all the other journalists had easily passed through, only to have a policeman pat the gun in his holster and turn me around.) These experiences are aggravating. They are not life-threatening.

I am not Michael Brown. But then Michael Brown wasn't Michael Brown before he was shot dead and had his body left on the street for four hours; Eric Garner was just a man trying to sell cigarettes in the street before he was choked to death in Staten Island; Tamir Rice was just a boisterous kid acting out in a park before a policeman leaped out of his squad car and shot him within seconds.

Being shot dead by the police or anyone else is not the daily experience of most Black people in America. But what became clear following the Department of Justice report into the Ferguson police force was just how extreme and commonplace the aggravations I have both faced and witnessed could be. To cite just a few examples: between 2007 to 2014, one woman in Ferguson was arrested twice, spent six days in jail and paid $550 as a result of one parking ticket, for which she was originally charged $151. She tried to pay in smaller instalments – $25 or $50 a time – but the court refused to accept anything less than the full payment, which she could not afford. Seven years after the original infraction, she still owed $541 – this was how the town raised its revenue. It was not a glitch in the system; it was the system.

Then there was the fourteen-year-old boy that the Ferguson police found in an abandoned building, who was chased down by a dog that bit his ankle and his left arm as he protected his face. The boy says officers kicked him in the head and then laughed about it after.

Me, Myself, I

The officers say they thought he was armed; he wasn't. Department of Justice investigators found that every time a police dog in Ferguson bit someone, the victim was Black.

Then there was the man pulled out of his house by the police after reports of an altercation inside. As they dragged him out, he told them, 'You don't have a reason to lock me up.'

'Nigger, I can find something to lock you up on,' the officer told him.

'Good luck with that,' the man responded. The officer slammed the man's face into a wall and he fell to the floor.

'Don't pass out, motherfucker, because I'm not carrying you to my car,' the officer is claimed to have said.

This was the same month Brown was killed. Were it not for the disturbances following Brown's death, there would have been no investigation – not only would we have heard nothing of these things but, because no light had been shone on them, the Ferguson police would be carrying on with the same level of impunity. This was a small Midwestern suburb few had heard of – unremarkable in every way, which is precisely what makes the goings-on there noteworthy. If it was happening there, then it could be happening anywhere.

It is exhausting. When the videos of brutality go viral, I can't watch them unless I have to write about them. I don't need to be shocked – which is just as well, because these videos emerge with such regularity that they cease to be shocking. Were it not for the thrill of seeing an unjaded younger generation reviving the best of the nation's traditions of anti-racist resistance, I would be in despair.

The altercations in the park, the rerouted walks to school – the aggravations of daily life are at the lower end of a continuum, a dull drumbeat that occasionally crescendos into violent confrontation and even social conflagration. As spring turns to summer, the volume keeps ratcheting up.

'Terror', the anthropologist Arjun Appadurai writes in his book *Fear of Small Numbers*, 'is first of all the terror of the next attack.'

The terrorism resides not just in the fact that it happens, but that one is braced for the possibility that it could happen to you at any moment. Currently, seven children and teenagers are shot on an average day in the US. I have just finished writing a book in which I take a random day and interview the families and friends of those who perished. Ten young people died on the day I chose. Eight were Black. All of the Black parents said they had assumed that this could happen to their sons.

As one bereaved dad told me: 'You wouldn't be doing your job as a father if you didn't.'

My mother's small island taught me what independence really means

As Barbados neared the fiftieth anniversary of its independence, I thought of my mother, who died at forty-four, and my relationship to her island of birth.

Guardian, 26 November 2016, London

My mother never made it to fifty. She was forty-four when she came home from a day of shopping in Stevenage town centre, went to sleep on the floor and died. Her death was sudden. She didn't leave a will – but she did leave a wish. She wanted to be buried in Barbados, the island of her birth, 'not this cold place'. I was nineteen, my brothers twenty-four and twenty-three. None of us had proper jobs or any money – but once we realised we had access to sufficient funds, we made it happen.

This was the second time my mother had gone back to Barbados since she left, as a teenager. The first was in 1974, with my brothers. Mum said she wanted to test the waters, see if she might come home. We returned after six weeks and stayed for good. While England had yet to deliver on its promises, she had yet to exhaust its possibilities. Because she didn't know that the next time she'd come back would be fifteen years later in a box; because she valued her independence.

Dead mother in the mother country. She didn't make it to fifty – but Barbados will, at the end of this month. Bajans gained full citizenship around the same time much of the planet did, in that sweet spot after Nelson Mandela had been convicted but before Martin Luther King had been assassinated – a time of hope, resistance and confidence. Smaller than the Isle of Man, with a population at the time approximately the same as the city of Derby today, it was now set free to stake out its place in the world. Audacious, timely, necessary – a village with a flag, an island with an anthem.

318   Dispatches from the Diaspora

Independence is not the same as freedom. There are lots of countries that are independent but aren't free. Barbados would not have been the first country to rid itself of one undemocratic overlord only to replace it with another. But independence is a prerequisite for freedom. How can you be free without running your own affairs and controlling your own resources? In what sense can one truly talk of liberty without first establishing autonomy?

But freedom is no guarantor of success. There are lots of countries that are free where people live without hope, food or support. If freedom means anything, it must mean the freedom to fail. No one who contemplates independence without also contemplating failure is taking independence seriously.

Herein lies the audacity, the tenacity, the perspicacity of the independence project: to take the leap, to take the risk, to meet the challenge.

When my mother died, this was my challenge. I was about to start exams at the end of my first year at university in Edinburgh. I had a long summer ahead of me, with no real sense of where to go. I had lost my lodestar. Edinburgh was not my home. But the place I had called home could not serve that role in the absence of my mother.

A year earlier, shortly before university, I had gone to Barbados with a friend in that well-worn pilgrimage of the children of immigrants, hoping to find a sense of security, a warm national welcome, where the racial response in Britain had been frosty. The country had my name on it: I was called Gary after Garfield Sobers, the nation's most imposing cricketer, whose name now graces a roundabout and pavilion on the island. Instead, like most, I found I was more British than I had realised. Barbados had not been waiting to envelop me in its embrace; rather, it was indifferent. I had not been expecting bunting, but nor had I anticipated ambivalence.

But my mother was home. As we laid her in the ground by St Martin's, beneath soil that could, on a windy day, be sprinkled by the sea breeze and then dried by the Caribbean sun, she had ended her journey not far from where she had started it, even if earlier than she had bargained for. And I was homeless – bereft of the things that make home possible and meaningful, reinventing my place in the world from scratch.

Everything about the funeral in Barbados reinforced this sense of displacement. My hair, which I had been wearing in plaits for several years, was out. The day before, Reverend Small had told me I couldn't attend the funeral with my hair like that because plaits were for women. He said it was in the Bible. Reverend Small. Small-minded. Small island. I did not know the hymns. Beyond immediate family, I did not know most of the people there.

I came back to an empty house in England and struggled to rebuild my life with the only indigenous resource I had: me. This independence was born of hope, yet had been forced upon me by fate. But the journey had to be undertaken nonetheless. Such was the audacity and tenacity of my project. It was a hard task to heave my teenage self into adulthood alone – until I finally realised that I was not doing it alone. I had brothers, aunts, friends, parents of friends, lecturers, the state – an assortment of hands to catch me if I fell, shoulders to lean on if I wept, bank accounts to draw on if I was broke. I couldn't have done it on my own.

'No man is an island, entire of itself,' wrote the poet John Donne. Barbados is an island, but not entire of itself. It could not have done it on its own. The trouble with national projects, even when they emerge from struggles against colonialism, is that they can degrade into nationalist projects. What starts as resistance based on the notion that all people are equal and should have the right to run their own affairs can descend into the notion that we can run our affairs better than others because we, who adhere to this flag and anthem, are better people. 'We' are not.

The fact that Barbados was independent did not excuse it from also having to be interdependent. From cricket to currency, it sought to join forces with the rest of the English-speaking Caribbean at various

Dispatches from the Diaspora

times. What does it mean to be independent in a neoliberal, globalised age of climate change and trade deals, terrorism and mass migration? That's the debate that Britain – bigger, richer, more powerful – keeps avoiding at its peril. It cannot escape Barbados. Nor should it. Having exported its people across the globe and stood in the historical crosswinds of slavery, colonialism and imperialism, its small size belies its inherently cosmopolitan nature.

My mother never made it to fifty. But Barbados did. And she lies within it. And it lies within me: independent, interdependent, autonomous, connected.

In these bleak times, imagine a world where you can thrive

My last Guardian *column reflected on the life lessons my mother taught me and how they informed my work and my life.*

Guardian, 10 January 2020, London

When I was a child, my mother used to put on the song 'Young, Gifted and Black' by Bob and Marcia, put my feet on hers and then dance us both around the living room. 'They're playing our song,' she'd say. It was the early 1970s, she was barely thirty, and I was the youngest of three children she was raising alone. Struggling to believe there was a viable future for her children in a country where racism was on the rise and the economy was in the tank, she had seriously considered returning to Barbados. But after a six-week family trip back, she decided we'd struggle to keep up academically: at school in England I played; in Barbados we sat in rows and recited times tables. I think this was partly cover for the fact that after more than a decade of self-reliance and relative anonymity, fitting back into island life would have been difficult. So we danced around the living room, singing ourselves up, imagining a world in which we would thrive, for which we had no evidence, though we did have great expectations.

In my interview for a *Guardian* Scott Trust bursary to study a post-graduate course in journalism, I was asked what kind of job I would aspire to if I ever got to work at the paper. 'A columnist, like Hugo Young,' I said.

'There's only room for a handful of columnists on a newspaper,' I was told.

'And why shouldn't one of them be me?' I asked.

From another applicant that question might have come from a sense of entitlement. But it was a genuine enquiry. I was merely

Dispatches from the Diaspora

articulating the logic that had got me that far: imagining a world in which I might thrive, for which I had no evidence.

This is my last column. After twenty-six years as a staff writer and twenty years – on and off – as a columnist, I'm leaving the *Guardian*. In April, I take up a post as professor of sociology at Manchester University. I have not given up journalism. I may appear in this paper (if they'll have me) and others very occasionally. But I will be liberated from having to have a thought every Thursday, and you will be liberated from having to read or avoid, enjoy or be enraged by it every Friday.

Much of the politics that has informed my writing in this space came from my mother. It is partly rooted in her experience. She came to Britain just a month after the Commonwealth Immigrants Act 1962 – branded by Labour's then leader Hugh Gaitskell as a piece of 'cruel and brutal anti-colour legislation' – was passed. She came because the then health minister, Enoch Powell, had embarked on a colossal programme of NHS restructuring that required more nurses. She was living proof of the immigrants that the British economy needs but that its political culture is too toxic to embrace. For her, sex, race and class were not abstract identities but forces that converged to keep her wages low and her life stressful.

But my politics is also rooted in what she made of those experiences. She was an anti-colonialist and an anti-racist, an internationalist and humanist who would have never used any of those words to describe herself. Race-conscious as she was, most of her community activism – youth clubs, literacy classes, discos in the church hall – took place in the working-class white community. They were her people, too.

She made me stay up and watch the *Holocaust* mini-series (which freaked me out) when I was ten and took me to watch *Gandhi* (which was way too long) during the holidays when I was thirteen. Both times she told me: 'This is your story, too.' She believed the world she wanted to create was never going to come to her, so she would have to take the fight to it. I saw her confront the local National

Front candidate, the police and her union – to name but a few. She took me on my first rally (Help the Aged) when I was four, my first demonstration (the Campaign for Nuclear Disarmament) when I was fourteen, and first picket (the South African embassy) at seventeen.

Even in her sudden and untimely death there were valuable lessons: that life is too short to waste time on people you don't care about, but long enough to make a difference if you want to. She was forty-four; I was nineteen. She never got to read my columns. My presence on these pages would have been, I think, as unlikely to her as anything else she hoped I might achieve as a child, as we padded around our living room.

No amount of self-image reinforcement could have defied those odds. The space where those politics could be shared and the route through which I would come to it were paved by others whom I didn't know and (mostly) never met. 'Men make their own history,' wrote Karl Marx in *The 18th Brumaire of Louis Bonaparte*. 'But they do not make it as they please; they do not make it under self-selected circumstances, but under circumstances existing already, given and transmitted from the past.'

The bursary I was awarded emerged in the early 1990s and was a response to the uprisings among Black youth in the 1980s. Black people were always in the news, but rarely in the newsrooms. The Scott Trust, which owns the *Guardian*, wanted to offer a correction and so gave bursaries to under-represented groups in journalism. Without it, I would have chosen another profession.

In 1999, the Macpherson report into the racist murder of Stephen Lawrence made the concept of institutional racism mainstream. That was the year my first column appeared here, Yasmin Alibhai-Brown's column began appearing in the *Independent*, my first book was published and Steve McQueen won the Turner Prize. The year before, Chris Ofili won the Turner Prize; the year after, Zadie Smith's *White Teeth* came out. The relationship between these events was not causal but contextual. This detracts not one iota from these people's creative

Dispatches from the Diaspora

abilities or the hard work that made their success possible. (Only the privileged and the naive believe people's achievements are purely the product of their own genius.) It simply acknowledges that there have been others who were similarly able and hard-working for whom space had not been cleared.

'Ingratitude' is the accusation launched by racists at Black people in the public eye who have the audacity to highlight the racial injustice they see and have experienced. So I'd like to take this opportunity to express my gratitude to the youth who took to the streets, and bereaved families who took to the courts, and made my career possible.

I sign off from this column at a dispiriting time, with racism, cynicism and intolerance on the rise, wages stagnant and faith that progressive change is possible declining even as resistance grows. Things look bleak. The propensity to despair is strong but should not be indulged. Sing yourself up. Imagine a world in which you might thrive, for which there is no evidence. And then fight for it.

Acknowledgements

Pulling this book together has demanded the support of a significant number of wonderful people to whom I am truly grateful. Colin
Robinson of O/R books, a great friend with whom I first shared the
idea and who is publishing it in the United States; Laura Hassan,
my UK editor at Faber, whose enthusiasm for the pieces encouraged
me greatly; and Hannah Knowles, who deftly took the baton when
Laura went on maternity leave. Jonny Geller, Viola Hayden and
Ciara Finan of Curtis Brown were always on the other end of the line
if and when I needed them; the indomitable Frances Coady, at Aragi
in New York, found corners I never knew I had and fought them for
me; and Taya Kitman of TypeMedia, who has supported me and my
work, both personally and through the Alfred Knobler Fellowship.

I stayed at the *Guardian* for twenty-five years, in no small part
because it was a great place to work. I also wish to thank *The Nation*,
the *New York Review of Books* and *The New Statesman*, all gracious
enough to give permission to include articles here without me paying
for the pleasure of republishing my own work.

As an anthology spanning twenty-eight years, the publication of
the book marks but a moment in a long journey that is not done yet
and which I could never have made on my own. Since 2007, many of
the datelines in this book denote time away from my children.

Beyond the home front, my career in journalism would not have
been possible without a countless number of people who backed me
when they had no self-interested reason to do so: colleagues and elders
who saw something in me and were prepared to give me a break;
editors who trusted my judgement; sub-editors who saved me from
embarrassment; readers who cheered me on. It is not merely the fear
of missing someone out that prevents me from naming them – they
know who they are and I hope I have acknowledged them already in

real life. It is also the fact that the list of names feels less important than the spirit in which they acted. Their encouragement was not transactional, and so I feel my responsibility – human, karmic, what have you – is to pay it back by paying it forward and encouraging and supporting others to make their own journeys, in the hope that their ride will be at least as joyful as mine, and that they, too, will pay it forward.

Index

Labour Party: 1996 conference, 162; Black Lives Matter solidarity, 167; Stormzy on, 263, 264–5

Laden, Osama bin, 102

Lake Charles, Louisiana, 178

Lambert, Margaret, 255

Lammy, David, 264

Lamotte, Phillipe, 292–3

Lanza, Adam, 108

Lapsley, Michael, 239

Larbalestier, Carmen, 271

Larsen, Nella: *Passing*, 204

Laslett, Rhaune, 34, 35–6, 37

Latino, Juan, 193

Latinos, 125, 311

Lauda, Niki, 275

Laura, Hurricane, 178

Lawrence, Stephen, 26, 27, 124, 166, 168

Lawrence family, 26, 27, 29

Le Castellet: French Grand Prix (2021), 272, 277

Le Pen, Jean-Marie, 147

Lee, Spike: *School Daze*, 204

Leeds, 178

Lee-Potter, Lynda, 39

Lenin, V. I., 137

Leopold II, King of the Belgians, 167, 179, 185

Levy, Amy, 248

Levy, Andrea, 5, 245–51; *Every Light in the House Burnin'*, 245, 246; *Fruit of the Lemon*, 245, 246; *The Long Song*, 247, 249–51; *Never Far from Nowhere*, 245, 246; *Small Island*, 245–6, 247–8, 250

Levy, Winston, 248

Lewington, Michael, 32

Liberia, 136, 138

Libya, 297

life expectancy, 122, 156

Life magazine, 153

Lincoln, Abraham, 98, 99, 137

Lindqvist, Sven, 127

Liuzzo, Viola, 150

Liverpool, 146, 192

Livingstone, Ken, 175

London: Black experience vs Stevenage, 271–2; Black immigrants, 192; fourth plinth, 175–7; George Floyd protests (2020), 167, 172; Lyceum, 34; Mandela statue, 182; National Portrait Gallery, 266–7; Notting Hill 'nigger-hunting' (1958), 31, 32, 33; pre-multicultural city (Levy), 248–9; pro-Mandela picketing, 1; Raikes statue, 181; St Pancras town hall Caribbean carnival (1959), 31, 34, 35; Seymour Hall, 34; South African embassy picket, 324; Stormzy's identity, 262; *see also* Notting Hill carnival

London School of Economics, 78

Lorde, Audre, 166

Lott, Trent, 43, 313

Louis, Joe, 50, 256

Louis D. Brown Peace Institute, 89

Louisiana, 122, 178, 209, 285

McAlpine, Sue, 34–5

McCain, Franklin, 258, 269–70

McCain, John, 52

McCarthyism, 32, 34

McClain, James, 230

McConnell, Mitch, 97

McFadden and Whitehead: 'Ain't No Stoppin' Us Now', 50

Machel, Graça, 240

Machel, Samora, 77

MacIntyre, Alasdair, 149–50

McIntyre, Renford, 120

Mack, Janet, 95

McLaren F1 team, 277

McLaurin, Virginia, 104

Macozoma, Sakumzi, 61–2, 69, 71

Macpherson report (1999), 26–30, 124, 130, 324

McQueen, Steve, 188, 324

mad cow disease, 286

Magee, Ruchell, 230

Mahabir, Ray, 40

Mahogany (costume company), 41

Malcolm X: Angelou works for, 218, 220; on brotherhood towards US Blacks, 167; and John Carlos, 252, 253, 254; murdered, 222, 223, 224; on NAACP, 226–7; Parks as devotee, 187, 211; on Uncle Toms, 141

Malik-Shabazz, Malcolm, *see* Malcolm X

Manchester, 178

US, 287–8; effect of Macpherson report, 26–30; as factor in Obama's victory, 52; Hurricane Katrina lays bare, 84–7, 122; interdependence with class, 86, 122, 130; lacks scientific/biological basis, 149; Lewis Hamilton on, 273–5, 276; and meaning of King's speech, 157–8; and Notting Hill carnival, 38; Obama's lack of engagement, 100–1, 234